The Exegetical Imagination

The Exegetical Imagination

On Jewish Thought and Theology

Michael Fishbane

HARVARD UNIVERSITY PRESS
Cambridge, Massachusetts
London, England
1998

Printed in the United States of America
Page 232 constitutes an extension of the copyright page.

Library of Congress Cataloging-in-Publication Data

Fishbane, Michael A.
The exegetical imagination : on Jewish thought and theology / Michael Fishbane.
p. cm.
Includes index.
ISBN 0-674-27461-X (cloth: alk. paper)
ISBN 0-674-27462-8 (paper: alk. paper)
1. Midrash—History and criticism. 2. Bible. O.T.—Criticism. interpretation, etc., Jewish. 3. Spiritual life—Judaism. I. Title.
BM514.F57 1998
296.3—dc21 98-12599
CIP

ציון לזכר

אא״ז יהודה לייב ב״ר משה נ״ע

for my grandfather
LOUIS MALTZMAN
in loving memory

Contents

Preface

My thinking about the content and form of this volume has evolved over several years. Initially, my intent was to write a poetics of Midrash; but after much work and thought, it became clear that the schematic and abstract structures of such a project would not do justice to the concrete complexity of the actual sources. More precisely, I became less confident that the isolation of separate units of exegesis would accurately capture the dynamic and composite character of the whole teaching. This holds true as much for any specific teaching as for larger anthological wholes. Indeed, the meaning of Midrash lies in the interrelation and contextualization of its diverse features. A formal or structural analysis could thus do little more that point to these matters—and then only in a static way and without conveying the actual unfolding and layering of Midrash, which are constitutive of its character.

My interests in Jewish hermeneutics therefore turned to "thick" descriptions of actual cases, and to their literary, exegetical, and theological modalities. The present volume thus provides several forays into midrashic thought, with an emphasis on the interrelationships between exegesis and religious ideas or values. Many students of Jewish thought tend to move quickly past the exegetical phenomena to the ideational content that may be deduced; my interest here is to examine how these ideas arise hermeneutically, and how they intersect with others in particular units. Only in this way, I believe, can we hope to retrieve the inner texture of classical Jewish thinking as an ongoing exegetical process. This process is not found in any given text or complex, but in the unfolding of ideas around key biblical texts over the course of millennia. The examples treated in this book thus afford a perspective on the history of religious ideas as exegetical trajectories; and comparisons of various points in the sequence, or between related trajectories from different periods, lay the groundwork for an inner-cultural, comparative Midrash.

In the evolution of this book I am indebted to the friendship and counsel of Ms. Peg Fulton, Senior Editor at Harvard University Press. Her interest in my work and her patience with my reformulations of this project are a debt that I happily acknowledge. In later stages of composition, Ms. Anita Safran put a keen eye to my words and a blue pencil to potential infelicities. I owe her many thanks.

Finally, I acknowledge a debt of life-long standing, and that is to my grandfather, Mr. Louis Maltzman, whose stubborn insistence many years ago that I master each week's "Rashis" instilled in me an old-fashioned commitment to exegetical thought. I owe him for much more than that, and not least for his Solomonic counsel, endlessly emphasized, that "A wise man has his eyes in his head, whereas a fool walks in darkness" (Ecclesiastes 2:14). For him this was a teaching of prudence and piety—prudence, insofar as it insists on focus and direction in earthly matters; and piety, insofar as it teaches that true wisdom stays connected to the divine source. My grandfather thus interpreted the phrase "in his head" *(be-rosho)* to mean "that which is above him," as have spiritual masters before him. May his soul be bound in the bond of everlasting life. I dedicate this book to his memory, in gratitude.

The University of Chicago
Shevat 5758/February 1998

The Exegetical Imagination

Introduction

Rabbinic thought and theology are quintessentially Bible-based—whether they are explanations, interpretations, or allegories of their scriptural source. Through such means and methods, the written words of Hebrew Scripture have been been extended since antiquity and given new voices for new times. For the latter-day interpreter of interpreters, it is precisely these modes of re-voicing that must be studied in order to understand how a second-order discourse derives from the first. This involves close attention to the texture of Scripture and to all the verbal conditions and nuances that elicit the exegetical imagination. Any jot or tittle may provide the occasion, just as any sound or image in the text may engage the inventive mind. The results follow their cause: the new "biblical" teachings are not abstract propositions, but forms of concrete discourse inspired by the shapes of Scripture. Change the citation and you change the exegesis; exchange the exegesis and new theology is the result. In another context, Thomas Mann spoke of *zitathaftes Leben*, of a textualized existence. The notion is applicable to Jewish exegetical thought as well. It too lives among the quotations.

As the ensuing discussions explore in detail, the exegetical imagination in Judaism rises and falls to the cadence of citations. For a given speaker, the words from one context call to mind like-sounding words from another, and new meanings are generated through their intertextual association. Another teacher may recontextualize the same words in an entirely different way. Exegetical locution is therefore locative from beginning to end, marking ever new tracings in the space of the text.

Culture calls these traces tradition and inhabits them as its latent or living mind.

There are many ways to approach the practical imagination of Jewish exegesis. For present purposes I wish to highlight the notion of *poesis* and the principle of similarity. The two are intertwined and constitutive elements of the exegetical theology to be examined in this book. By using the term *poesis* I mean to emphasize the fact that rabbinic exegesis is always "made," that every exegetical act is a conscious construction of meaning through the verbal conditions of Scripture. Indeed, for rabbinic culture, the sense of Scripture is never predetermined; rather, everything depends on creative readings of its inherent, God-given possibilities. Perceiving in this process the profound core of their own sacred universe, Jewish mystics in medieval times rightly said that interpretation creates a new heaven and a new earth for human habitation—again and again. The old masters of Midrash would agree; for them, too, the prolongation of scriptural speech through the exegetical imagination renews the world and gives it divine meaning. With this attitude Judaism elevates the creative act of interpretation to a type of *imitatio dei*.

The principle of similarity or equivalence is different, being a specific feature of the exegetical constructions themselves. Taking their stand within Scripture, separate acts of biblical interpretation are completed when one thing (be it a word or a phrase) is explained by means of another. This is the fundamental equation of exegetical procedure. At the micro-level of lexical sense, the guiding formula of equivalence is often stated explicitly: "this is (like) that"; but even on higher and more complex levels of textual interpretation, the goal remains the same. When one phrase is explained by another, despite all apparent differences at the verbal surface, the concluding prooftext is introduced by the words "this is what Scripture says," or their formulaic variations. Similarly, when a pentateuchal homily "opens" (as the texts say) with a particular passage from the Writings (the book of Psalms, for example, or Proverbs), the apparent remoteness or difference of this passage from the target verse in the Torah only teases the listener to anticipate a closure of this gap through mediating rhetorical strategies. This sense of expectation is one of the many pleasures of Midrash.

At the macro-level of interpretation, then, intertextual dissimilarities are adduced in order to reveal deeper scriptural correlations. Similar letters in different words serve as the outer signs of more profound links;

verbal tones elicit unexpected puns and semantic possibilities; numerological patterns and anagrammatical features yield surprising connections; and metaphors used for human purposes may be transmuted into concrete images of divine affect or action. In all, a vast network of convergences allows parts to explain wholes, and vice versa. Significance is thus omnipresent in the textual signs, and only awaits attentive discovery (or recovery) for older teachings to be renewed or altered. By these means Scripture interprets Scripture, as the sages said; and a related dictum in the Jerusalem Talmud follows the principle that words poor in possibility in one place may be enriched by others from other places. The intertextual linkage between all parts of the canon is an essential truth for the rabbis, and they show it again and again through endless chains of equivalents.

Similarity is also the constitutive feature of such rhetorical genres as the parable or the example. Woven into an exegetical discourse, these analogical forms function to explain something in Scripture (whether the text itself or its interpretation) by a fictive episode that is said to "resemble" it. The rhetorical question, "to what does this matter compare?" opens up a hermeneutical space in which similarity is imagined. It does not matter that the elements compared may be on fundamentally dissimilar planes of existence—as when divine acts are compared to those of a human king, or divine pathos is expressed through even more humble life forms. Rather, a dynamic correlation is established between the analogy and the text that not only bridges the space between them but allows features of the earthly episode to penetrate the realm of theology. In this way the emotional or dramatic realism of the parable affects the meaning of Scripture in unexpected ways. The significance of a similitude is thus that life serves to explain the text, and it gives a concreteness or directness to the text which it might otherwise not have. In a parable on parables found in the Midrash, analogies are said to be like ropes that lower a bucket into a well: without explanatory images the interpreter would often be stymied by the text, and the waters of Torah would be inaccessible. The strategy of likeness thus serves to explicate Scripture—and even to draw a connection between its truths and those of everyday reality.

Seen in terms of the principle of similarity, the work of exegesis may be said to create strategies of intertextual conversion. But a higher conversion remains: the exegetical construction of reality and the transformation of the culture into the images produced by that exegesis. Thus, beyond the strategies of law and legal practice, interpretation redefines the theological values of Scripture and orders them as ideals for life. Love and death and joy are not just aspects of one's natural being, but values to be enacted in idealized ways. The shapes in which one may imagine death and regard it as a goal or value are therefore constructed by the exegetical imagination; in a similar way, the ideals of joy are articulated and transmitted through theological interpretation. Consequently, the world of the text serves as the basis for the textualization of the world—and its meaning. Through exegesis new forms arise, and the content varies from one teacher to another. What remains constant is the attempt to textualize existence by having the ideals of (interpreted) Scripture embodied in everyday life. This process of world-making is the ultimate *poesis* of the exegetical imagination, even as the conversion of the biblical text into life is the culmination of the principle of similarity.

There is one further point to be addressed here, and that is the attempt to retrieve past acts of exegetical imagination by later interpreters. Several paragraphs earlier I referred to the need for attentiveness—attentiveness to the texture of the text the exegetes interpret, along with its patterns and forms, so as to understand the exegetical imagination at work. This involves a two-tiered notion of *Verstehen,* or understanding of the text. At the first level, the modern interpreter of interpreters must let the discourse being analyzed determine his understanding of its sense. The *poesis* of the older exegetes must be the guide here. To by-pass this process is to ignore the patterns of exegetical thinking preserved in the text, and thus, possibly, to misconstrue its emphases or degrees of literalness. The task for the interpreter is therefore to examine carefully the exegetical reasoning manifest in the text at hand—in the thickness of its citations and expression—and re-imagine the earlier exegete's habit of mind. Only thus will a truly historical theology be retrieved.

I emphasize the imaginative aspect of the scholarly task because the modern interpreter is already engaged in a third-order discourse. This is the other aspect of *Verstehen* that needs to be specified. The new voice of the contemporary scholar is no more the voice of the old interpreters than theirs was the primary voice of Hebrew Scripture. Like its predecessors, this new voice is also engaged in prolonging the words of the ancient text—despite the new language and contexts in which it speaks. Scholarly discourse may therefore rightly be seen as a kind of supercommentary, analyzing texts with the ideas and methods of one's own historical situation, and integrating them into new orders of significance. Accordingly, the ideal may be to approximate an authentic double-voicedness: to speak about the text with an intimacy and understanding achieved through philological persistence, but in a voice that is also shaped by the conceptions and concerns of one's own time and place. I do not believe that the older interpreters did any less, in their own way. It is therefore a renewal of their double-voicedness that I have tried to achieve in this book, and in so doing, to prolong the voices of Scripture through my own exegetical imagination.

The chapters of this book follow a double course. Broadly speaking, the first part (Chapters 1–6) offers a series of studies in ancient Jewish speculative theology, which takes its form through midrashic exegesis and mythopoeic images. Both are concrete features of this textual thinking. They arise from the texts and speak between them. Without this guideline, so to speak, the teachers would not speak authentically and their teachings would not be biblical. For that is the pivotal paradox: the sages produce Jewish theology as the meaning of Scripture. This rabbinization of Torah is thus one side of a double mirror; the other is the biblicization of Judaism. Accordingly, it seemed right to open with a chapter dealing directly with the hermeneutics of Midrash and how meaning is made in Scripture. Subsequent chapters give examples of how ancient rabbinic theology is generated and justified by exegesis. Each chapter is typical of the concerns of the rabbis and takes up a selected topic: divine pathos for Israel (Chapter 2); divine dramas at the beginning and end of time (Chapter 3); speculations on the status of Israel and the mystery of God (Chapter 4); and theologies of messianic pathos (Chapter 5). As many of these essays reveal different layers of mythic theology, dramatizing divine concern and action in concrete ways, this part concludes with a more conceptual discussion of the stages of mythmaking in Jewish thought and its textual assumptions (Chapter 6). This discussion also serves as a bridge to the chapters that follow, where diverse layers of exegetical theology are taken up in a different way.

While the separate discussions of this first Part may be read independently, they are nevertheless integrated at several levels. First and foremost, these chapters demonstrate the thick texture of ancient Jewish theology and the integration of exegesis and thought. As I had stressed earlier, Jewish exegetical thought is not propositional but concrete through and through. It does not follow, however, that the constructions are either simple or simply arrived at. To the contrary, midrashic composition is at once deceptively naive and highly elliptical. It is the former insofar as the pattern of thought seems to be merely a play of passages, clever correlations, or the need to work through all the phrases of a verse. But on closer inspection one must attend precisely to the concrete implications of a series of interpretations, for they often reflect dialectics or tensions of a complex sort (Chapter 4). In a similar manner, strings of images or homilies can reveal patterns of redaction in which new narrative or theological cycles are constructed for ongoing tradition (Chapters 3 and 5).

On the other side, midrashic thinking and compositions are also highly elusive—both deliberately so, because of the concern of the teacher to treat esoteric or delicate topics circumspectly (if not practicing self-censorship); and accidentally, because of our historical distance from the common assumptions embedded in the terms of the text (Chapters 4 and 5). Sometimes it is hard to separate these two factors; but all in all, the texts often need comparative perspectives, from within the midrashic corpus and beyond, for their full elucidation. In this way, certain oblique theological ideas or terms may be nuanced or filled in on the basis of formulations found elsewhere; in other instances, historical disturbances causing self-censorship, suppression, or distortion in the texts require the interpreter to look afield and catch glimpses of meaning in refractions of the topic preserved in Talmudic manuscripts, Karaite polemics, the New Testament, the Church Fathers, or even Gnostic sources of late antiquity (see Chapters 2, 4–5). Paradoxically, such scholarship becomes a second-order *poesis* where the later interpreter makes sense of tradition.

The second Part (Chapters 7–11) takes this book in a complementary direction. While similarly rooted in the exegetical constructions of theology, and closely attentive to diverse patterns of instruction, the ensuing essays deal more with the exegetical construction of ritual reality. There is thus a move from what I earlier called speculative theology to something like a Jewish practical theology—insofar as the concern here is to take account of, advocate, and even give normative expression to certain types of ritual practice. What is notable, however, and what keeps this

Part aligned with the first one, is that the *praxes* discussed are by and large theological. That is, I have chosen to explore how theological attitudes or thoughts become practical theological actions through forms of meditation or right attitude. This is of course not to deny that they are embedded in public practices, but rather specifically to emphasize the interior process through which certain exegetical theologies are actualized and embodied.

In order to explore these matters, I have again chosen distinct but typical cases. Paralleling the opening essay on Midrash in the first Part, this section opens with a study of the hermeneutics of the *Zohar*, the classic work of medieval Jewish mystical exegesis. In the course of analysis, special attention is given to the transfer of certain speculative intepretations to the service of meditation in prayer. A focus on the language of certain words in the book of Genesis, for example, and through them to their deep theosophical structure, provides the occasion to reveal a similar structure behind the language of the great proclamation of faith in Deuteronomy 6:4 (Chapter 7). Established through exegesis, these structures are recapitulated in the liturgical recitations of ritual. The result is that a given verbal theology (the proclamation) and mental theology (mystical chains of being) are correlated and enacted in worship. Meditations on Deuteronomy 6:5 (the subsequent verse) are also considered—but only, of course, on the basis of its transformed exegetical sense (see Chapter 9).

In addition to this meditative feature, the chapters in the second Part focus on other mental dimensions that have been part of the normative ritual life of Judaism for millennia; specifically, the use of mental or ritual-mental substitutes for concrete behaviors when these are not possible, owing to historical or other exigencies (Chapters 8–9). Thus the inner life of the worshipper is of intense concern in these essays, and in particular where the concern is to cultivate certain forms of attention and attitude (Chapters 8–10). The singular fact is that such cultural cultivation derives from textual exegesis and is justified by it. The result is that patterns and clusters of concern emerge that become stable topics over the centuries, nurturing diverse behaviors for public or private expression. I have therefore sought to indicate their structure by linking theological theories (so to speak), or emphases, with their practical enactment (see the relation between Chapters 8–9 and between 10–11). My choice of such topics as penitential acts or substitutes, meditation on aspects of death or dying, and the necessity for joy in the fulfillment of the commandments has been guided both by their inherent value and because they are all central topics of Jewish spirituality. These theological practices developed over time and constitute major elements in the historical theology of Judaism. They exemplify how, through exegesis, life imitates (and interiorizes) texts. This is *zitathaftes Leben* in its full embodied sense.

It is my view that Jewish thought and theology arise in the thickness of exegesis and are carried by its forms. The theologians thought with these elements, and the rabbinic editors regularly compiled them into anthologies for religious instruction. Yet it is remarkable how often studies of Jewish belief and behavior ignore or neutralize this fact. The present work therefore seeks to show that Jewish historical theology lives among the citations—and to offer various specimens as proof.

1

Midrash and the Nature of Scripture

An old tradition told in the *Midrash Sifre Deuteronomy* (343) presents a powerful image of the giving of the Law: God's word appears as a fire that emerges from His right hand, encircles the nation, and returns; the fire is then transferred by God from His left hand to His right, whereupon it is inscribed upon the tablets of Moses.[1] In this way the sages gave mythic realism to the scriptural phrase *mi-yemino 'esh dat lamo,* "from His right hand [there emerged] a fiery law for them [the nation]" (Deut. 33:2). Another passage, stating that "the voice of the Lord carves out flames of fire" (Psalm 29:7), is expressly added to indicate the world-encompassing power of divine speech. This verse from the Psalms serves here to reinforce the main teaching that the tablets were chiseled by tongues of fire (the verse was thus presumed to say that God's "voice . . . carves out *the Decalogue by* flames of fire"). Elsewhere, Rabbi Akiba gave just this explication as an independent account of God's fiery words at Sinai.[2] The editor of our *Sifre* passage has chosen to subordinate this teaching to his interest in the heavenly arm as an agent of the inscription.

In our midrashic myth God's word emerges from the divine essence as visible fire and takes instructional shape as letters and words upon the tablets. The written Law is thus an extension of divine speech—and not merely its inscriptional trace. This identification of God's utterance and Torah is the hermeneutical core of Judaism. Midrash works out the details.

The sages were alive to this point. In a teaching joined to a version of the aforementioned myth, R. Azariah and R. Yehudah bar Simon (in the name of R. Yehoshua ben Levi) pondered the question of how much the

Israelites actually learned at Sinai (*Songs Rabba* I.2:2). They proposed that the people learned *all* the 613 (principal) commandments of (rabbinic) Judaism at that time. This interpretation links the Words of the Ten Commandments to all the teachings that will emerge through Jewish discourse. Such a notion is first found explicitly in Philo;[3] but something of it can already be found in Tannaitic teachings of the first two centuries (C.E.). Thus, in a variation of the above-noted *Sifre* teaching, we learn that the meaning of the word *yevoneneihu* in Moses' song—"He [God] instructed him [Israel])" (Deut. 32:10)—is that Israel learned "how much Midrash was in it [each word of the Decalogue], how much Halakhah was in it, how many *minori ad maius* arguments were in it, and how many textual analogies were in it."[4] Significantly, this phrase also appears in *Songs Rabba* in connection with what the angel of the Law (according to Rabbi Yoḥanan) or the Word itself (according to the rabbis) addressed to each Israelite as they heard each of the Ten Commandments.[5]

The Decalogue is thus a paradigmatic text, and Sinai a paradigmatic moment, for Midrash: not only is something of the mysterious fullness of divine speech infused in the letters of the Decalogue, but its revelation is accompanied by a prolepsis or encapsulation of the future achievement of rabbinic interpretation. The written text thus mediates between the original verbal revelation of God at Sinai and the ongoing discourses of the sages in history. Paradoxically, the divine Word unfolds through human speech. As exegetical act and event, this human speech is Midrash.

And more: as a field of totality, the tablets metonymically represent the truths of the whole culture. They may therefore be compared to the shield of Achilles, which was fashioned for the hero by the god Hephaestus (*Iliad*, Book 23). The sea-like border design indicates the boundaries of civilization, and the images on the various panels depict its achievements and values. The shield is therefore more than battle armor for a day: rather, it depicts the world for which the hero fights, the entire symbolic order rescued from chaos by human industry and virtue.

Similarly, to understand the shapes on the tablets is to understand the truths of God's teachings for all generations—which are the truths of Judaism insofar as the tradition is truly based upon a scriptural foundation. As a fixed and final formulation, the tablets are therefore a canon-before-the-canon. That is to say, just as the closing of Scripture in later times meant that "all" was "in it" (as an old epigram put it) and nowhere else, so too is "everything" already on the tablets. In this sense, divine instruction was virtually complete at Sinai. Ongoing interpretations (of these or other words) do not therefore add to God's original voice, but rather give it historical and human expressions. This is an essential postulate of the sages, and it is fundamental to the work of Midrash.[6]

In its broadest sense, biblical Scripture is a complex system of written signs, put into words that interrelate to make sense in their primary context—beginning with the phrase and including the sentence, the paragraph, and so on. As an anthology of cultural materials spanning a millennium, a good many of the units were originally independent of each other, and they circulated in distinct circles of instruction and tradition (such as the priestly or wisdom schools). Because of the long period of literary development, many of the materials allude to predecessor traditions and rework them in a number of ways.[7] In these cases, a new network of intertextual relations is produced, and the context of the second biblical text is greatly expanded.

In terms of structural linguistics, we may restate this as follows. The texts of Scripture derive from any number of conditioning linguistic factors; and these, as the set of open possibilities, constitute the potential of biblical "language" (*langue,* to use Saussure's terminology). By contrast, the realization of these possibilities in actual expression (and by this is meant the meanings constructed from the potentials through the conjunction of specific letters, words, or syntax) is biblical "speech" *(parole)*—though, of course, this does not mean oral speech only (even if the written text is derived from an oral expression, purports to quote it directly or indirectly, or has special status when recited aloud).[8] Naturally, as a document of great historical and cultural range, Scripture is made up of many such speeches—now collected in units and genres. The books *(ta biblia)* of these anthologies constitute the Bible.

The word "torah" is indicative of these matters. At one end of the spectrum it marks very specific, short instructions of law in the priestly sources, which are attributed to Moses as speaker of divine speech; but Torah also marks, eventually, the entire book of Deuteronomy as Moses' summary instruction of divine speech voiced through him (along with historical details); and finally, by the post-exilic period, the Torah of Moses serves as an even more comprehensive designation (as in Malachi 3:22).[9] By contrast, in wisdom circles the term "torah" originally indicated some didactic instruction—grounded in experience of the natural world—which was then written down as a cultural maxim. On the surface, such instructions have nothing whatever to do with Moses' divine speech. Indeed, the task of the moral teachings is to make one worldly wise—not holy or pure. The incorporation of gnomic and priestly torahs in one cultural anthology shows just how diverse Scripture is.

The closure of the scriptural canon (by the beginning of the common era) changes matters fundamentally. It is a transformative event, for with this closure there can be no new additions or supplementations to the biblical text. Indeed, there is now an "in" and an "out"—a within and a without, so to speak. And since God's Word *(speech)* is deemed comprehensive and sufficient for human culture in all its historical diversity, it is only within the existent divine words that new meanings can arise. Accordingly, the effect of the closure is to transform the many separate units (and contexts) of biblical speech into the *one* speech (and context) of Scripture. Everything must be found in it.

The result is that the extended (but bounded) speech of Scripture is reconceived as the multiform expressions of divine revelation—beginning with the individual letters of its words, and including all the phrases and sentences of Scripture. These all become the constituents of possibility in the opening of Scripture *from within.* In the process, to return to our structuralist diction, the speech or *parole* of Scripture becomes the language *(langue)* of each and every midrashic statement *(parole)*. In other words, Scripture becomes a closed and unified system of language with particular possibilities for linking words and phrases. Midrash is the name for the speech-acts that arise from this system. Hence, just as every speech of Moses is an actualization of the divine *langue* through him, so each midrashic *parole* (properly) spoken by the sages is an actualization of the divine *langue* of the scriptural canon. Thus is the midrashic word inscribed within the language of Scripture.

The opening of Scripture from within radically transforms the grammaticality of the text: the ordinary connections between the letters of a word and between the words of a sentence are broken. These components now become extra-ordinary.[10] Indeed, each letter has (virtual) anagrammatical significance; each word may encode numerous plays and possibilities; and each phrase has any number of potential correlations within Scripture. Midrash determines the sense of each component through extending the context of the component to the entirety of Scripture (thus the original setting or sequence is often immaterial). Letters in one place may therefore be related to letters in another; and words or phrases from a given part of Scripture are revealed through midrashic methods to refer to the same thing as words and phrases found elsewhere. The emergent enchainment *(ḥarizah)* of possibilities thus dramatizes what is always the presupposition of midrashic exegesis: that all Scripture is one interconnected whole. Accordingly, the use of the word "torah" in the book of Proverbs not only means that its epigrams may be correlated with teachings of the Torah of Moses, but also means that the divine elements in Moses' words are related to the wise words of Solomon. Both Solomon's Proverbs and Moses' Torah are aspects of the divine *langue*—which is Scripture. Midrash establishes these correlations or equivalences again and again.

Historically considered, Ezra is the first master of the midrashic *parole*—for he "inquires" *(doresh)* of the Torah of the Lord (in Ezra 7:10) as former generations "inquired" of God for a living oracle (2 Kings 22:5, 8). His act (and those of his rabbinic heirs) thus conjures new meanings from God's *langue.*[11] No part is too small to become a whole. Come and hear.

The account of creation in the book of Genesis is framed by a prologue and epilogue. It opens with the words *be-reshit bara':* "in the beginning" God "created" the heavens and the earth (Gen. 1:1); and it concludes with the coda about the heavens and earth *be-hibbar'am,* "when they were created" (Gen. 2:4a). Struck by the form of this last word, the midrash in *Genesis Rabba* (12.10) ponders the agency of the divine creation. Grammatically, *be-hibbar'am* combines the preposition *be* (used in the temporal sense of "when") with an infinitive absolute form of the verb *bara'* (in the *niphal* form) and a plural suffix. And precisely because of this grammatical form, some sages intuited a parallel with the phrase *be-reshit bara'* in Genesis 1:1.

Genesis 1:1 had long since been interpreted to suggest that God "created" *(bara')* the world "with" or "for the sake of" *(be) reshit* (variously deduced as Torah, the Throne of Glory, Moses, and so on).[12] A similar anagrammatical construction (though of more esoteric import, as we shall see) was proposed for the word *be-hibbar'am* in Genesis 2:4a by R. Abbahu in the name of R. Yoḥanan. In his view, we may find (encoded) here the teaching that God "created" *(bara')* the heavens and earth "with" or "by means of" *(be)* the letter *he*. The meaning of this reading emerges from the whole teaching, as follows.

> *be-hibbar'am*. Rabbi Abbahu [interpreted] in the name of Rabbi Yoḥanan: "with [the letter] *he* He created them. Just as this *he* is the only non-lingual letter [being merely aspirated], so did the Holy One blessed be He create His world merely 'with the word of YHWH' [Psalm 33:6]—and immediately 'the heavens were made' [*ib.*]."
>
> Rabbi Yudan Neshiy'a inquired of Rabbi Shemuel bar Naḥman, and asked: "Since I have heard that you are an expert in Aggadah, explain the meaning of [the phrase] 'Extol Him who rides the clouds; the Lord [*be-YaH*] is His name' [Psalm 68:5]." He answered: "There is no place in [all] His dominion [*biyah;* Greek *bia*][13] without an appointed authority—[thus] the *ecdicus* [public prosecutor] is responsible for the dominion in his city,[14] [and] the *agba bastes* [*apparitor*] is responsible for the dominion in his city.[15] Similarly: Who is responsible for the dominion [*biyah*] on High? *Be-YaH* is His name, *biyah* is His name." [Rabbi Yudan] answered: "O woe for those [sages] who have died but are not forgotten!" for I had [also] inquired of Rabbi Eleazar, and he did not explain it so, but rather [interpreted the word with reference to Isa. 26:4] "for in YaH [*be-YaH*] the Lord [YHWH] you have an everlasting Rock [*tzur 'olamim*]." [Meaning:] With these two letters [*Y(od)* and *H(e)* of His name] the Holy One, blessed be He, created [*bara';* but rendering *tzur* as *tziyyer*] His world."[16]
>
> Now we do not know if this world was created with [the letter] *he* and the world to come with the *yod;* but on the basis of the way Rabbi Abbahu in the name of Rabbi Yoḥanan explained *be-hibbar'am* as *be-HE bera'am,* surely this world was created with the [letter] *he*. And whereas from the [graphic] shape of this *he,* which is closed on all [three] sides but open from below, we have an indication that all the dead descend to Sheol; [so too] from the tip on the upper side we have a hint of their resurrection; and from the spatial gap in the upper corner we may [also] learn [a lesson of hope] for penitents. [Thus we may conclude:] the world to come was created with the *yod*. And just as its stature is bent over, so [will] the stature of evildoers be bent over and their faces darkened in the world to come—as we read [in Scripture]: "Then man's haughtiness shall be humbled" [Isa. 2:17].[17]

This teaching appears as a typical midrashic construction, combining a variety of voices and opinions (let us call each of them a microform) into one integrated piece (let us call the whole a macroform). First we have Rabbi Abbahu's (received) teaching that God created the world with the letter *he*. This point is supplemented with the linguistic comment that *he* is an aspirant. The point is apparently indicative of the ease of God's creation; but the prooftext (from Psalm 33:6) adduced in support of this is perplexing, since it seems to speak of creation "by the word of the Lord [YHWH]." But appearances are deceiving in Midrash. I am inclined to suppose that this scriptural proof was initially cited to extend the view of creation through the letter *he*. For a close reading of that phrase (in light of the ensuing discussion) suggests that it was understood quite concretely to mean that "the heavens were created [by God] by means of the [letters of the] word YHWH [the Lord]"—*he* being one of those letters. And because this citation also goes on to say that "all the hosts [were created] by the breath of His mouth," the primary teaching was supplemented by a second one about aspirants. The prooftext now does double duty: it links R. Abbahu's teaching to the discussion of the letters of God's name, and it mentions the hosts who reappear as the regents of God's dominion. As is typical, the midrashic teaching is laconic. It springs from Scripture and is reanchored in Scripture. Between these poles of authority the sage mediates his message.

The ensuing queries of R. Yudan seem to be an abrupt *non sequitur* after R. Abbahu's teaching—a shift which even the citation of Psalm 33:6 (as meaning that God created the world with His name) only partially mitigates. Moreover, though R. Shemuel's teaching of *be-yah* as a Greek homonym is consistent with multilingual puns in the Midrash,[18] it is certainly irrelevant to this macroform as a whole. The discussion of Psalm 68:5 is adduced merely as a prelude to R. Eleazar's exegesis. The editor then cleverly brings the discussion back to the opening teaching by reconciling R. Eleazar's position (that God created the world with the letters *yod* and *he*) with that of R. Abbahu (who asserted that the world was created with the one letter *he*). The differentiation of the letters (one for this world, the other for the world to come), leads to a bit of graphology. The letters are now viewed as iconic forms—replete with religious significance. Thus does the midrashist follow God and inscribe theological truth into the depth of existence. Axiology recapitulates ontology.

The teaching in *Genesis Rabba* thus appears as a hierarchy of voices—beginning with Scripture itself, and descending, through a chain of teachers, to the anonymous editor. Indeed, beginning with the opening lemma (the word *be-hibbar'am*), the string of teachings is knotted by several scriptural citations. The editor seems to direct this midrashic theatre with consummate legerdemain, introducing and resolving microforms to produce a teaching that begins with the creation and ends with eschatology. But we would hardly suspect the degree to which this editor has manipulated his traditions in the process. This editorial activity only becomes clear when we examine the homily of Rabbi Abbahu and the exegesis of Rabbi Eleazar in *yerushalmi* (Jerusalem Talmud) *Ḥagigah* 2.1, their original context.

In this Talmudic context the teaching of Rabbi Abbahu comes after traditions about the meaning and shape of the letter *bet,* the first letter of the creation account. He offers a new proposal. In view of what may be learned about how Midrash is formed and reformed, the matter deserves closer scrutiny.

> Rabbi Abbahu [said] in the name of Rabbi Yoḥanan: "With two letters were two worlds created—this world and the world to come: the one with *he,* the other with *yod.* What is the proof? 'For *be-YaH* [with *yod/heh*] the Lord *tzur 'olamim* [formed, *tziyyer,* worlds; literally, is an everlasting Rock]' [Isa. 26:4]. And [from this verse] we do not know with which letter he created which world. But since it is [also] written, 'These are the generations of the heavens and the earth *be-hibbara'am'* [Gen. 2:4], [we may infer that] He created them with [the letter] *he.* Thus: this world was created with the *he,* and the world to come was created with the *yod.* And whereas *he* is open below, this is an indication to all creatures that they will descend to Sheol; [and] whereas *he* has a point at its top, [this is to indicate that] from the moment they descend they [may] ascend; [and] whereas *he* is open at [nearly] every side, so [God] opens a passage for penitents; [and] whereas *yod* is bent, so will all creatures be bent over—[as is written], 'and all faces will turn pale' [Jer. 30:6]. When David perceived this, he began to praise [God] with [the same] two letters: 'Hallelu-yah [Be praised, *yod* and *he*] O servants of the Lord, give praise; praise the name of the Lord'" [Psalm 113:1].

> Rabbi Yudan Neshiyya inquired of Rabbi Shemuel bar Naḥman: "What is [the meaning of] this scripture?: 'Extol Him who rides on the clouds; the Lord [*be-Yah*] is His name. Exult His presence' [Psalm 68:5]." He

> said to him: "There is no place without an authority apppointed over its dominion [*biyah*]. And who is responsible for the dominion of them all? The Holy One blessed be He: *Biyah* is His name, for Yah is His name." [Rabbi Yudan] replied: "Your master Rabbi [E]leazar did not interpret [*doresh*] so; but rather [explained it by way of a parable] of a king who built a palace in a place of sewers [*bivin*], dumps, and waste.[19] [Now] if anyone would come [by] and say that the palace is built in a place of sewers, dumps, and waste, would he not malign [both king and palace]? Just so: if one were to say that the world was originally water within water, he would surely malign the garden of the King and the roof built above it. He should therefore look and not touch."

It is clear that we have here two separate microforms: a teaching of R. Abbahu regarding the two letters of the divine name used to create this world and the next; and teachings by R. Shemuel and R. Eleazar regarding the lower and upper worlds. All three sages develop interpretations of the word *be-yah,* but they do so on the basis of different texts. R. Abbahu uses Isaiah 26:4, and divides the letters anagrammatically, while the teachings of R. Shemuel and R. Eleazar explain Psalm 68:5 via Greek puns (*bia,* "dominion"; and *ouai,* "woe").[20] In many ways the macroform in *yerushalmi Ḥagigah* is more streamlined than the one found in *Genesis Rabba,* and presents each of the microforms as a distinct exegetical unit. For example, R. Abbahu's homily opens with a teaching about the letters *heh* and *yod,* and proceeds to ponder the specific employment of each (resolving the issue through reference to Gen. 2:4). By contrast, the version in *Genesis Rabba* has separated R. Abbahu's remark regarding the letter *he* from its use to resolve the quandary as to which letter (*he* or *yod*) was used for the creation of which world (this one or the next).

In comparing the two, reference to the *yerushalmi Ḥagigah* demonstrates that *Genesis Rabba* transforms the tradition completely. For now (in *Genesis Rabba*) Rabbi Abbahu's teaching seems limited to a comment on Genesis 2:4; and his interpretation of Isaiah 26:4 (in the *yerushalmi*) is given to Rabbi Eleazar (whose parable is totally dropped). Moreover, the ensuing query about which letter was used in the different worlds *now* seems to be the voice of the editor, since it invokes Abbahu's first teaching by name in order to clarify what is *now* presented as R. Eleazar's exegesis. The subsequent theology of the letters also reappears as the editor's voice, and not part of the extended homily of R. Abbahu as presented in the Jerusalem Talmud.

Obviously, the editor of *Genesis Rabba* desired to privilege Rabbi Abbahu's comment on the letter *he* in the context of a midrash on Genesis; but this resulted in a total relocation of interpretations and the insinuation of his own voice into a prominent position. In contrast to the redactor of the *yerushalmi Ḥagigah* pericope, whose voice is absolutely absent, the anonymous editor of *Genesis Rabba* 12.10 speaks loud and clear as an impresario of traditions. By dividing the original homily of R. Abbahu in two, and transferring one part to the end, the teachings of R. Shemuel and R. Eleazar are now incorporated into the discourse on the letters of the creation. In the *yerushalmi,* rather than being subordinate interpretations of the word *be-yah,* they are simply included for the sake of the completeness of tradition. Thus while both macroforms show midrashic tradition as complex acts of tradition-building, they do so in different ways. For example, the passage in *yerushalmi Ḥagigah* has grouped its traditions in a static chain of authorities. This stands in sharp contrast with the more dynamic process of enchainment found in *Genesis Rabba.* Here the voice of the editor actively enters the hermeneutical fray. Little wonder that at one point he even took the words of Rabbi Abbahu right out of his mouth.

The hierarchical chain of voices that constitute midrashic pericopes is also a chain of memory. Scripture is remembered first and foremost—and then the teachers, who are remembered by the anonymous editor by their own names and those of their teachers. Thus Midrash swings between the temporal poles of a memorialized past of instruction and the present moment of re-presentation. Indeed, as a linear process, time is marked by the teaching of Scripture. Meanings accumulate as one "other thing" *(davar 'aher)* brings up "another"—and these are even edited into stylized series and structures for the sake of further instruction. From the myriad phonetic and grammmatical possibilities of connection, passages throughout Scripture are combined in ever new ways: "as it is written" here, says one teacher; or "this is what Scripture says," notes another. Exegetical discourse thus speaks from the fullness of God's canonical *langue,* revealing ever new iterations of its truth. Our collections of midrashic *paroles* bear witness to this messianic project.

But the rabbinic sage also works under the sign of myth. For every scriptural interpretation is a reenactment of the revelation at Sinai—the paradigmatic time of Instruction. Indeed, each midrashic *parole* participates in God's canonical *langue* and revitalizes it for new generations.

The divine "word is fire," reports the prophet Jeremiah, "like a hammer splitting a rock"; and his rabbinic heirs understood this as the Sinaitic sparks that are released from Scripture through human interpretation.[21] Every sage is thus a disciple of Moses and may be compared to Ben Azzai, who was once interpreting Scripture "and a flaming fire encircled him." His colleague Rabbi Akiba thought him to be in the heat of mystical passion, but Ben Azzai explained that he "was rather sitting and (exegetically) enchaining *(ḥorez)* the words of Torah, Prophets, and Writings to each other—and the words rejoiced as when they were given at Sinai, and were as pleasant as when they were first given" at Sinai in fire.[22] King Solomon may himself have had a similar sense of the renewal of Sinai through exegesis, suggested an anonymous sage, when he spoke of his beloved's "cheeks as beautiful in ringlets" (*torim;* but hinting at the oral and written Torahs), and her "neck in chains of gold" (saying *ḥaruzim,* but alluding to the process of linking the words of Scripture).[23] Indeed, this passage even seems to reveal something of the spiritual eros that animates midrashic exegesis—an eros in which the Bride (Torah) is adorned by her rabbinic lovers through re-citations of her very essence (the words) in endless combinations.

Now if all interpreters may be compared to Ben Azzai, let us exemplify the point through a teaching of Rabbi Berekhiah, who linked the opaque phrase "To the leader: [concerning] *'al mut la-ben*" in Psalm 9:1 to the words of Kohelet in Ecclesiastes 3:11. In this way, he allowed the two passages to interact and clarify each other reciprocally. Thus, in the course of a gnomic maxim, Kohelet said that God created each thing for its proper time, "and even put the world [*ha-'olam*] in their hearts [*be-libbam*]." Reading *ha-'olam* in the second passage as *ha-'elem* ("the youth"), Rabbi Berekhiah re-read Ecclesiastes to mean that God has even put fathers' "love for their children [*'olelim*] in their hearts." By so doing, he thereby hinted that David's words in the Psalm should also be understood in this manner (that is: he construed *'al mut la-ben* as *'alamut [be-]libban,* "youth in their hearts"'). Others, however, preferred to interpret Kohelet as meaning that God "concealed [*he-'elim*] the day of death [*mavet*] and judgment from His creatures"—and thus likewise the words of David. That is, Psalm 9:1 is now midrashically interpreted to mean that "God [the Leader] hid [*he-'elim*] the time of [*'al*] death [*mavet*] from the hearts [*libban*] of His creatures [*la-ben,* "the son," construed as a collective noun]."[24]

And to whom may Rabbi Berekhiah be compared?—to yet other

teachers who interpreted David's words to refer to how God cleanses *(melabben)* the hidden (meaning unintentional) sins *(ha-'alumot)* that His sons *(ben)* commit on the Day of Atonement; or with respect to the death *('al ha-mavet)* decreed by God against Israel (His firstborn son, *ben*; citing Exod. 4:24) for his sins, though God will cleanse him *(malbino)* of all iniquity when he (the son, Israel) returns in true repentance. Other sages added "another thing" when they suggested that these words even taught how God's own heart *(libbo)* was cleansed of retributive anger with the atoning death of His sinning sons (who failed to repent in their lifetime).[25]

Surely in all these ways and a myriad more the words of Scripture are renewed through new correlations, redivision, and repointing. And surely this process also reanimates the consonants of Scripture with new sounds and senses drawn from like-minded texts. The enchainments thus dramatize the unity of Scripture and *reveal it as a rabbinic work*. Indeed, this is ultimately the great achievement of midrashic exegesis. For in endless variations the sages show that the Written Text is one interconnected instruction; and that all the values of rabbinic Oral Tradition (as, for example here, divine providence and justice, sin and judgment, or repentance by deed or death) are present in it, explicitly or implicitly. By activating the *langue* of Scripture, rabbinic *paroles* keep the fiery speech of Sinai aflame. What is more: re-animated by human breath, the old words rejoice—and not least because they reveal the "laughing face" of God (*Pesiqta de-Rav Kahana* 12.25).

The messianic dimension inherent in the midrashic desire to reveal the fullness of the divine *langue* leads to a last question. Is there a limit to this endeavor?

The answer is threefold, at least. First and foremost are the limitations imposed by spiritual or intellectual capacity. They may be inferred from Rabbi Akiba's reply to Rabbi Ishmael's query as to how his (Akiba's) hermeneutical techniques could help explain the meaning of the seemingly senseless accusative particles in Genesis 1:1 (since by his own principles and tradition such elements could not be interpreted).[26] R. Akiba answered by way of Deuteronomy 32:47, "For it [Scripture] is not something [*davar*] of little worth [*req*] for you [*mikkem*]"—meaning, as he pointedly says, that "if it is senseless [*req*], it is your fault [*mikkem*, lit., "from you"]—for you do not [therefore] know how to interpret"! By cleverly playing on the noun *davar* as the "word" of Scripture, and semantically restructuring the clause, R. Akiba hermeneutically rebukes his interlocutor and meta-communicates the truth that the horizon of interpretation may be extended both by sufficient exegetical techniques and by the individual's ability to use them. The limits of the *langue* are determined by the *parole* of the interpreter.

Another limitation to Midrash aims to thwart mean-spirited and potentially anarchic readings of Scripture. The first of these two is what the sages call *haggadot shel dofi,* midrashic interpretations which are designed to malign or mock the teachings or teachers of Scripture (*b. Sanhedrin* 99b).[27] Jeroboam is the paradigmatic offender, and his like are silenced lest they use the tradition to traduce it. At the other extreme are those who show little self-restraint for their position as teachers, or those who push theology to its public limits. One thinks here of Rabbi Pappius, whose exegeses hang on gnostic horns. Rabbi Akiba senses the danger, and issues a recurrent command of "Enough!" *(dayyeka).*[28] The fact that other times and teachers might regard the interpretations as acceptable is irrelevant. The principle of *dayyeka* (like the danger of *dofi*) is always a matter for social regulation.

A final consideration may be offered here by way of conclusion—and that is the limits which sin places on faithful interpretation. Indeed, this factor subverts the very possibility of Midrash. Let us learn: when the Holy One, blessed be He, gave the tablets to Moses on Sinai, their physical weight was lightened because of the holy letters inscribed thereon. Only thus could Moses bear their heavenly weight—until the moment the people sinned before the Golden Calf. Descending with God's Law to see the people's apostasy, the letters flew off the tablets and ascended to their heavenly source. The stones were then too heavy for Moses to bear, and they fell from his hands to the earth, as it is written, "And he cast the tablets from his hands, and he broke them at the base of the mountain" (Exodus 32:19).[29]

For the sages, the fiery words of God's speech transform the world of nature—elevating it towards their supernatural source. But sin confronts this truth with earthly instinct, and the holy letters fly upward. Their loss is not only the end of revelation, but of all the traditions to come. One may suspect that this myth was told with a shudder.

2

"The Holy One Sits and Roars": Mythopoesis and Midrashic Imagination

Among the historical religions, classical Judaism is often characterized by its apparent break with mythology. Indeed, if one nostrum is widely accepted it is just this: that the foundation document of Judaism, the Hebrew Bible, reflects a primary rupture with the world of myth and mythmaking; and that this break has widened appreciably over the centuries. But such assessments are often based on self-serving assumptions and the restriction of admissible evidence to only part of the stream of tradition. Thus it is argued that the creation account in Genesis 1, with its schematic structure and implied critique of Near Eastern theomachies, is telling proof of the nonmythological temper of ancient Israel. I am not convinced. Priestly theologies of 25 lines or so may have their say; but it is a long way from this to a denial of the mythic imagination overall. Let us simply call to mind that biblical Scriptures are replete with instances of mythic drama which strongly resembles the ancient battle between Marduk and Tiamat (from Mesopotamia) or Ba'al and Yam (their Canaanite counterparts); and that this monotheistic myth remained vibrant throughout the Babylonian exile and long thereafter.[1] Indeed it is quite possible to trace the continuity of biblical accounts of a mythic strife at *Urzeit* and *Endzeit* (like Isa. 51:9—11 and 27:1, respectively) well into rabbinic times, and to observe their new variations in the Pseudepigrapha and Midrash. The anthology of mythic theomachies preserved in the Babylonian Talmud (*b. Baba Bathra* 74b–75a) is a striking case in point.[2] Assorted details now known from ancient Ugarit resurface in this literary source long after their eclipse or obfuscation in the intervening biblical tradition.[3] Other aspects of our mythic theme recur in the liturgical prayers of the great synagogue poet, Eleazar be-Rabbi Qallir;[4] and some of these survive into the high Middle Ages. Thus Qallir's depiction of Leviathan in a curved form, with the tip of his tail in his mouth,[5] takes on iconographic form in the so-called Bird's Head Haggadah.[6] The idea that this primordial serpent encircles with his body the sea that surrounds the world is also preserved in the biblical commentary of Rabbi David Kimḥi (*ad* Isa. 27:1).[7]

Now the historian of religion is understandably intrigued by this extensive evidence of mythic transformation, and particularly by the creativity of its monotheistic reception. Such a multimillennial accommodation to mythic types certainly changes the appearance of rabbinic culture for even the most wary. But one must go further, and wonder whether this panorama captures either the more primary or most characteristic aspects of rabbinic mythmaking. By this I mean, first, the movement from natural experience to its mythic dramatization; and then, as a further feature, the mythological reformulation of a received linguistic tradition through exegesis. To explain this more fully, let me briefly review the theories of mythic origins proposed by Johann Gottfried Herder and Max Müller.

As is well known, Max Müller championed the philological origins of myth. For him, language is the primary process from which myth is derived. Or to put it slightly differently: mythic formulations have their roots in concrete metaphors which have decayed or are misconstrued. And since all linguistic denotation is fundamentally ambiguous, the inevitable "paronymia" of words lies at the source of mythology. Why, for example, are men and stones related in the Greek myth of Deucalion and Pyrrha? Is it not because the words *laoi* and *laas* are assonant? And is not the transformation of Daphne into a laurel to escape the clutches of Apollo clarified when we learn that the word *daphne* means "laurel" in Greek, and that this word can be traced to a Sanskrit cognate meaning the redness of dawn? "Mythology is inevitable," concludes Müller; "it is an inherent necessity of language." And further, "[m]ythology, in the highest sense, is the power exercised by language on thought in every possible sphere of activity."[8]

How different is the romantic perspective of Johann Herder, for whom mythology is primary and language its faded echo. In his prize essay on the origin of speech, he wrote: "As all nature sounds, so to Man, creature of sense, nothing could seem more natural than that it lives, and speaks, and acts . . . The driving storm, the gentle zephyr, the clear fountain and the mighty ocean—their whole mythology lies in those treasure troves, in *verbis* and *nominibus* of the ancient languages; and the earliest dictionary was thus a sounding pantheon."[9] In Herder's view, language itself is a "faded mythology" and not its source; for we first experience the sounds of the "stirring godhead" and only then tell its story.

But for all the pleasure we derive on hearing these mythic genealogies, neither moves us as a comprehensive theory. And yet even if we grant that myth is not *au fond* a philological puzzle, may we not agree that, here and there, verbal assonances or details have inspired mythic narratives? This is no idle query, as it bears decisively on exegetical mythmaking found in Gnostic and rabbinic literature—where the mythological constructions regularly turn on philological forms embedded in a received tradition. Conversely, even if we grant that myth is not, in all cases, the cultural record of the sounds of nature, are there not some cases where experiences of this sort have produced mythic features? And so, rather than try to mediate between Müller and Herder on the relative priority of nature and language as the ground of myth, I would rather regard each theory as a typical mode of mythopoesis. The one case allows us to focus on the primary processes of nature which are heard and reported as the acts of the gods; the other, more philological perspective, starts with a given philological tradition and transforms its polysemy into mythic exploits. Both theories help reveal important modes of the rabbinic mythic imagination. To order our attention I shall focus upon a compelling feature of the larger rabbinic motif of divine sorrow—the roar of God. By this means we shall work our way from nature to myth, and from the mythopoeic exegesis of Scripture in ancient Midrash to the mythic transformations of medieval Jewish mysticism.

Let us begin with a striking *sugya,* or literary unit, found in the Babylonian Talmud (*b. Berakhot* 59a). The context is an elucidation of a mishnaic teaching that rules as follows: "On [the occasion when one experiences] comets, or *zeva'ot*, or lightning, or thunder, or violent storms, one says—'Blessed [is He] whose power and might fill the world'" (*M. Berakhot* IX.2). For later tradition, the word *zeva'ot* is a problem; for while it occurs several times in the Bible (see Isa. 28:19), it seems to mean nothing more than "dismay" or some form of personal "quaking." No clear relation to natural wonders is evident; hence the following discussion:

> What does *zeva'ot* mean? Rav Qaṭina said: "earthquake" [*guha'*]. Once Rav Qaṭina was on a trip and passed the home of a necromancer when an earthquake shook. He mused [aloud]: "Might this necromancer know the meaning of this quake?" The latter then called out: "Qaṭina, Qaṭina! Don't you know [what it is]? Whenever the Holy One, blessed be He, remembers His children who are in distress among the nations of the world, two drops fall from His eyes into the Great Sea and His voice resounds from one end of the world to the other—and that is the earthquake." Rav Qaṭina responded: "[This] necromancer and his explanation are deceitful, for were he correct I would have expected a double tremor [*guha' guha'*]; but this did not occur." But the real reason why Qaṭina did not acknowledge this interpretation was to prevent the people from being led astray after the necromancer. [Thus] Rav Qaṭina explained [the phenomenon as]: "God clapping His hands," as is stated [in Scripture], "I, too, shall clap My hands together and abate My anger" {Ezek. 21:22]. Rabbi Nathan explained [it as]: "God groaning," as is stated, "I shall abate My fury against them and be calm" [Ezek. 5:13]. And our sages have explained [it as] "God stamping in the heavens," as is stated, "a shout echoes throughout the earth like the sound of those who trample the vats" [Jer. 25:30]. Rav Aḥa bar Ya'akov [also] explained [it as] "God squeezing His feet under His Throne of Glory," as is stated, "The heavens are My throne and the earth My footstool" [Isa. 66:1].

This remarkable pericope is composed of several layers of tradition. At the outset, a lexical observation on the meaning of *zeva'ot* is proposed and reinforced by an episodic encounter between Rav Qaṭina and a necromancer, who interprets the earthquake as a sign of divine sorrow for the travail of Israel. This semiotic explanation is then rejected by the sage, Rav Qaṭina, in order not to encourage a following for the mantic. After this comes a variety of other rabbinical opinions, collected along with prooftexts from Scripture. It would seem that all of the suggestions attempt to account for the earth tremor, and that virtually all of them do so on the basis of an accompanying sound made by God: there is handclapping, foot-stamping, and groaning, among others. From this perspective, one may suspect that the gist of the necromancer's explanation is that it was the roaring of God in sorrow that produced the quake, not the two tears, but it was the latter that R. Qaṭina picked on to cavil with the mantic's proposal, as the Talmudic redactor already hints. Indeed, I would even suggest that the basis of the necromancer's explanation of the roaring voice as the divine cause of earthquakes lies in a folk etymology of the strange word *guha'*. It will suffice here merely to recall that this Aramaic noun derives from the monosyllabic **g(u)*, which means "voice" in Ugaritic.[10] The Hebrew verb *hagah* and noun *hegeh* mean "to emit a sound" (Ps. 1:2) and "groan" (Ezek. 2:10), respectively.[11]

But let us not allow lexicography to obscure what is so remarkable about our passage from the viewpoint of religion, and that is that a highly rational mishnah, which collects various *mysteria tremenda* of nature and proposes a fixed blessing praising each *tremendum* of God, is explained by later sages and the necromancer in purely mythic terms. That is, earth tremors are presented as the terrestrial expression of a divine pathos. In this way, irrational terrors in the natural world are domesticated and rationalized. Note further that, for all the historical pathos implied in the necromancer's interpretation, he does not invoke a biblical prooftext. This fact underscores the primary aspect of the mantic's mythopoesis, and suggests that the proofs accompanying the views of R. Qaṭina and company are the later addition of a redactor. Indeed, it is just his voice that dominates the organizational structure of the pericope and provides the hermeneutical rationale for why Rav Qaṭina rejected the necromancer's reading of the signs of nature.

Taking these several strata of Talmudic evidence into account, I would reconstruct the following ideal-typical stages of mythic progression. In the beginning there were the unnamed and unknowable terrors of nature, which were subsequently mythicized as divine acts. The motivation ascribed to such behavior could be entirely ahistorical, as in Rav Aḥa's view that earthquakes are the effect of God squeezing His feet under His Throne; or it could be passionately historical, as in the view of the necromancer. At a later point, these diverse mythic episodes were linked to scriptural proofs. This development gave the human dictums traditional authority, and set the stage for subsequent mythicizations of the sacred text. If the mythopoesis of the necromancer invokes the shade of Herder, mythical elaborations of the literary tradition conjure with the wand of Max Müller.

To appreciate this development, let us turn back to folio 3a in the same tractate. We find here a more exegetical use of the scriptural text than those noted earlier. Once again the Talmudic discussion is halakhic; but now the topic is the mishnaic dictum of the same Rabbi Eliezer who said that one is permitted to recite the credal prayer of *Shema'* (Deut. 6:4) in the evening until the conclusion of the first watch. The later sages queried whether Rabbi Eliezer had three or four evening watches in mind, and thus whether the *terminus ad quem* of the first was four or three hours. The ensuing speculation is terminated by quoting from a non-mishnaic dictum of Rabbi Eliezer, who said: "The night consists of three watches, and during each and every watch the Holy One, blessed be He, sits and roars like a lion, as is stated [in Scripture]: 'The Lord roars [*yish'ag*] from on high, and thunders from His holy dwelling; yea! He roars mightily [*sha'og yish'ag*] against [*'al*] His habitation' [Jer. 25:30]."

From the prooftext cited in conclusion, it is clear that the mythic pronouncement recited at the beginning is based on the threefold repetition of the verbal stem *sha'ag*, "to roar" in the Jeremian prooftext; and it is just this hermeneutical procedure which marks the difference between the myth of Rabbi Eliezer and that of the necromancer, who brings no prooftext and does not specify the time or times of divine pathos. He merely states that "when" or "whenever" the Holy One thinks of His suffering people He cries and groans. One may suppose that just this is the core moteme of the myth, and that the temporal specificity of Rabbi Eliezer is the result of the odd conjunction between a myth (of the divine voice) and a halakhic rule (concerning the nightly watches). It may be added that whereas the necromancer's version is historically unspecific, Rabbi Eliezer's teaching invokes the reality after 70 C.E., when the Temple was destroyed. This is done hermeneutically, by a bold rereading of Jeremiah 25:30. In its ancient context, this oracle is a prophecy of doom by the God of Israel who roars "from on high . . . against [*'al*] His habitation [*navehu*] . . . against all the dwellers of the earth." It might be suggested that Jeremiah has himself mythicized this doom topos, since in Amos 1:2 the prophet announces that the Lord roars from Zion and Jerusalem—not from His heavenly dwelling—and "the pastureland [*ne'ot*] of the shepherds shall lie waste."[12] But Rabbi Eliezer has gone further. For him, the Lord does not roar in anger (against the nations) but in anguish "over" or "because of [*'al*] His [destroyed earthly] abode [that is, Temple, *navehu*]."[13]

By so transforming the particle *'al* from a prepositional ("against") to an etiological ("because of") sense, and by giving the pastoral word *naveh* a sacral focus, Rabbi Eliezer has dramatically shifted the oracle from prophecy to pathos—from a proclamation of doom to a divine lament evoked by the fate of Israel and the Temple. The deeper cultural dimension of the halakhic discussion is therewith underscored. With the Temple in ruins, the sages no longer recall the correct periods of nocturnal priestly watches in order to fix the upper time limit for reciting the *Shema'* in the evening. This forgotten tradition is then reconstructed by the mythic teaching of Rabbi Eliezer. It is thus not interpretation which saves the myth, as in the well-known passage from Plato's *Phaedrus* (229D ff.), but rather a mythic interpretation which saves history—and gives it new life.

Later tradition pondered the divine roar. In what appears to be an explication of Rabbi Eliezer's myth, the Talmud goes on to note that "Rav Yitzḥak b. Shemuel taught in the name of Rav: "The night is composed of three watches, and over each watch the Holy One, blessed be He, sits and roars like a lion, and says, 'Alas for the children [*'oy la-banim;* namely, Israel], on account of whose sins I destroyed My Temple, burnt My Shrine and exiled them among the nations.'" You will note, first of all, that this version presupposes the prooftext from Jeremiah (with the threefold use of the verb *sha'ag*), but has elided it; and that the divine roar gives way to a statement of sympathy and theodicy. God at once avers the justice of His destructive acts and acknowledges its consequences. With this, we have moved considerably from the mythic act of divine sympathy which produces earth tremors *(zeva'ot)* "whenever" the memory of Israel's suffering recurs, to the routinization of divine pathos (expressed thrice daily) and a moralizing reflection. Both developments appreciably weaken the mythic dimension involved.

A further move in this direction is evident in the version of this *mythos* preserved in the name of Rabbi Yose. In this case, the lament "Alas for the children" *('oy la-banim)* is heard by a traveler who secretes himself in a ruin to pray. By contrast with Rabbi Eliezer's account, the voice here is not God's roar but a divine echo resounding like a cooing dove; and there is also no reference to either earth tremors or priestly watches. Nevertheless, the comment made to R. Yose by Elijah the prophet, that this cooing sound recurs thrice daily during the times of required prayer, does suggest that some mythicizing exegesis (presumably of Jer. 25:30) underlies this account as well—though it has lost its bite. A similar defanged mixture of myth and morality concludes the pericope, when Elijah goes on to say that "Whenever Israel enters synagogues or study houses and answers [the preceptor with the words] 'May His exalted Name be blessed,' the Holy One, blessed be He, moves His head from side to side and says, 'Happy is the king who is praised in his palace; so what [woe] then to a father who has exiled his children? and alas for the children [*'oy la-banim*] who have been exiled from their father's table!'"

An even stronger example of the theologization and moralization of the myth at hand is found in the Jerusalem Talmud (*Berakhot*, IX, hal. 2, 64a). Here, without any mythic fanfare, the query as to why *zeva'ot* occur is answered legalistically: because of the sin of improper handling of priestly donations.[14] This, it is said, resolves the scriptural contradiction at issue; though an appended opinion states that this is not the "core" of the matter. The old myth is saved by a new etiology of *zeva'ot*. We read: "Whenever the Holy One, blessed be He, looks [down] at the [Roman] theaters and circuses existing in safety, rest and tranquility, while His Sanctuary lies in ruin, He threatens to destroy His world, as [Scripture] says: 'He roars mightily over [*'al*] His Temple;' that is, because of [*bishviyl*] His Temple."[15] In this form, the prooftext from Jeremiah does not support any halakhic decision but provides another mythicizing explanation of the divine pathos which produces earthquakes. The lexical gloss is of considerable interest in this regard, since the explanation of *'al* by *bishviyl* makes it perfectly clear that the divine pathos is self-directed: God roars because of His own ruined Shrine, and not because of Israel's religious loss. Such a conclusion, clearly based on the prooftext from Jeremiah 25:30, suggests that we rethink the traditions of Rav and Rabbi Yose, in whose name we read that God cries out, "Alas for the children." To do so, we must turn to the medieval reception of our Talmudic myth by various Jews and Christians.

In comparing the different versions of God's roar collected in the Babylonian and Jerusalem Talmuds, we have observed a tendency to rationalize or moralize the *mythologoumenon* of earth tremors. I am even tempted to speak of a palpable trend towards demythologization—bearing in mind that the core mythic moteme here (the divine roar) is never directly delegitimized in any of the traditions. Such is not the case, however, among some latter-day readers of these rabbinic texts. For example, when Hai Gaon, the head of the Babylonian academy in Pumbedita in the early eleventh century, answered a responsum concerning the tears of God in *b. Berakhot* 59a, he explained that the depiction had no substance, but was merely "a figure of speech [*be-torat mashal*]."[16] Similarly, his contemporary in Kairouan, Rabbenu Ḥananel, commented on the same topos and asserted that its entire purport is "to demonstrate to Israel that the Holy One, blessed be He, has not abandoned them" and "to strengthen their hearts that they not despair of the redemption."[17] Not satisfied with explaining the figure, Ḥananel attacked the trope directly. "God forbid," he says, "[that the image refers to actual] tears from the eye, but rather [to] drops [that seemed] like tears." To this docetic rationalization he added the further caveat that there is also no groaning or clapping or kicking by God—but rather that "the Holy One, blessed be He, commands an angel" to do this, in each case. The author of the *'Arugat ha-Bosem* also transmits this position, and sums up the whole with the remark, "Everything [was done] by an angel."[18]

The Church Fathers were less inclined to literary legerdemain in these cases, as we can see from the comments of Petrus Alfonsi of Huesca, a Spanish contemporary of Hai and Ḥananel. In his *Dialogus* with a literary interlocutor, Moises the Jew, Petrus criticizes the "sages" for expounding the "prophets rather superficially" and for ascribing corporeality to God.[19] In sum, *"dicta sunt,"* he says, *"ad litteram solam exponere"*—the Jews expound Scripture in its most literal way.[20] For example,

> They say that once every day He weeps, and two tears drop from His eyes and flow into the Great Sea . . . This same weeping which they shamefully ascribe to God is, they say, because of the captivity of the Jews, and because of His sorrow they assert that three times a day He roars like a lion and shakes the Heavens with His feet like heels in a press, or emits a sound like a humming dove, and He moves His head from side to side, and says in a lamenting voice: "Alas for Me! Alas for Me! [*heu mihi, heu mihi*] that I have made My house into a desert and have burned My Temple, and exiled My children among the nations. Alas for the father who has exiled his children, and alas for the children [*heu filiis*] who have been exiled from their father's table!"[21]

This tradition is remarkable in several respects. Not least striking is that, in the very process of criticizing the myth-making of the Jews, Petrus has reworked the various teachings from *b. Berakhot* 3a and 59a into a continuous mythic discourse. By deleting the various tradents—from the necromancer and Rav Qaṭina to Rabbi Yose and the prophet Elijah—Petrus has paradoxically provided a myth of even greater force than that of the Talmudic anthology itself. Added to this is the literary-critical value of his comments; for one will easily notice that the divine lament here is "Woe to Me" *(heu mihi)* and not "Woe to the children because of whose sins I have destroyed My Temple." That is to say, Petrus has articulated a self-directed divine lament and not a theodicy; and it is just this divine reflexivity which appears to be the primary force of the mythicizing reinterpretation of Jeremiah 25:30. When God roars "over" His Temple, therefore, He laments to Himself "because of" its loss and destruction.

This mythic layer of divine pathos is thus literarily and phenomenologically separate from both the lament over children who have been exiled from their father's table and the rabbinic justification for earthquakes. Its authenticity is confirmed by an earlier, tenth-century Karaite polemic[22] in which Salmon ben Yeruḥim confronts his Rabbanite counterparts with their Talmudic "abominations."[23] He first refers to the mythos of God roaring thrice nightly, and then adds: "Rav Yitzḥak ben Shemuel ben Martha taught in the name of Rav: 'The night consists of three watches, [and] over each one the Holy One, blessed be He, sits in His Temple and cries for the exile and says, Alas for Me! [*'oy li*] for I have destroyed My Temple, and burnt My Shrine and exiled My children throughout every land.'"

On the basis of this evidence (confirmed by several manuscript sources)[24] and the Latin rendition of Petrus (taken over by Peter Venerabilis),[25] it stands to reason that we have recovered the original divine lament of our rabbinic mythos, and may confidently assume that *'oy li* ("Alas for Me") was subsequently changed to *'oy la-banim* ("Alas for the children") in the later versions of our received Talmud.[26] This change was either the result of a deliberate demythologization of the lament, or, as seems more likely, the direct result of an accommodation to Karaite criticisms. The reading "Alas for Me" is already mentioned in Al-Qirqisani's ninth-century polemical treatise *Kitab 'al-'Anwar* (The Book of Lights).[27]

It remains to add that the virulent anti-Rabbanite polemic in Salmon's *Sefer Milkhamot Ha-Shem* (The Book of the Wars of the Lord) puts Petrus' own Talmudic reception in a new light; for a comparison of the midrashic features criticized in chapter 14 of the *Sefer Milkhamot* with the pertinent sections of the *Dialogus* reveals a remarkable concordance between the two.[28] While it is, of course, entirely possible that the arguments of the convert Petrus of Huesca were drawn from the fanatical Benedictine monks from whom he received baptism (before Alfonso I of

Aragon) or even that similar religious attitudes may independently produce similar polemical agendas, it is also likely that the Karaites then in Spain served (directly or indirectly) as the tradents of this bill of theological particulars. In another parallel, later attacks on the Talmud by another convert, Abner of Burgos, were themselves indebted to a stock of arguments drawn up by Nicholas Donin. This Jewish apostate, who denounced the Talmud to Pope Gregory IX after being excommunicated by the French communities for denying the validity of the Oral Law, provided excerpts of it to the ecclesiastical tribunal for examination. As Yizhak Baer already observed, the arguments of the Christian inquisitors, when the Talmud was subsequently put on trial (in Paris, 1240) and condemned to be burned, "were substantially the same as those [used] by the Karaites."[29]

Let us now return to the original Talmudic reading *'oy li* ("Alas for Me") in *b. Berakhot* 3a, and give one more turn to the mythological wheel. The purpose is to provide a striking variation on our theme of divine lamentation (with tears) and earth tremors, and therewith a transition to its hypostatic form in the mystical mythology of the later Kabbalah. The place to begin is *Midrash Eikha Rabba, petiḥta'* 24.[30] In the course of a supplemental comment on Isaiah 22:12 ("My Lord God of Hosts summoned on that day to weeping and lamenting"), we read:

> When the Holy One, blessed be He, intended to destroy the Temple, He said: "As long as I am [present] in it [the Temple], the nations of the world cannot harm it; so I shall remove My [protective] eye from it and shall swear that I shall have no need of it until the endtime—and then the enemies shall come [in] and destroy it." Thereupon the Holy One, blessed be He, swore by His arm and put it behind Him [*heḥezirah le-'aḥorav*]; as it is written, "He withdrew [*heshiv 'aḥor*] His hand before [*lifnei*] the enemy" [Lam. 2:3]. At that moment, the enemies entered the Shrine and burnt it. Once it was burnt, the Holy One, blessed be He, said: "Once again I have no dwelling [place] on earth; [thus] I shall remove My *Shekhinah* from it and ascend to My first dwelling" . . . At that moment the Holy One, blessed be He, was crying and saying: "Alas for Me [*'oy li*], what have I done?! I have caused My *Shekhinah* to dwell below for Israel's sake; and now that they have sinned, I have returned to My first dwelling. Never indeed shall I be a mockery to the nations or a [subject of] derision to humans!"

In this allomorph of the lament motif in *b. Berakhot* 3a, the Holy One cries *'oy li* as an expression of despair over the destruction of the Temple and the consequent withdrawal of His *Shekhinah* from the earth. As in the Talmudic variant, the lament is a self-directed statement of loss—though here it is supported with an expression of divine pride and dignity. Another difference between our midrashic text and the tradition of Rav Yitzḥak (in *b. Berakhot* 3a) is that the lament here is a spontaneous outcry at the realization of the destruction, and not a near-liturgical recitation of woe thrice nightly. Indeed, in the *Eikha Rabba* passage the divine cry follows a deliberate decision to destroy—dramatically reinforced by an oath to withdraw the protective arm of the Lord. In this form the episode further accentuates the passive-aggressive divine act enunciated in Lamentations 2:3, though with one major difference. In the later text the biblical metaphor of withdrawn protection has been literalized and mythicized. The earthy consequence of this divine drama is doom and the ascension of the *Shekhinah* to the heavenly heights (from which it has gradually descended).[31]

In response to the burst of divine woe (*'oy li*), the supreme angel, Metatron, volunteers to cry in God's stead. This request is strongly rejected, and God invites the angels, with Jeremiah at their head, to view the destroyed Temple. At this sight, the Holy One again bursts into tears and cries: "Alas for Me [*'oy li*] because of My Abode!" Now God requests Jeremiah to invite the three Patriarchs and Moses to lament, "for they know how to cry." Thereupon, Moses leads the Patriarchs in tears and lamentation; "and when the Holy One, blessed be He, saw them He too turned to keening and crying, and said: "Alas [*'oy lo*] for the king who succeeded in his youth and failed in his old age." With this remarkable statement of self-deprecation, the pericope ends. As a divine testament to depleted authority, nothing like it occurs in midrashic literature. The obliquely worded cry *'oy lo* (literally, "Alas for him") recurs in all versions of the tradition. By contrast, the sheer pathos of the personal lament *'oy li* (twice) is omitted both in the parallel version of *Midrash Eikha Zuṭṭa* and in the *Yalquṭ Shimoni*, which depends upon it.[32]

Phenomenologically speaking, *petiḥta'* 24 of *Eikha Rabba* bears comparison with the pseudepigraphic composition 3 Enoch 48 A.[33] For if the former shows a significant step towards a mythic hypostatization of the divine arm in the context of divine lamentation, this process is all but complete in the Enochian passage. Here, God's arm is one of the cosmic mysteries in the seventh heaven (along with the source of snow and fire, the heavenly curtain, the holy Names, etc.) shown to Rabbi Ishmael by Metatron, his heavenly guide.

> Rabbi Ishmael said: Metatron said to me: "Come and I shall show you the right arm of the Omnipresent One *(maqom)*, which is thrust behind [Him] [*nishlaḥat le-'aḥor*] because of the destruction of the Temple. All manner of splendid lights shine from it; and by it 955 heavens were created. Even the *seraphim* and *ophanim* are not permitted to view it until the day of salvation comes."
>
> [So] I went with him; and he took me by the hand, bore me up on his wings and showed it [the arm] to me with all manner of praise, jubilation and psalm—[though] no mouth can [fully] speak its praise, nor any eye view it because of the extent of its greatness, splendor, glory, honor and beauty. Moreover, all the souls of the righteous who merit seeing the joy of Jerusalem stand beside it, praising it and entreating mercy—saying thrice daily: "Arise, arise! Put on strength, arm of the Lord" [Isa. 51:9]; as it is written, "He made His glorious arm go at the right arm of Moses" [Isa. 63:12]. At that moment, the right arm of the Omnipresent One would cry, and five rivers of tears flowed from its fingers into the Great Sea, making the whole world quake; as is written, "The earth will split apart, the earth will be rent in ruin; the earth will surely stagger like a drunkard and totter like a lean-to" (Isa. 24:19 f]—five times, corresponding to the five fingers of the great right arm.[34]

In its hypostatic splendor the arm of the Lord is a *mysterium tremendum*, a heavenly mystery in whose might is the salvation to come. Its centrality in the ultimate eschatological drama is indicated both by Rabbi Ishmael's comments and by the prayer of the righteous souls. Indeed, the salvific manifestation of the arm is the subject of the ensuing paragraphs which bring both this chapter and 3 Enoch as a whole to climactic conclusion.[35] As in the preceding *petiḥta'* from *Eikha Rabba*, the theme of the divine arm is dramatized here by a midrashic reading of Lam. 2:3—though in 3 Enoch its withdrawal is portrayed as a *post-factum* occultation of providential power (*mipnei ḥorban*, "because of the destruction"; not *mipnei 'oyev*, "because of the enemy['s advent]"). Moreover, in the Enoch passage, it is the thrice-daily evocation of the arm by the righteous which elicits tears. This liturgical ritual in the highest realms stands in stark contrast with the *ex eventu* mourning of God in the Midrash.

A final point of comparison lies in the lament topos in 3 Enoch, which is not a cry of woe but the silent flow of divine tears through the fingers of the glorious arm. Forming five streams of sorrow that fall into the Great Sea, these tears produce five earth tremors in a manner strikingly reminiscent of Rav Qaṭina's explanation of *guha'* in *b. Berakhot* 59a. In that passage God roared upon recalling the destruction of the Temple, and His tears fell into the Great Sea. No prooftexts were adduced by the necromancer in support of the divine roar, though we did see how the threefold repetition of the verb *sha'ag* ("roar") in Jeremiah 25:30 was used to support Rabbi Eliezer's teaching of the nightly watches in *b. Berakhot* 3a. With this in mind, we may observe that the prooftext from Isaiah 24:18–19 provides a similar scriptural support for the teaching of five tremors in 3 Enoch—since the noun *'eretz* ("land") recurs five times in that prophetic passage. This midrashic point has been obscured, somewhat, in the transmission of our apocalypse; for the biblical phrase *va-yir'ashu mosdei 'aretz* ("and the foundations of the earth will shake") from Isaiah 24:18b has been rendered here *u-mar'ishot 'et ha-'olam kulo* ("making the whole world quake")—deleting one instance of the word *'eretz* just before citing v. 19, and its fourfold repetition of that word.

With this hermeneutical refiguring of Lamentations 2:3 and the lament of God, we have moved from mythical Midrash (in *Eikha Rabba, petiḥta'* 24) towards a mythopoeic imagination which finds hypostatic realities encoded in Scripture (3 Enoch 48 A). Indeed, in this shifting upward of the scene of sorrow from a descriptive metaphor to mythic drama and mystic vision, there is a corresponding shift from the *historia sacra* of the Hebrew Bible to the *historia divina* of Midrash and apocalyptic literature.

An even more dramatic transformation of the myth of divine pathos is achieved by the medieval kabbalists. Their theosophical hermeneutics transpose the entire focus to the Godhead, so that all the scriptural references dealing with divine woe symbolize processes taking place within Divinity as a result of human sin. In this way, the sorrows of God mark complex diminishments of divine power due to the disruptions of earthly transgression; and the heavenly lamentations expressing grief over the loss of the "Sanctuary" indicate disasters in that symbolic gradation of the Godhead. History as we know it has thus been absorbed into a mystical symbology, and the ultimate narrative is the myth of God's inner Being.

In the book of *Zohar* (III. 74b), the combination of the biblical verse from Jeremiah and the lament features from the Talmud results in highly esoteric hermeneutics. Briefly, its content and character is this. Starting from the assumption that the biblical rule prohibiting illicit consanguinity has a secret sense ("You shall not uncover the nakedness of your father or the nakedness of your mother" [Lev. 18:7]), Rabbi Shim'on bar Yoḥai proceeds as follows.[36] He begins by citing the verse from Ezekiel 11:13, in which the prophet cries "Alas!" *('ahah)* over the threatened destruction of Israel. On the basis of the orthography of this cry *('ahah='aleph-he-he)*, we are taught that as a result of Israel's sins a profound division is effected in the supernal Godhead—symbolized by the divine Name YHVH, the Tetragram, *yod-he-vav-he*. For when Israel sins, the lower feminine gradation of the Godhead (the *Shekhinah*, symbolized by the second letter *he* in the Tetragram and in the word *'ahah*) is separated from the palace of the King (denominated as the Holy One, blessed be He, or *Tiferet*, and symbolized by the letter *vav* in the Tetragram). The result is that the upper feminine gradation (*Binah* [Understanding], symbolized by the first letter *he* in the Tetragram and in the word *'ahah*) cannot transmit the transcendental flow of blessing to the lower powers in the divine totality *(kol)*. This teaching of divine disaster is seconded by citing Jeremiah 25:30, "The Lord roars from on high and gives voice from His holy Shrine, He roars mightily over His *naveh*." Rabbi Shim'on explains the passage as follows: "'His *naveh*,'" precisely; which is the Matrona [the *Shekhinah*], and that is certain! And what does He say? 'Alas [*'oy*] that I have destroyed My Temple, etc.' 'My Temple,' [this being] the conjunction with the Matrona.'"

Let me gloss this hermeneutical process. For Rabbi Shim'on, the Hebrew Bible is not a product of ordinary language but the precipitate of divine Speech. This means that its exoteric laws and narrative are but an outer garment of sense, and that, in truth, the Torah is an esoteric teaching about the divine reality. Accordingly, the law against incest in the book of Leviticus contains a secret warning of the theosophical consequences of human sin, as do the aforementioned prophecies of Ezekiel and Jeremiah. Indeed, when properly decoded, the verbs and nouns of Scripture constitute allusions to hypostatic realities in the divine realm—where there is a King and a Queen [the Holy One and the *Shekhinah*], and a sacred marriage or union that can be disrupted by sin. In a similar way, the very letters of certain words (like *'ahah*) may symbolize the same theosophical truth. This helps us to understand the remainder of Rabbi Shim'on's teaching, which provides a mystical meaning to the content of God's roar (*'oy li,* "Alas for Me!") as stated in the original Talmudic tradition.

The ensuing explication begins with the mystical philology of the final two components of the cry *'oy* ["Alas"; written *'aleph-vav-yod*], the letters *vav* and *yod.* The esoteric excursus goes as follows:

> We have learned: When the King is separated from the Matrona, and blessings are not to be found, then He is called *vav-yod.* What is the meaning of this designation? It has been taught: The initial [letter] of the [divine gradation called] *Yesod* [Foundation] is a *yod,* since *Yesod* is a minuscule *vav* and the [gradation called the] Holy One, blessed be He [*Tiferet*] is a majuscule *vav,* above [it]; therefore, [this latter *vav*] is written [out for pronuciation] *vav-vav,* [viz.] two *vavs* together; and the initial letter of *Yesod* is *yod.* Now when the Matrona is removed from the King, and the conjunction does not occur through the beginning of *Yesod* [i.e., *yod*], the upper *vav* [*Tiferet*] takes the beginning of *Yesod* [which is *yod*], and draws it to itself, and then [the result] is *vay* [i.e., *vav-yod*]—*vay* [woe] for the totality, the upper and lower [gradations].

The issues involved in this alphabetical arcana require some explication. First, Rabbi Shim'on is expounding the meaning of the second two letters *(vav-yod)* of the divine lament *'oy* in *b. Berakhot* 3a. These letters combine to yield the reading *vay,* which, according to an ancient midrashic teaching based on the Greek lament word *vai,* means "alas."[37] Rabbi Shim'on integrates this tradition into his esoteric exegesis, and provides a mystical parallel to the cry of woe *'ahah* in Ezekiel 11:13. Whereas the letters *he-he* of that word symbolize the upper and lower feminine gradations of the Godhead (*Binah* and *Malkhut* [the *Shekhinah*]), as noted earlier, the letters *vav-yod* of the word *'oy* symbolize the two masculine gradations of *Tiferet* and *Yesod.* When there is harmony in the supernal realm, and a dynamic conjunction between the masculine and feminine potencies is in effect between the King *(Tiferet)* and his Queen *(Malkhut),* these two masculine potencies are normally symbolized by the letter *vav* (written *vav-vav*)—the first being understood as the majuscule form of it, the second as its minuscule version (since, orthographically, the *yod* is deemed a diminished *vav*). It is important to add here that this compound *vav* is symbolized by the letter *vav* of the Tetragram YHVH. However, when Israel sins, the sinfulness causes a disruption of the supernal conjunction marked by the divine Name. The result is that the lower female gradation (the Matrona-*Shekhinah*, symbolized by the final *he* of the Tetragram) is separated from her masculine consort (the King-*Tiferet;* symbolized by the *vav* of the Tetragram) and he withdraws from her. In this situation, the supernal gradation of *Yesod* (the virile element of the King) contracts from a minuscule *vav* to a *yod* and is drawn upward to the Holy One (the upper *vav*).[38] The subsequent combination of these two letters (*vav-yod* marks a profound disjunction within the divine totality, and is symbolized by the resultant word *vay,* "alas."

Rabbi Shim'on then goes on to wonder why the lamentation *'oy* (spelled *'aleph-vav-yod*) occurs in Jeremiah's teaching, and not its synonym *hoy* (spelled *he-vav-yod*). His explanation is that the word *hoy* is used "when the matter [involved] is dependent upon repentance and the people do not do so." On such occasions, the divine principle of Repentance, symbolized by the first *heh* of the Tetragram, draws the letters *vav* and *yod* to itself and the word *hoy* is the result. By contrast, when Israel does not repent, the King recedes into the divine hierarchy. He then becomes inaccesible to human prayer and is absorbed into the divine *absconditus* called *'eheyeh,* which draws the letters *vav* and *yod* to it. The result is the combination of the initial *'aleph* of the divine Name *'eheyeh* ("I shall be"; the divine self-nomination in Exod. 3:14) with the letters *vav* and *yod* of the Tetragram. This produces the more profound lament word *'oy.* It symbolizes both the loss of all hope in repentance and the fateful withdrawal of the flow of divine blessing from all vital conjuctions to a most recessive point in the divine mind.

The mystical hermeneutics of Rabbi Shim'on bar Yoḥai thus symbolize profound mythic dramas within the Godhead. Put graphically, the supernal union of the masculine and feminine gradations (*Tiferet* and *Malkhut*) is a scene of cosmic procreation that is disrupted when the child, Israel, disobeys the will of the divine parents and enacts improper liaisons on earth below. Such sin, in this case called "uncovering the nakedness of your father and mother" (the incest prohibition of Leviticus 18:17, cited at the outset of the teaching), produces an interruption of unity within the divine Being. This causes the female gradation (the Queen) to separate from her masculine consort and, correspondingly, for the masculine gradation (the King) to withdraw his virile potency from the blessed conjunction, so to speak. In this state of separation, the divine reality cannot be inseminated with blessing and is in a state of woe. Continued failure of the child to repent results in a more dire diminishment of the nurturant female potencies of the divine Being and a reabsorption of the vital fluids of divinity into the brain of the supernal Anthropos.

Through this mystical hermeneutics, the older *mythologoumena* of divine sorrow in classical Midrash have undergone a qualitative shift. A one-time historical event of sin, whose consequences are remembered by God with a groan of woe, is transformed in the *Zohar* into a recurrent cosmic drama in which the sins of Israel produce divine disaster. But for all that, three lines of continuity between the earlier and later exegetical phenomena can be traced. The first focuses on the ongoing correlation between myth and history; for what is striking about the midrashic and mystical features considered here is the recurrent connection between them. In all cases, historical sin has its reflection or correlation in the supernal realm. A two-tiered perspective is thus envisaged, whereby human acts variously effect a state of woe or lack in the divine. Put differently: (Israel's) history is not dissociated from meta-history; on the contrary, it is significantly valorized as its vital catalyst.

A second trajectory that may be traced between the mythic tropes of ancient Midrash and the dramas of Zoharic mysticism is the relationship between divine speech and mundane disaster; for whether the divine sound is a wordless roar of sorrow or an explicit cry of *'oy* (with historical or hypostatic significance), there are natural repercussions to God's cry. In one case, the roar results in earthquake; in another, divine despair signals doom and the diminishment of earthly blessing. These moments of disaster in the natural realm are signs of a supernatural response to human events. Irregularities in the world of nature are thus theologically interpreted as expressions of divine sorrow.

A final observation serves to link the mythopoesis of classical Midrash with its cogeners in later mystical sources. As we have seen it, the rabbinic "work of myth" is a profound hermeneutical process. This holds whether one is dealing with the interpretation of natural processes as reflections of a divine drama; with the reworking of the Bible through creative philology and semantics; or with the revision of a midrash itself by means of hypostatic symbolism and linguistic permutations. To appreciate these exegetical procedures is thus to enter the inner-cultural realm of Jewish mythmaking and its protean forms of creativity. It has been the essential purpose of our discussion to sharpen this very point, and to suggest that, in no small measure, midrashic mythopoesis has been a mainspring of the concrete Jewish theological imagination.

3

The Great Dragon Battle and Talmudic Redaction

The "Great Dragon Battle" is an old story, widely diffused in various versions throughout the scriptures and mythologies of the world. The surviving records from the ancient Near East confirm this point, preserving interconnected evidence that spans three millennia. One of the earliest representations appears on a Mesopotamian seal cylinder from Tell Asmar in the Akkad dynasty (ca. 2400 B.C.E.), where two gods are in combat with a monster with seven heads (four are slain, three raise their ugly heads).[1] This same motif surfaces more than a millennium later in old Canaanite literary sources. According to one version, it is apparently Baal who slays the monster Lotan (Leviathan), "the mighty one of the seven heads" *(šlyṭ . d . šbʿt . rašm)*.[2] And a millennium and one-half after that, a visionary beheld the apocalyptic spectacle of a "great seven-headed monster" coming out of the sea (Rev. 12:3; 13:1).[3] In the light of this long-standing tradition, it is intriguing to recall a prophecy of Isaiah, in which he depicts a future event of redemption when the Lord "will raise His hand over the river [Euphrates] with a piercing wind and smite it into seven streams [*shiv'ah neḥalim*]" (Isa. 11:15). One suspects that this eighth-century (B.C.E.) prophet has adapted an ancient mythic image to new circumstances.

Echoes of a primordial battle against a sea monster reverberate in Hebrew Scriptures. One setting for synopses of this mythic event is in prologues to Psalms, where the speaker entreats God to manifest again His ancient powers over chaos and disorder. Greatly condensed, these appeals nevertheless portray with verbal vigor the results of an old theomachy. "It was You who drove back [the] Sea [*yam*] with your might, smashed the heads of Tannin-monsters [*rashei tanninim*] in the waters; [and] it was You who crushed the heads of Leviathan [*rashei livyatan*], leaving him for food for the dwellers of dry land" (Psalm 74:13–14). Reflecting a similar scene of strife, another psalmist also praises God for His rule over the swelling of the sea, and adds in praise how "You crushed [*dik'ita*] Rahab like a corpse, with Your mighty arm You scattered Your enemies" (Psalm 89:10–12).[4] With these words of remembrance and entreaty, the speakers do not so much historicize this myth as contextualize events of divine power. Ancient mythic themes have thus been thoroughly nativized into the context of Israelite monotheism.

This process of nativization is further expressed in literary figures, which allude to the myth to underscore feelings of victimization. Thus in Psalm 44:20 the speaker asserts abiding loyalty in God and His ways "though You have crushed us [*dikiytanu*] like the sea-monster [*tannim*],[5] and covered us with the darkness of death." Similarly, Job, in a paroxysm of grief, bemoans the overwhelming force of his destruction and says "Am I Yam (Sea) or Tannin, that You place a guard [*mishmar*] over me?" (Job 7:12). This allusion recalls just such a "guard" *(maṣṣaru)* placed over the slain sea monster Tiamat in the Babylonian creation epic *Enuma elish*, so that her waters might be contained (IV. 139–140).[6] Such ironic personalizations push metaphor to its limit, where the self identifies with old images of mythic suppression. Their pathos would make no sense if they were merely faded residues of ancient motifs.

The enormous impact of the old dragon story extends even further afield, surviving in diverse regions and times of late antiquity. One need only mention the monumental portrayal of the battle motif on the Temple of Bel at Palmyra in the first centuries of the common era,[7] or the reference to the defeat of "Leviathan the dragon" *(levyatan tenina')* in Jewish magic bowls from the Babylonian city of Nippur several centuries later,[8] to realize the vibrancy of the motif in religious consciousness long after the official end of the Babylonian academies and temples. Indeed, remnants of the Babylonian creation epic were similarly preserved elsewhere in antiquity. One Greek version of a portion of the theogony is found in a Neo-Platonic treatise entitled *Difficulties and Solutions of First Principles* by Damascius (b. ca. 480 C.E.);[9] in another, an account by the Babylonian priest Berossus (originally published around 275 B.C.E.) was transmitted via Alexandor Polyhistor (first century B.C.E.) and the Church historian Eusebius (ca. 340 C.E.), and preserved in the early

Middle Ages through the agency of an eighth-century monk in Constantinople named Synkellos.[10]

Given this range of evidence, it is hardly a surprise to find diverse mentions of the dragon battle reported and commented on in the Babylonian Talmud (fifth century C.E.). What is rather unexpected is the form these traditions take. On first view, one is inclined to suppose that the cluster of these traditions in *b. Baba Bathra* 74b–75a is just an appendix to the series of (primarily) fantastic fish tales told by Rabbah bar Bar Ḥana (73a–74b)—tales of rich and amusing color, with motifs reminiscent of the later tales of Sinbad the Sailor. But this common perception fades on closer examination, when one attends to details of theme, order, and style. What emerges is no casual collection of traditions but a coherent anthology that has all the characteristics of a new myth. Indeed, the scholastic redaction has constructed from its mythic fund a living *rabbinic myth,* a cultural palimpsest of ancient motifs and contemporary ideals. To appreciate this point, the traditions are presented here as a literary whole (with paragraphing and enumeration added).

> "And God created the great sea-monsters [*tanninim*]" [Gen. 1:21]. Here [in Babylon] they translated: the sea-gazelles. Rabbi Yoḥanan said: This refers to Leviathan the slant serpent and Leviathan the twisting serpent, as it says: "On that day the Lord will punish with his harsh [and great and strong] sword [Leviathan the slant serpent and Leviathan the twisting serpent]" [Isa. 27:1]. ([Mnemonic:] 'All,' 'Time,' 'Jordan')
> *I.* Rav Yehuda said in the name of Rav: All that the Holy One, blessed be He, created in His world He created male and female. Even Leviathan the slant serpent and Leviathan the twisting serpent he created male and female; and had they mated one with the other they would have destroyed the whole world. [So] what did the Holy One, blessed be He, do? He castrated the male and killed the female preserving her in salt for the righteous in the world to come; as it is said: "And He will slay the dragon [*tannin*] in the sea" [Isa. 27:1]. And also "Behemoth on a thousand hills" [Ps. 50:10] He created male and female; and had they mated with one another they would have destroyed the whole world. [So] what did the Holy One, blessed be He, do? He castrated the male and cooled the female and preserved her for the righteous in the world to come; as it is said: "Behold, his strength is in his loins" [Job 40:16]—this refers to the male, "and his force is in the muscles of his belly" [*ib.*]—this refers to the female.
> —There also, [in the case of Leviathan], He should have castrated the

male and cooled the female; [so why did He kill her]?—Fish are dissolute. Why [then] did He not do the opposite [and kill the male but preserve the female]?—If you want, say: A salted female [fish] is tastier; or, alternatively, say: Because it is written: "There is Leviathan whom You have created to sport with" [Ps. 104:26]; and with a female this is not proper. Then here also [regarding Behemoth] He should have preserved the female in salt.—Salted fish is tasty; salted meat is not.

II. And Rav Yehuda said [further] in the name of Rav: When the Holy One, blessed by He, wished to create the world, He said to the Prince of [the] Sea *(Yam)*: "Open your mouth and swallow all the waters in the world." He said to Him: "Master of the world, it is enough that I stay with my own [kind]." Immediately, He kicked him with His foot and killed him; as it is said: "With His power He stilled Sea *(Yam)* and with His skill He smote Rahab" [Job 26:12].

—Rav Yitzḥak said: From this we infer that the name of the Prince of [the] Sea is Rahab; and had the waters not covered him no creature could have stood his [foul] odor, as it is said: "They shall do neither harm nor hurt on all My holy mountain, etc., as the waters cover the sea" [Isa. 11:9]. Do not read "cover the sea [*la-yam*]" but "cover the Prince of [the] Sea."

III. And Rav Yehuda said [further] in the name of Rav: The Jordan issues from the cave of Paneas. It has also been taught: The Jordan issues from the cave of Paneas and passes through the sea of Sibkhay and the sea of Tiberias and rolls down in the Great Sea and on until it reaches the mouth of Leviathan, as it says: "He is confident because the Jordan rushes into his mouth" [Job 40:23].—Raba bar 'Ulla objected: This [verse] is written of "Behemoth on a thousand hills"!—Rather [understand it thus] said R. Abba b. 'Ulla: When is "Behemoth on a thousand hills" "confident"?—When the Jordan rushes into the mouth of Leviathan. ([Mnemonic:] 'Seas' 'Gabriel' 'Hungry')

IV. When Rav Dimi came, he said in the name of Rabbi Yoḥanan: What [means] that which is written: "For He has founded it upon the seas and established it upon the rivers" [Ps. 24:2]?—These are the seven seas and four rivers which surround the land of Israel. And these are the seven seas: The sea of Tiberias, the sea of Sodom, the sea of Ḥelat, the sea of Ḥilta', the sea of Sibkhay, and the Great Sea. And these are the four rivers: the Jordan, the Jarmuk, the Keramyon, and Pigah.

V. When Rav Dimi came, he said in the name of Rabbi Yonatan: In the future Gabriel will arrange a hunt of Leviathan; as it is said: "Can you draw out Leviathan with a fish hook, or suppress his tongue with a rope?" [Job 40:25]. And if the Holy One, blessed be He, does not help

him, he will be unable to prevail against him; as it is said: "Only his Maker can draw the sword against him" [Job 40:19].
VI. When Rav Dimi came, he said in the name of Rabbi Yoḥanan: When Leviathan is hungry he emits [fiery] breath from his mouth and causes all the waters of the deep to boil; as it is said: "He makes the deep boil like a cauldron" [Job 41:23]. And if he did not put his head into the Garden of Eden, no creature could stand his [foul] odor; as it is said: "He makes the sea like a spiced jar" [*ib.*]. And when he [Leviathan] is thirsty he makes many furrows in the sea; as it says: "He makes a path shine after him" [Job 41:24].
—Rav Aḥa bar Ya'akov said: The deep does not return to its strength until [after] seventy years; as it is said: "One thinks the deep to be hoary" [*ib.*], and hoary age is not [attained at] less than seventy years.
VII. Rabbah said in the name of Rabbi Yoḥanan: In the future, the Holy One, blessed be He, will make a banquet for the righteous from the flesh of Leviathan; as it is said: "The associates [*ḥabarim*] will make a banquet [*yikhru*] of it" [Job 40:30]. *Keirah* must mean banquet; as it is said: "And he prepared [*va-yikhreh*] for them a great banquet [*keirah*], and they ate and drank" [2 Kings. 6:23]. Associates [*ḥabarim*] must mean scholars; as it is said: "You who dwells in the gardens, the companions [*ḥaverim*] hearken to your voice; cause me to hear it" [Songs 8:13]. The remainder [of Leviathan] will be distributed and sold in the markets of Jerusalem; as it is said: "They will divide it among the *kena'anim* [Job 40:30]. And *kena'anim* must mean traders, as it is said: "As for *kena'an,* the scales of deceit are in his hand, he loves to oppress" [Hos. 12:8].—And if you wish you learn it from the following: "Whose merchants are princes, [and] whose traders [*kena'aneha*] are the honorable of the earth" [Isa. 23:8].
VIII. Rabbah said in the name of Rabbi Yoḥanan: In the future, the Holy One, blessed be He, will make a tabernacle [*sukkah*] for the righteous from the skin of Leviathan; as it is said: "Can you fill his skin with *sukkot* [tabernacles; lit., darts]?" [Job 40:31]. If one is worthy, a tabernacle is made for him; if he is not worthy [of this] a covering [*tziltzel*] is made for him; as it is said: "And his head with a *tziltzel*" [*ib.*]. If one is worthy [of this] a covering is made for him. [However,] if he is not worthy [even] of this] a necklace is made for him; as it is said, "And necklaces around your neck" [Prov. 1:9]. [And finally,] if he is not [even] worthy [of this] an amulet is made for him; as it is said: "And you will bind them for your maidens" [Job 40:29]. The remainder of [the skin of] Leviathan the Holy One, blessed be He, will spread upon the walls of Jerusalem, and its splendor will radiate from one end of the

world to the other; as it is said: "And nations shall walk by your light, and kings at the splendor of your shining" [Isa. 60:3].

In this long anthology of mythic traditions and interpretations, a remarkable cultural achievement is preserved—spanning several centuries and including sages from both Israel and Babylon. The structural character of the pericope is clear from the outset. The collection begins with reference to one of the primordial acts of God, cited from Genesis 1:21: "Elohim created the great sea monsters *(tanninim)*." At first it is the meaning of the word *tanninim* that draws comment. Two explanations are offered. Beginning with the Babylonian context ("here") in which the materials are collated and discussed, the redactor offers an Aramaic rendering ("sea-gazelles"). This is immediately followed by a report that Rabbi Yoḥanan had identified the creatures with the Leviathans, described as "slant" and "twisting" serpents in Isaiah 27:1.[11] This is itself a notable innovation, for it reads the parallelism in that passage (where one Leviathan is given a double attribution) as depicting *two* distinct dragons called Leviathan. Following this piece of exegesis, whose specific consequences are developed in the sequel, there follow eight separate groups of tradition, subdivided into two triads and one concluding pair. The first two triads are each preceded by mnemonic markers that indicate the three incipits of each group, thus specifying the fixed sequence of the unit. The final pair has no mnemonic marker. Moreover, as regards the coherence of each triad, the three units of each triad follow a set pattern of attributions and are formulated in a distinctive style. Interspersed throughout these main traditions are characteristic rabbinic discussions, proposing queries and alternate interpretations. Some of these are cited verbatim in a (reported) speaker's own name, while others are the words of the anonymous editor.

The first triad reports three mythic traditions, each with the introit: *'amar Rav Yehudah 'amar Rav,* "Rav Yehuda said in the name of Rav." The first item (*I*) states that "everything that the Holy One, blessed be He, created was created male and female" and goes on to speak specifically of Leviathan (citing the double reference in Isa 27:1) and Behemoth (on the basis of Job 40:16). We learn that had these monsters mated with their kind, "the entire world" would have been "destroyed" because of their unrestrained proliferation—and so God intervened. He castrated the male Leviathan and killed (and salted) the female; whereas with respect to the two Behemoths, the male was castrated and the female "cooled off."[12] In both cases, the female of the species was set aside "for the righteous in the world to come." In the meantime, God sported with the living male Leviathan—a matter not unseemly, as would have been the case had the female one been preserved (Ps. 104:26).

Tradition *I* thus presents a primordial event in which the Creator maimed and killed sea and land monsters for the sake of the well-being of the creation as a whole. This is presented as a unilateral divine act; no battle or resistance is mentioned. By contrast, the second myth of this group (*II*) states that when the Holy One "desired to create the world," he told the tutelary Prince of [the] Sea (whom Rav Yitzḥak identifies as the sea monster Rahab) to "swallow all the waters of the world." However, the latter rebelled against the "Master of the world" and was duly killed (as mentioned in Job 26:12) and also buried underwater, so that the stench of his corpse would not befoul the earth. An appropriate verse is therewith adduced, one presumed to contain an oblique reference to that event (Isa. 11:9). By further contrast, the third tradition (*III*) reported by Rav Yehuda gives a brief geographical notice that the Jordan river flows from its headwaters in the north. This Babylonian synopsis is forthwith given in a more expanded form, preserved in a Tannaitic tradition from the Land of Israel. In this account, the Jordan flows through several seas down to "the Great Sea," whence it flows "into the mouth of Leviathan." This mythic conclusion is adduced on the basis of Job 40:23 ("He is confident because the Jordan rushes forth to his mouth"); but Raba b. 'Ulla properly observed that the subject of Scripture here is Behemoth.[13] R. Abba b. 'Ulla then saves the day with a synthetic position (namely, that "*Behemoth* is confident because the Jordan rushes into the mouth of Leviathan").[14] With this reinterpretation of the pronouns the mythic allusion in Job 40:23 is restored and the problem put to rest.

The second triad of mythic traditions now follows, each with the same patterned introit: *ki 'ata' Rav Dimi 'amar Rabbi Yoḥanan/Yonatan,* "When Rav Dimi came [back from the land of Israel], he said in the name of Rabbi Yoḥanan/ Yonatan." In the printed edition of the Talmud, the first and third traditions are given in the name of Rabbi Yoḥanan, whereas other versions read either Rabbi Yoḥanan or Rabbi Yonatan throughout.[15] Presumably, two distinct chains of authority (or orthographically similar names) have been fused. Whatever the case, the content of the fourth tradition (*IV*) is a list of the seas and rivers "that surround the Land of

Israel," including the Jordan River and the Great Sea. In this context, such information seems merely to provide geographical specificity to the scriptural citation "for He (God) has founded it upon the seas and established it upon the rivers" (Ps. 24:2), where "it" is interpreted as referring to the Land of Israel ("the land" in v. 1 being construed nationally). But the plain sense of Scripture is otherwise: the "land" clearly means the "earth," and the verbs evoke primordial acts of creation. There is thus an old mythic allusion embedded in the citation, long since metaphorized by poetic or geographical perspectives.

The ensuing two traditions are more manifestly mythic. The fifth (*V*) has Rav Dimi say (in Rabbi Yonatan's name) that "in the future," the angel Gabriel will perform an animal hunt *(qenegi'a)* of Leviathan,[16] a gamesome challenge initiated by God's query, "Can you draw out Leviathan with a fish hook?" (Job 40:25), which the angel is not up to without divine aid (for "only his [Leviathan's] Maker can draw the sword after him," Job 40:19). This fantastic scene is followed by another tradition (*VI*) that dramatizes the awesome monstrosity of Leviathan and Behemoth. The Leviathan, when hungry, has such ferocious breath that "he makes the deep boil like a cauldron" (Job 41:23a); whereas Behemoth, when thirsty, gulps huge quantities of water and leaves a furrow-like "path" in his wake (v. 24a). Rav Dimi adds that Leviathan's breath is so smelly that if he had not put his head among the perfumes of Eden, his stench would overwhelm the world. Proof is found in a creative reading of Job 41:23b.[17] Rav Aḥa b. Ya'akov showed corresponding ingenuity in deducing from v. 24b that Behemoth's rampages leave a "hoary" *(seivah)* foam on the deep for seventy years (v. 24b)—since the traditional age of a greybeard *(seivah)* is in fact three-score and ten.[18]

Following the two triads is a final pair of traditions dealing with sea monsters. Each begins with the formulaic introit: *'amar Rabba 'amar Rabbi Yoḥanan,* "Rabba said in the name of Rabbi Yoḥanan," and each goes on to say that "the Holy One, blessed be He, will in time to come make" something "for the righteous from the" body "of Leviathan." According to the first of these traditions (*VII*), that something is a "banquet" from the monster's flesh.[19] Job 40:30 is used to prove the point through a clever midrashic reading of the phrase "traders shall traffic him" *(yikhru 'alav ḥabarim)* as "[the scholarly] companions [*ḥaverim*] shall eat of him [Leviathan]."[20] The paired variant (*VIII*) announces that the righteous will also be tabernacled by the skin of Leviathan, through an equally astonishing exegesis of Job 40:31a (for once the "darts [*suk-kot*]" of destruction are read as the *sukkot* [tabernacles] of the righteous, the aggressive image of the source yields the promise of eschatological reward). The less righteous enjoy lesser gifts, as various passages come to prove (from Job 40:31b and 29, respectively; and from Isa 60:3).[21] As earlier, the rabbinic myths are linked to Scripture in sundry ways.

But what manner of sea menagerie does our Talmudic text contain here? A casual glance through the traditions may see nothing special in the foregoing Leviathan myths, and even suppose that the sequence is haphazard. At most one could suppose that the eight dragon stories have been placed *after* the reference to the luminous eyes of a sea-monster in the deep (in *b. Baba Bathra* 74b) and *before* a medley of traditions that preserve sundry wonders that will accrue to the righteous "in the future." Seen thus, the myths are merely part of a chain of traditions—thematically clustered, to be sure, but without any overall coherence. But such a perspective misinterprets the details.

Viewed formally, the foregoing materials are clearly distinguished by three clusters of patterned introits that, in the case of the first two, even have a fixed, mnemonic sequence. These traditions are thus clearly marked off from the less patterned Rabbah bar Bar Ḥana fish tales on the one side and the thematic medley of heavenly rewards on the other. What is more, the beginning and end of the series have a thematic cohesion that distinguishes them from the whole setting: tradition *I* speaks of the preservation of the female Leviathan (and Behemoth) "for the righteous for the future" *(la-tzaddiqim le-'atid la-bo');*[22] and this is exactly what is fulfilled in traditions *VII* and *VIII*, where the flesh and skin of Leviathan are enjoyed by the righteous. The temporal sequence of the pericope thus has a mythic span—from *Urzeit* to *Endzeit*, where first things correspond to last things.

Once this overall framework is noticed, the role of Rabbi Yoḥanan's teaching prior to the collection of dragon traditions is clear. It will be recalled that he interpreted Genesis 1:21 ("Elohim created the great sea monsters") in the light of Isaiah 27:1, so that the primordial monsters *(tanninim)* of the first text are identified with the "slant" and "twisting" Leviathans mentioned in the other. There are two Leviathans here, not one dragon with two synonymous epithets. This interpretation of the identity of the monsters serves as a prologue to *I*, which cites that very passage in order to prove that God created the primeval sea monsters (and all other living things) "male and female."[23] What is more: in relation to the succeeding pericope as a whole, virtually every element of Isaiah 27:1 has a proleptic function. We may start with v. 1a: "On that day, YHWH will punish [*yifqod*], with His fierce, great, and mighty sword, Leviathan the elusive serpent—[and] Leviathan the twisting serpent." According to the plain sense of the passage, "that day" is the future time when the Lord will "punish" or requite the monster(s). But why? The prophet Isaiah does not say, and if he has some myth in mind, we do not know it from Scripture. The rabbis filled this mythic gap. For them, the passage was construed (midrashically) to mean that in the end of days God will "remember" *(yifqod)* the (female) monster that he had "appointed" or "accounted" for the righteous,[24] and will kill her consort with "his sword" *(ḥarbo)*. This very act is accomplished in our tradition *V*, when the male Leviathan is killed by God with "his sword" *(ḥarbo)* before the final banquet.

Isaiah 27:1b assumes an equally proleptic function in this editorial context. From Rabbi Yoḥanan's exegetical perspective, it is precisely the whole of v.1 that permits his identification of the *tanninim* ("monsters") in Genesis 1:21 with the Leviathans in Isaiah 27:1a, in that the phrase "He [God] will slay [*ve-harag*] the Dragon *(tannin)* in the sea" (v. 1b) occurs just after the punishment forecast against the Leviathans (v. 1a). Indeed, this narrative conjunction suggests that the two phrases are really one prophecy (doubly rendered by synonomous parallelism, with no special significance to be attached to the different dragon terms). But other mythic readings were possible. Disconnected from the first clause, the verb *ve-harag* need no longer double *yifqod* (with a future sense) but could be construed as a simple perfect and refer to a past event when God "killed" the *tannin*. Notably, this is precisely how Isaiah 27:1b is interpreted in tradition *I*, where this is cited as a separate phrase. From a redactional perspective, therefore, Rabbi Yoḥanan's opening prooftext anticipates both this (past) event and another one yet to come.

The patterning of traditions reviewed so far suggests that the overall scheme of the collection is temporal. This sense is reinforced by tradition *II*, which refers to a rebellion by the tutelary Prince of [the] Sea at the beginning of creation. This monster refused God's command to swallow the waters and was duly destroyed. The prooftext evokes an echo of this mythic death from elsewhere in Scripture—with due allowance for the slight softening of the mythic antagonist Sea *(Yam)* into the Prince of [the] Sea. Perhaps, at first glance, the very refusal of the Prince to obey explains the ensuing tradition (*III*) about Leviathan, who *does* swallow the waters. Viewed thus, the very next tradition (*IV*) seems merely to be a thematic doublet dealing with the identity of several streams of water. We shall reconsider this matter later on, but for now let us group traditions *III* and *IV* and observe the following overall sequence in our pericope: (*I*) the creation and mating of primordial monsters at the beginning of time, with one Leviathan killed and set aside for the future; (*II*) the primordial rebellion of the Prince of [the] Sea and his death; (*III* and *IV* seem merely to be parenthetical references to seas and rivers throughout the Land of Israel); (*V*) the future hunt of the living male Leviathan and his death; (*VI* provides parenthetical traditions about the monsters' gastric and gustatory vices); and (*VII–VIII*) portray the events dealing with the use of Leviathan's body by the righteous in the future to come.

Thus together with its movement from past to future, the pericope develops toward thematic fulfillment: the two Leviathans at the beginning are slain—the female at the outset; the male in due time, after the *qenegi'a.* Given this sequence linking the initial and final traditions, the double sea references in traditions *III* and *IV* seem interruptive. But they are placed in the center of this overall development, and their conjunction is deliberate. Indeed, the mnemonic markers manifest a clear editorial intention to join the two before resuming the opening thematics. Further reflection on this arrangement reveals the following chiastic structure.

A (*I*)	*Urzeit:* a Leviathan prepared for the righteous
B (*II*)	Death to the Sea dragon, in the beginning (Sea is buried under water because of its stench)
C (*III*)	The Jordan river and its flow
C′ (*IV*)	The seas and rivers of the Land of Israel
B′ (*V*)	Death to a Leviathan, in the future (*VI:* Leviathan's stinking breath gets perfumed)
A′ (*VII–VIII*)	*Endzeit:* the righteous partake of Leviathan

The linguistic and thematic connections of the outer frame (A/A′) were adduced earlier. We may now observe that the inner frame (B/B′) is similarly related. First and foremost are the two battle scenes—against the rebellious Sea and the wily, hard-to-catch Leviathan. God slays both monsters: the first by trampling it;[25] the second by the sword.[26] But subsidiary themes also link the units. For example, in the first part of *II* we read that "when" *(besha'ah she-)* God began to create the world, He commanded the Prince of [the] Sea to "open your mouth" *(petaḥ pikha)* and swallow the waters. The monster refused, was killed, and was left to rot. The second section adds that "were it not" *(ve'ilmale')* that God buried it in the sea, "no creature would have been able to withstand its stench" *('ein kol beriyah yekholah la-'amod be-reḥo)*. Correspondingly, at the other end, we read first in *V* about the *qenegi'a*, and that "were it not" *(ve'ilmale')* that God intervened, the appointed angelic slayer "would have been unable" *('ein yakhol lo)* to succeed. The ensuing tradition *VI* adds that "when" *(besha'ah she-)* Leviathan is thirsty, a foul odor comes out "from his mouth," and "were it not" *(ve'ilmale')* that his breath was perfumed with the spices of Eden, "no creature would have been able to withstand its stench" *('ein kol beriyah yekholah la-'amod be-reḥo)*. These terms and phrases are virtually restricted to this frame, so much so that the trace of some editorial hand seems assured.[27] Presumably, tradition *VI* is itself a fragment of the final battle between Leviathan and Behemoth known from other midrashic sources.[28] This episode is omitted in our pericope, except for the characterization of some of the vile features of the contenders. The Talmud has transmitted it here in language that echos and balances tradition *II*.

Before proceeding to consider the middlemost pair of the pericope, it is important to note the pattern of prooftexts found in our pericope. Quite remarkably, citations are drawn from Job 40:16 (a+b), 25, 29, 30 (a+b), 31 (a+b); and 41:23 (a+b), 24 (a+b). Evidently we have before us part of a lost Midrash on Job 40–41, reworked into a myth spanning *Urzeit* to *Endzeit*.[29] Taken together, the traditions encompassed by these passages are *I*, *III*, *V*, *VI*, *VII*, and *VIII*. This too is notable, for it will readily be observed that only traditions *II* and *IV* are unmarked by a phrase from the Book of Job. Most likely this is because neither deals with a dragon called Leviathan. In addition, one may even suggest that the theomachy (against the Sea) in *II* is not required by the themes of this cycle and that the river geography in *IV* is redundant, given the immediately preceding tradition about the Jordan. What, then, might account for the inclusion of traditions *II* and *IV* in our Talmudic myth?

Two considerations suggest an answer: the first is that tradition *II* is about a combat occurring after the initial tradition about the mating of primordial sea dragons and before the ensuing account of the Jordan's flow throughout the land; the second is that tradition *IV* links its reference to a total of 11 seas and rivers to Psalm 24:2 ("For He [YHWH] has established it [the earth] upon the seas . . ."). Now, in and of themselves, the foregoing thematics of *II* and *IV* seem merely to add two more "sea" traditions to a string of Leviathan myths. But a comparative perspective raises another possibility, namely, that the final redaction of our Talmudic pericope has been influenced by structural and topical features known from Mesopotamian sources.

The Babylonian creation account of *Enuma elish* is most pertinent in this regard. The myth begins with the mating of the primordial sea-gods Apsu and Tiamat and later Laḫmu and Laḫamu (I:1–10); the ensuing noisy commotion of the offspring led to a cycle of antagonisms and revenge that, in due course, pitted the divine Marduk against Tiamat and her horde (IV:20–32); the battle resulted in Marduk's victory (IV:33–120), and the splitting of Tiamat's watery hulk to establish the upper and lower realms, including the founding of water springs and releasing "the Tigris and Euphrates through her eyes" (V:54–55);[30] and finally, Marduk built a temple and convened a banquet for the gods (VI:67–75). With this background, our Talmudic traditions take on new coherence; for it is now evident that the sequence of mating waters, theomachy, and earthly order are part of an ancient mythic pattern. Indeed, in the light of the Babylonian myth, the placing of traditions about the waters that flow through the land *after* the slaying of the sea monster makes structural and thematic sense, and what is more, this very nexus explains the citation and use of Psalm 24:2. No mere praise, the statement that "[YHWH] has founded [the earth] *upon* the seas and established it *upon* the rivers" is now redolent with mythic implications.[31] One may even ponder whether the geographical notice of 11 seas and rivers mentioned alongside this prooftext is a mere gratuitous detail, since this is precisely the number of monsters who fight alongside Tiamat.[32] In any case, the overall redactional result is that traditions *I–IV* (death and the world order) + *VII–VIII* (booths and banquet) conform in structure and content to a celebrated and long-enduring mythic pattern from the ancient Near East. The mnemonic markers in the Talmud are thus more than an *aide-mémoire*. Rather, they impose the invariance of a specific mythic sequence on all future tradents. The inclusion (and position) of traditions *II* and *IV* was absolutely necessary to this end.

The tradents mentioned in the Talmudic pericope allow us to suggest further possibilities about the mythic traditions and their redaction.[33] To begin with, it is notable that a preponderance of traditions reported here derive from the Land of Israel: Rabbi Yoḥanan bar Nappaḥa (d. 279) was head of the academy in Tiberias in the mid-third century C.E., and Rav Yitzḥak II was his student. What is more, Rav Dimi visited the west on several occasions, and was known as a *neḥuta'* who "came [back] down" to Babylon with traditions from Israel. On the other hand, it is also striking to note that all of the traditions in our pericope are associated with sages active at the Babylonian Academy of Pumbeditha: Rav Yehudah (d. 299; a contemporary of Rabbi Yoḥanan, with whom he consulted)[34] founded this school, and Rabbah (d. 330) was a subsequent director (and a tradent of Rabbi Yoḥanan);[35] in addition, Rav Dimi was associated with this academy (reporting to Abayye; d. 339),[36] and Rav Aḥa b. Ya'akov lived nearby (in Pafunya). Accordingly, while it is evident that some features (and even clusters) of the previously mentioned Near Eastern mythic pattern existed or circulated in certain forms in the west,[37] both the diversity of materials in our Talmudic pericope *and* the provenance of its various tradents strongly suggest that this is a (new) rabbinic reformulation of ancient mythic traditions, worked out at Pumbeditha, using local but also western (especially Tiberian) traditions.

The redactor of our Talmudic pericope has thus created a composite myth from a series of separate and distinct traditions. Overall, these traditions appear to be primary and the scriptural proofs secondary—even where these latter may actually derive from old Israelite mythical fragments (like Isa. 27:1 and Job 26:12)—the reason being that the prooftexts do not stand alone as a coherent narrative, *and* many of them depend on midrashic readings to work as myth. Accordingly, the effect of the proofs on the pericope is to biblicize the mythic narratives and give the impression that the narratives depend upon an underlying (though broken and dispersed) biblical myth. But the contradictory and harmonizing character of many of the subtraditions in the pericope reinforces the dominant sense that we have a *constructed* myth, and not a reconstructed one.

The constructed character of our unit is reinforced by the anonymous voice of the editor. His voice appears first in each of the various subunits, when he introduces the tradents in whose name(s) the myths and prooftexts are given (or contested). What is more, his voice is the continuous coordinator of the complex Talmudic chorus in the various units. In this way the myth topics are aligned and emplotted such that the (local) debates are subordinated to the (larger) narrative development. The work of rabbinic myth-making is thus inseparable here from the process of tradition-building so central to the Talmud overall, and indeed to its construction of a hierarchy of authoritative teachings and values.

A quite different hierarchy governs the spatial components of the pericope. In ascending order, these are sea, earth, and heaven, together with their corresponding inhabitants: monsters and tutelary powers, human beings, angelic agents, and God. This hierarchy not only moves along a natural-supernatural axis (with humans in the middle), but reveals the central value of our rabbinic myth: obedience to divine authority. Thus potentially uncontrollable or clearly rebellious natural forces must be contained or killed, even as controllable or variously obedient natural elements and human beings are variously celebrated or rewarded.[38]

The value scale of obedience is concretized around the mouth and ingestion. Thus in tradition *I*, the instinctual (and thus inherently uncontrollable) female Leviathan is set aside as food for the righteous (who obey God); in tradition *II*, the Prince of the Sea is commanded by God to "open your mouth *(pikha)*" and is killed for his refusal; in tradition *III*, the Jordan flows into the mouth *(piv)* of Leviathan (or Behemoth), thus serving the habitable earth in an orderly way; in tradition *V*, the resisting and over-playful male Leviathan cannot be hooked by "his tongue" and must be slain; in tradition *VI*, we learn that when the monster Leviathan is hungry, he emits a foul odor from "his mouth" *(piv)*, which God must deodorize with the spices of Eden (Behemoth also swallows water in gross gulps); and finally, in tradition *VII*, the righteous eat of the flesh of Leviathan, as promised long before.

From another angle, this obedience/disobedience split reveals the even deeper tension between nature and culture in our myth. The two are most dichotomous at the outset (in tradition *I*), where primitive desire (the monsters) and cultivated virtue (the righteous) are completely differentiated. Nevertheless, these poles are ultimately integrated at the end (in traditions *VII–VIII*). Indeed, through their ingestion of the erstwhile creatures of instinct (sacrificed by God for the sake of the creation), the righteous symbolize the transformative potential and ultimate triumph of (rabbinic) culture over nature. Seated at their banquet under the luminous skins of Leviathan, the righteous are the Adamic figures of this myth—glorified in an aura of light.[39]

4

The Measure and Glory of God in Ancient Midrash

The old Aggadah holds many surprises for the discerning eye—and not least because of the way the sages viewed Scripture and infused it with new theological meaning. Texts which at first sight sing high praise of God are exegetically revealed to laud Israel and give it God-like status; and passages proclaiming divine omnipotence can be inverted to aggrandize the powers of the worshipper. These turns of interpretation become key factors in the presentation of theological ideas whose origins lie beyond the text. Little would we know of such rabbinic views without such evidence; but, if truth be told, it is often hard to fathom the gist of the hermeneutical hints that have been preserved. The language of midrashic exegesis is often so densely wrought and so darkened by allusion that the full intent of the sages is obscured. Later readers can only wonder what the ancient rhetors had in mind in many cases, and what their more untutored listeners could have understood. This is particularly the case where the terms used in a comment or homily derive from esoteric traditions. Full comprehension of such cases may now require comparison with terms embedded in sources long lost or largely misunderstood. The following discussion provides just such an instance. Beginning with the mythic formulation of God's advent in Deuteronomy 33:26, its transformations in the *Midrash Sifre Deuteronomy* are explored and precious traces of ancient Jewish spirituality recovered. In the process, a bit of the complex relationship between early Jewish mysticism and aggadic Midrash is revealed.[1]

* * *

The great "Blessing of Moses" in Deuteronomy 33 reaches its climax in vv. 26–29, with an extended paean to Israel's God of salvation. The coda begins at v. 26.

> O Jeshurun, there is none like God!
> Who rides through the heavens to help you *(be-'ezrekha)*
> And in His majesty *(ube-ga'avato)* on the high vaults.

The exclamation proclaiming God's incomparability in the first line is followed by an explanation of this supremacy in the next two versets. God's greatness is presented in terms of His beneficent aid to Jeshurun (Israel), and formulated in terms of the ancient theme of a storm god who rides to battle upon the clouds of heaven.[2] This mythic scenario derives from early Canaanite patterns and recurs throughout the Hebrew Bible (Ps. 18:10–11; 68:5, 34–35).[3] It is balanced in the present instance by the conclusion in v. 29, where an assertion of Israel's incomparability ("who is like you?") is followed by phrases exalting the warrior deity, who is the people's "shield of protection *('ezrekha)*" and "sword of triumph *(ga'avatekha)*." This repetition of terminology (in vv. 26 and 29), along with the double invocation (to Jeshurun and Israel) and assertions of incomparability ("none like God"; "who is like you?"), achieve a celebratory finale that proclaims God's routing word and Israel's restful inheritance of the land (vv. 27–28).[4] In addition, the entire unit (vv. 26–29) forms a grand thematic balance with the prologue to the blessing (vv. 2–5). Here, too, Israel is called Jeshurun, and the divine advent is envisaged as that of a storm god flashing fire (v. 2).[5]

This complex of biblical traditions is radically revised in *Midrash Sifre Deuteronomy* (*pisqa* 355), in which the syntactical coherence of Moses' blessing is reformulated to serve entirely new purposes.

> "There is none like God, O Jeshurun!" [Deut. 33:26]:[6] Israel says, "There is none like God," and the Holy Spirit responds, "except Jeshurun!"[7] Israel says, "Who is like you, O Lord, among the mighty?" [Exod. 15:11], and the Holy Spirit responds, "Happy are you, O Israel, who is like you?" [Deut.33:29]. Israel says, "Hear, O Israel, the Lord our God, the Lord is one" [Deut. 6:4], and the Holy Spirit responds, "And who is like Thy people Israel, a nation one in the earth" [1 Chron. 17:21]. Israel says, "As an apple-tree among the trees of the wood, [so is my Beloved]" [Songs 2:3], and the Holy Spirit responds, "As a lily

among thorns, [so is my love] [Songs 2:2]. Israel says, "This is my God, and I will praise Him" [Exod. 15:2], and the Holy Spirit responds, "The people which I formed for Myself [shall recount My praise]" [Isa. 43:21]. Israel says, "For you are the glory of their strength" [Ps. 89:18], and the Holy Spirit responds, "Israel, in whom I will be glorified" [Isa. 49:3].

"Who rides through the heavens to help you" [Deut. 33:26]: When Israel is upright and performs the will of God, He "rides through the heavens to help you"; but when they do not perform His will, [then]—if one may say so—"and in His majesty on the high vaults" [*ibid.*].

"And in His majesty on the high vaults": All the people of Israel gathered around Moses and said to him, "Our master Moses, tell us about the Glory [of God] on high." He replied, "You may know about the Glory [of God] on high from [the appearance of] the lower heavens." A parable: To what may this be likened? To one who said, "I wish to behold the glory of the king." He was told, "Go to the capital city and you may see him." He came [there][8] and saw a curtain set with precious stones and pearls and spread out at the entrance of the city. He could not take his eyes off of it, until he collapsed in a swoon. They then said to him, "If you could not take your eyes off of a curtain set with precious stones and pearls and spread out at the entrance of the city, until you collapsed in a swoon, how much more so had you entered the city [and beheld the glory of the king]." Therefore it says [in Scripture], "And in His majesty on the high vaults."[9]

The midrashic pericope opens with the first phrase of Deuteronomy 33:26, "There is none like God, O Jeshurun!" As noted, this is a proclamation of divine uniqueness: God (who rides the heavens to rescue His people) is beyond compare. The point is stressed with semantic decisiveness. A strong negative assertion precedes the contrast ("there is none like God"), and the disjunction between this theological assertion and the addressee ("O Jeshurun!") not only differentiates the God of Israel from all other gods, but from everything else as well—Jeshurun included.[10] But if this is the plain sense of the scriptural citation, the whole force of the midrashic exposition is employed to transform this assertion through a whole series of citations. Indeed, it is precisely the *likeness* or similarity of God *and* Jeshurun that is now emphasized. This unexpected concordance is achieved by a de-semanticization of the biblical phrase, so that the negative assertion and the vocative are construed as two parts of a dialogue. Israel speaks standard biblical theology ("There is none like God!"), and the Holy Spirit subverts it with a new Jewish teaching ("*except* Jeshurun!"). One may assume this innovation long preceded its midrashic justification, since no straightforward reading of Scripture would have led to such a conclusion. In fact, the textual support for this theology requires a clever (but partial) doubling of the main theological element *'el* ("God"). Israel says, *'ein ka'el yeshurun* ("There is none like God"), while the Holy Spirit answers, *'el yeshurun.* This last phrase may be read either as an ellipsis for *'el[a'] yeshurun* ("except Jeshurun"),[11] or as the more daring assertion, *'el yeshurun* ("Jeshurun is [*like*] God").[12] In either case, the utter incomparability of God as enunciated in Scripture is effaced by the midrash, and a theological correlation of God and Israel is celebrated. Remarkably, the new voice whose authority subverts Moses' theological claim is none other than the Holy Spirit itself.

The second part of the midrashic passage ostensibly completes the scriptural citation (Deut. 33:26). It begins with the second verset ("who rides the heavens to help you") and ends with the third ("and in His majesty on the high vaults"). Between these two citations is the midrashic teaching: "When Israel is upright and performs the will of God, 'He rides the heavens to help you'; but when they do not perform His will, [then]—if one may say so—'and in His majesty on the high vaults.'" Once again a two-part structure has been introduced into the biblical passage, though here it is not to break up one phrase into two assertations, but rather to differentiate the parallelism of versets 2 and 3 into positive and negative valences, conditioned by the obedience of Israel to the divine will. On the face of it, the grounds for this exposition is far from obvious. A clue lies in the programmatic condition of the contrast: "When Israel is upright *(yesharim).*" The verbal similarity of *yesharim* and *yeshurun* (Jeshurun) suggests that the midrashist is not only punning on the name Jeshurun, but has cleverly constructed his condition around the opening phrase ("O Jeshurun, there is none like God!"). Thus when he says that if the people of Israel are *yesharim ("upright"), then* God will come to their rescue, he is transforming the positive assertion of the opening line into a conditional promise (and threat) by means of a bilingual pun: the (Hebrew) declarative *'ein* ("there is *no*") heard as the (Aramaic) particle *'in* ("if").[13] The result is a disruption of the theological assurance of the biblical text and its transformation into the two conditions of divine providence. The opening assertion is thus midrashically revised to say: *if ('in)* the people (Israel) are upright like God, then He will rescue them in His role as cosmic warrior (phrase two); but if they are *not ('ein)* upright, then (phrase three) *ube-ga'avato sheḥaqim* ("and in His majesty on the high vaults").

What does this conclusion mean? Since the midrashist reads the third verset in relation to the negative condition, it is unlikely that it is simply parallel to the salvific action recorded in the second verset. We must rather assume that the phrase *ube-ga'avato sheḥaqim* represents the reverse of God's advent to earth. Accordingly, the particle *waw (u-)* would not produce a conjunction of images, but rather construct a contrast ("then"). The sage teaches that, as a result of Israel's disloyalty, "His [God's] majesty [ascends/withdraws to] the high [heavenly] vaults": in this way, the utterly transcendent God of the passage, who graciously descends to save His people, is now midrashically presented as conditioned by Israel's covenantal behavior. The result nomicizes the conditions of divine salvation and concomitantly empowers Israelite practice. On an inner-midrashic level, therefore, the vertical axis of the second section of the midrashic discourse (God descending and ascending) revises the horizontal axis of the first one, in which God and Israel are put on an equivalent plane. This produces the notion that God descends to those who do His will, but withdraws to hidden heights on account of human sin.[14] It is presumably also from the heavenly realm called *sheḥaqim* ("high vaults") that God descends to ride through the *shamayim* ("[lower] heavens") for the salvation of Israel. A cosmology of different divine realms is thus presupposed here, as also in the third section of the midrash.

Ostensibly, the final unit of *pisqa 355* also comments on the phrase *ube-ga'avato sheḥaqim* ("and in His majesty on the high vaults"), since this portion of the passage is cited again. But the process is far from clear. To begin with, the midrash shifts from its exegetical style to present a scene in which Moses responds to a query by the people upon his descent from Sinai. According to a widespread theme found in both classical rabbinic sources and in the *Hekhalot* traditions, Moses' ascent of Sinai was the beginning of his heavenly voyage to receive divine wisdom. In some versions Moses ascends easily,[15] while in others he undergoes a titanic struggle with angelic powers who jealously guard the seven heavens from human encroachment.[16] Either way, Moses achieves his goal and descends with the law of God. Nothing of these ascent traditions is mentioned in our midrash, which begins with the hero's return. As the text states, the people surround their master and want to know the "measure of God's glory [*middat kabod*] on high." But Moses demurs. He then tells them that they may infer this splendor from the lower heavens. To support his point, Moses tells a parable of a person who wished to view the arrival of a (Roman) ruler.[17] Coming to the city to behold the splendor of imperial majesty, this person sees a bejeweled curtain hung at the entrance. He is utterly enthralled, and stands transfixed until completely overcome. The conclusion is easily inferred: if a mortal is so overcome by the relatively minor splendor of a royal curtain, how much more would he be dazzled by the radiance of the king (emperor) himself. The analogical application may be just as easily deduced. Since the people could never comprehend God's supernal Glory, they should be satisfied with "knowing" His splendor from its lower reflections. This point is not stated as such in our pericope, where the parable is completed by the *a fortiori* formula "how much the more so" and the apparently self-justifying conclusion: "Therefore it says [in Scripture], 'And in His majesty on the high vaults.'"

But what is the point? Is part three merely an associative extension of the previous section (namely, that the depiction of divine ascension is complemented by the reference to God's exaltation), or is it an altogether independent piece? The solution lies in both the structure of the piece and the background of its vocabulary.

The concluding section of the *pisqa,* like the previous one, is structured around a contrast between the lower *shamayim* ("heaven") and the higher *sheḥaqim* ("high vaults"), only now the latter is the focus of interest. The people want to know something about the divine reality on high, and they gather around Moses, who has just descended from this realm. We thus have a striking complement to the theme of human ascent to heaven to receive divine knowledge. In the one case, the hero vertically penetrates a divine plane where a scene of instruction unfolds; in the other, the sage descends from his heavenly journey to the foot of Sinai, where a special revelation is requested. All told, this latter feature occurs three times in *Sifre Deuteronomy:* once here, in *pisqa* 355, and twice more in *pisqa* 307 and *pisqa* 356. In *pisqa* 307 the request is to know "the measure [or nature] of judgment [*middat ha-din*] on high," whereas in *pisqa* 356 the people want to be informed of "the good which the Holy One, blessed be He, will give us."

The tenor of the request in *pisqa* 356 seems clear enough: it is a desire for soteriological knowledge. By contrast, the first query is much more obscure. Viewed in light of the prooftext ("The Rock, whose way is perfect . . .; a trustworthy God without iniquity," Deut. 32:4) and Moses' teaching (that God judges justly even when it seems otherwise), *pisqa* 307 leads some interpreters to suggest that it takes an anti-Gnostic (or anti-Marcionite) posture; namely, that the heavenly measure of judgment is not an evil dimension in God (the Demiurge), but an expression of His trustworthy justice.[18] However this may be, two important points are evident. The first is that both texts (*pisqa* 307 and *pisqa* 356) express the people's desire for theological secrets not revealed at Sinai, while the second is that Moses repeatedly avoids the people's formal request for information by his tautological repetition of the biblical citation (that is, the people are told that they can rejoice over a reward to come, or that God's justice is without iniquity despite appearances). Both considerations aid our investigation of *pisqa* 355, for there, too, the people's request for special knowledge (of God's Glory "on high") is summarily deflected by Moses. Indeed, on the basis of the foregoing parallels, we may even surmise that the key phrase *middat kabod* ("the measure of God's Glory") refers to some esoteric knowledge. But if so, of what kind?

The parable is an appropriate place to begin this inquiry, because the story of the person wanting to see the king is presented as an analogy to the people's theological request. Several features emerge from a consideration of its structure and terms. The first is that the initial query of the people, who wish to know "about the *middat kabod* on high," is a request for supernal knowledge. Moses tells the people: "You may know [*yode'im*] the *middat kabod* on high from the lower heavens." This contrast between "on high"/"lower heavens" further suggests that the request refers to the *middat kabod* in the upper heavens. Moreover, from the analogy (which speaks of one who wanted "to see the *kabod* of the king [Roman emperor]" upon his advent into the city), we may surmise that the people have asked Moses for knowledge about the King of Kings whom he saw in the high heavens. The *middat kabod* of God is thus apparently related to His "majesty on the high vaults [*sheḥaqim*]—the portion of the biblical passage that informs this part of the pericope. This supposition is confirmed not only by the (broad) synonymity of *sheḥaqim* and *shamayim* ("heavens") in Scripture, but also by the fact that *shamayim* is the designation for the third of seven heavenly realms according to several rabbinic traditions. Indeed, in the famous account of heavenly ascensions found in 3 Enoch (17:3, 33:5) and the esoteric lore preserved in the Talmud (*b. Ḥagigah* 12b), the lower *shamayim* is subtended by a layer called a *viylon*—precisely the word used in our text for the bejeweled curtain (Greek *bēlon*) hanging before the city entrance. As such terminology can hardly be accidental in this context, it is reasonable to suppose that the sages have used it in the parable to reinforce Moses' rejection of the people's request for heavenly knowledge.

Technical allusions to heavenly matters in the parable are further indicated by the remark that the visitor was unable "to take his eyes off [*la-zuz*]" the *viylon* "until he collapsed." On the one hand, this remark conveys the compelling yet numinous force of the spectacle, a matter known from many texts. Yet the singular oddness of the expression in the *editio princeps* makes one wonder whether the better (and original) reading is not preserved in the variant formulation that the pilgrim was not able "to feast [*la-zun*] his eyes" on the *viylon*.[19] This locution is a technical expression found not only in mystical sources[20] but also in several midrashic teachings that report how the angels on high are "sustained [*nizonim*]" by the spiritual light of God's presence.[21] In a striking comment, Rabbi Yitzḥak Nappaḥa adds that even these heavenly beings only "see" the form [*demut*] of God's Glory [*kabod*] "as through [the refraction of] a *viylon*"! (*Pesiqta Rabbati* 81).[22] Can it therefore be that the knowledge which the people in *Sifre* 355 desire is in fact the *middah* of God's *kabod* in heaven, namely, the supernal stature (or form) of the divine figure on high? The parallel of the person's falling into a faint before the radiant *viylon*, much like the prophet Ezekiel's collapse after his vision of the divine Glory *(kabod)* "in the likeness [*demut*] of a man" (Ezek. 1:26–28), enhances this possibility. The technical import of the term *middah* and its theosophical relation to God's supernal Glory will prove the point.[23]

As we have noted, the phrase *ube-ga'avato sheḥaqim* is cited at the beginning and end of the third part of *pisqa* 355. On the basis of the people's reference to the (hypostatic) divine Glory "on high," we may assume that this portion of Deuteronomy 33:26 was correspondingly understood to refer to an aspect of the same reality—namely, that God's heavenly Glory and Majesty are synonyms for the human-like image (or Anthropos) found in the *sheḥaqim*. Precise proof for this assumption can be adduced from the esoteric traditions preserved in *Midrash Mishlei* 10.[24] There, in the context of a consideration of the hierarchy of knowledge in rabbinic culture, the rabbinic disciple is asked whether he has gone beyond Talmudic learning and engaged in the supernal mysteries. "Have you viewed [*tzafiyta*] the [heavenly] throne [*merkabah*]," he is asked, "[and] have you viewed the [divine] Majesty [*tzafiyta be-ga'avah*]"?[25] Quite clearly, the *ga'avah* referred to here is a hypostatic reality on high. More precisely, as we may deduce from the sequel, such a vision involves knowledge of "the throne of My Glory [*kebodi*]" and the cosmic "measure" *(shi'ur)* of the limbs of the divine Glory (the so-called *Shi'ur Qomah*),[26] which is the heavenly Anthropos. This esoteric knowledge of God is again celebrated by the divine speaker in the resumptive finale of the text. "And surely this is My Glory, this is My greatness, this is My might, this is My splendor, and this is the splendor of My beauty,[27] that My children recognize My Glory [*kebodi*][28] in this measure [*middah*]!"

Further confirmation that the phrase *ga'avato sheḥaqim* was understood as the hypostatic Majesty of God on high, the anthropomorphic *kabod* in its full cosmic "measure," can be derived from the rendition of our *Sifre* passage found in the *Midrash Ha-Gadol*.[29] Commenting on the phrase *ube-ga'avato sheḥaqim*, it says: "All Israel gathered near Moses, and said to him: 'Our Master, Moses, tell us about the *middat kabod* on high.' He said to them: '*ein ka'el yeshurun*' ['There is none like God, O Jeshurun!']; for if one cannot look at the lower heaven, how much the less (could one look) at *middat kebodo* ['the measure of His Glory']!" Clearly, the textual tradition here has equated *ga'avato* with *kebodo*—God's Majesty with His Glory. Both are hypostatic realities in heaven; indeed, they are one and the same: the Anthropos on high. The mystical *Hekhalot* hymns of the heavenly palaces go further and, in one case, restate Deuteronomy 33:26 with the formulation: *ve-ga'avato ba-sheḥaqim* ["His Majesty *in* the high heavens"].[30] Even more compelling is the formulation in Ms. Oxford Opp. Add. 4o 183, fol. 1*a*, which states: *ve-'al kise' nora' yitbarakh ha-ga'avah ba-sheḥaqim* ("and on [His] awesome throne, may He be blessed, [sits] the Majesty in the high heavens").[31] Hereby the Majesty, like the Glory, is enthroned in supernal splendor.

To know the cosmic dimensions of the supernal Anthropos is thus the point of the people's query in *Sifre Deuteronomy* 355. But Moses refuses to devulge the "*middat kabod* on high," for it is an esoteric secret. Indeed, in related theosophical traditions, the supernal Torah also assumes a comparable esoteric form. This point is preserved in a striking liturgical poem composed by Eleazar be-Rabbi Kallir.[32] It opens with Job 28:23–27, where it is stated that only God knows the way and place of Wisdom (v. 23), only He has "seen it and gauged it" (v. 27). Kallir extends this description and transforms it completely when he says: "Then You saw and gauged . . . and measured *(u-maddadeta)* and set the extension *(ve-shi'arta)* . . . of every line . . . and measure *(medded)* and its extension *(shi'urav)*." But to what does this refer? Inasmuch as Jewish tradition had long since identified Wisdom with Torah, and even imagined the Torah as the King's (that is, God's) daughter,[33] one may safely surmise that the object of Kallir's computation is nothing less than the *middat bat melekh,* the heavenly "measure of the King's daughter" mentioned in the prayer. The context further supports the connection between this divine daughter and the supernal Torah (or Wisdom)—and this is precisely how an anonymous medieval commentary understood Kallir's words: "The King's daughter *is* the Torah."[34]

It is particularly noteworthy that the extension of this anthropomorphic Torah is called a *middah,* and not solely because the phrase *middat bat melekh* in the prayer is similar to the expression *middat kabod,* mentioned in *Sifre Deuteronomy* 355. Its value derives from the realization that the "measure" *(middatah)* of this configuration is said to extend about 2,000 cubits, "like the vision of the divine figure [lit., measure, *ha-middah*) which the messenger [Moses] saw." That is to say, Rabbi Eleazar alludes to a tradition in which Moses envisioned a supernal Being at Sinai—a hypostatic configuration—whose cosmic extension was referred to as a *middah!* Indeed, the almost self-evident way the poet refers to the esoteric figure as a *middah* should give us pause, for the prayer is not a secret hymn but one written for public recitation on one of the special Sabbaths preceding Passover. Equally striking is the graphic depiction of the *bat melekh* ("king's daughter") in this exoteric prayer. Quite certainly, Kallir has boldly combined old speculations on the cosmic extension of the supernal Anthropos (the *Shi'ur Qomah*) with ancient midrashic traditions concerning the anthropomorphic form of the heavenly Torah.[35] The use of the term *middah* to describe both realities gives us only a hint of the theosophies of Torah that circulated in late antique Judaism.

Additional confirmation for the interpretation of *middah* as the measure (or extent) of a divine configuration comes from a widespread theosophical tradition concerning the lower angels that serve or support the throne of the divine Glory. In the better known part of that tradition, the key Hebrew term for an angelic form is *tzurah*. Thus the later mystical book of *Bahir*, in the context of referring to angelic hypostases in the heavenly realm, speaks of *ha-tzurot ha-qedoshot*, "the holy forms."[36] Gershom Scholem noted that a similar description of the angelic court on high is preserved in an important remark by Maimonides.[37] In his *Mishneh Torah (Hilkhot Yesodei Ha-Torah*, VII. 1), the philosopher speaks of persons who enter the mystical meditations of the heavenly world *(pardes)* as those "whose knowledge is ever turned upward, bound beneath the Throne [in order] to understand the various holy and pure forms [*ha-tzurot ha-qedoshot veha-tehorot*]." Quite clearly, the word *tzurot* was one of the technical terms for the angelic "forms" in medieval Jewish speculations on the esoteric divine Chariot (the so-called *Ma'aseh Merkabah*).

But this usage was no late invention. It rather derives from a millennium-old tradition of theosophical thought fragmentarily preserved in various ancient sources, magical, Gnostic, and Jewish. One striking witness to its antiquity is an invocation to Thoth-Hermes in a Greek magical papyrus, where "holy Thauth" (whose true visage is hidden) is said to appear in various *morphais hagias*, "holy forms."[38] Another attestation is the reference to the 72 morphai (or divine "forms") of the heavenly realm mentioned in the Gnostic treatise known as *On the Origin of the World* (II, 5, 104–105).[39] As has been recently observed,[40] there is a remarkable correspondence between this text and the esoteric speculation on the 71 *tzurot* supporting the divine Throne found in the book of *Bahir* (in fact, 71 + 1 central figure).[41] Given the relatively clear computation found in the Jewish source (which speculates that the divine throne comprised 64 + 7 + 1 components), the abbreviated presentation in the Gnostic text is arguably derivative.[42] If this is so, the Gnostic source would be a precious witness to the antiquity of the full complex of such theosophical ideas (as preserved in a Jewish-oriented Christian milieu),[43] though it would be far from the earliest record of such speculations or vocabulary. In fact, comparable locutions can be recognized in the speculations on the divine Chariot preserved among the ancient scrolls found at Qumran. Moshe Idel has correctly stressed the importance of such expressions as *tzurot 'elohim ḥayyim* ("forms of the living God") and *tzurot kabod* ("forms of glory") for reconstructing the ancient Jewish mystical tradition.[44] Indeed, in one ancient midrash the term *tzurah* was used to depict the heavenly Anthropos on the throne, referred to in parallel passages as "the *demut* [form] of the Power on high."[45]

Further links in the present reconstruction of *Sifre Deuteronomy* 355 may be forged by returning to the theosophical traditions preserved in Gnostic sources. As noted, 72 divine *morphai* ("forms") in the heavenly world are mentioned in the treatise *On the Origin of the World*. In another document deriving from the same Jewish-oriented milieu, known as the "First Apocalypse of James,"[46] a reference is actually made to "72 measures" that "come forth from Him who is without measure" (V, 3, 26, 2–15).[47] It would seem that the reference here is to divine archons or powers that emanate from the Father, and although they are hostile forces, and not the constituents of the Chariot, it is notable that the author of this text uses the word "measure" (*shoshou* in Sahidic Coptic) to indicate both the divine beings and the Unmeasured Father.[48] One may thus suppose that we have here a later reflex of the older Jewish term *middah*, used to indicate the anthropomorphic measure of God on high.

A remarkable midrashic confirmation of this point is preserved in the *Abot de-Rabbi Nathan* (A, 37). In this old rabbinic treatise, seven *middot* ("measures") serve God before the throne of His Glory.

> Seven *middot* serve before the throne of the Glory *(ha-kavod)*, and they are Wisdom, Righteousness, Justice, Mercy, Kindness, Truth and Peace. As is said [in Scripture]: "And I [God] shall betroth you to Me forever; and I shall betroth you to Me with Righteousness and Justice, and with Kindness and Mercy; and I shall betroth you to Me with Truth and you shall know the Lord" [Hos. 2:21–22]). Rabbi Meir says: "Why does Scripture use [the words] 'and you shall know [*ve-yada'at*] God?"—To teach that whoever has [lit., has in him, *bo*] all these qualities [*middot*] knows the Knowledge of God [*da'ato shel maqom*]."[49]

There can be little doubt that these *middot*, which serve *(meshammeshot)* before the throne of God's *kabod*, are archangelic beings of the pleroma—much like the archangelic forms *(morphai; tzurot)* found in the Gnostic and later Jewish theosophies.[50] One may even suppose that speculation on this divine hebdomad developed quite independently of the Hosean prooftext, since only five of the hypostases are scripturally justified by it.[51] Indeed, there are grounds to suggest that traditions of these angelic beings were already part of ancient biblical throne theosophy. Best known, of course, are the theriomorphic and anthropomorphic *hayyot*, or "beings," which supported the divine throne upon which the prophet Ezekiel envisaged the *kabod* in the appearance of a human form (Ezek. 1:26–28). But similar images also occur in the book of Psalms, and a straightforward reading of several passages indicates that the beings that carried this throne and praised the divine King were hypostases of moral qualities. In Psalm 89:15, for instance, four of the potencies mentioned in the later rabbinic source form part of the heavenly retinue. Two help carry the throne and two serve before it: "Righteousness [*tzedeq*] and Justice are the supports of Your Throne; Mercy and Truth stand before You" (v. 15).[52] On the other hand, in Psalm 85:11 "Mercy and Truth meet; Righteousness [*tzedeq*] and Peace kiss"; nothing is said of the divine Throne. But we may nevertheless assume that heavenly hypostases are reflected here as well, since the text goes on to report that "Righteousness [*tzedeq*] looks down from heaven" (v. 12), and that "Righteousness [*tzedeq*] goes before [God]" (v. 14), on His earthly advent to save the needy. Indeed, this suggestion that *tzedeq* is a divine element in the ancient Israelite pantheon is reinforced by the finding that *tzdq* and *msr* (Righteousness and Equity) are recorded in a list of gods found in old Canaanite Ugarit,[53] and that *zydyk* and *misor* were considered divine hypostases among the Phoenicians (according to Philo of Biblos).[54] The angelic status of *tzedeq* is still clearly attested in the so-called War Scroll of the Qumran sectaries (1 QM XVII. 6–8).[55]

Let us return to the passage from the *Abot de Rabbi Nathan* and its prooftext from Hosea 2:21–22. If the role of these verses is not merely to provide scriptural support for the host of seven *middot* on high, what possible reason is there for connecting a speculation on divine hypostases with a biblical passage that speaks of God's espousal of Israel through qualities that result in knowledge of God? The nexus is explicated by Rabbi Meir. He begins with the all-important verb *ve-yada'at* ("and you shall know"), and asks just why Scripture should specify knowledge of God as a consequence of this espousal. His answer refers to the qualities *(middot)* of which the hypostases are composed, and in this way reveals his theosophical reading of Hosea 2:21–22. More specifically, Rabbi Meir interprets the biblical passage as a divine directive to incorporate the various attributes mentioned there in order to "know the knowledge of God." And since these moral *middot* are associated with the hypostatic *middot* in heaven, he makes the point that whoever is able to assimilate or interiorize ("who has in him [*bo*]") the essence of these divine realities will have gnosis of God. Rabbi Meir thus presupposes a profound correlation between the heavenly *middot* which surround the throne of God's Glory and their earthly actualization. Some mystical praxis of Jewish gnosis, involving the transformation of an adept through the interiorization of spiritual *middot,* is thus indirectly revealed. The intended result would presumably be a spiritual betrothal or unification with God. The Hosean prooftext ("I shall betroth you to Me") may thus indicate not only the program of the praxis, but also something of the erotic dimension of this intellectual perfection as well.

Rabbi Meir's exegesis is certainly related to the ancient Jewish mystical tradition. First, his use of the term *middot* to indicate the divine supports of the heavenly throne is echoed in later visionary traditions. Most striking is the reference in the *Hekhalot Rabbati* (XIII.2) to the *middot nose'ei kise' kebodo,* "the [angelic] forms which bear the throne of His Glory."[56] In addition, Meir's strong reading of the phrase *ve-yada'at 'et YHWH* ("and you shall know the Lord," Hos. 2:22) as the knowledge of God following the internalization of the heavenly *middot* shows that a profound esoteric wisdom was involved. Indeed the technical use of the verb *yode'a* ("knows") in the phrase *yode'a da'ato shel maqom* ("knows the knowledge of God") points to other midrashic passages where esoteric divine knowledge is mentioned. Just paragraphs after this text, we read that "because of sin, it is not given to man to know [*leyda'*] what is the 'likeness *(demut)* on high'; for were it not for this [viz., sin] all the keys would be given to him and he would know [*yode'a*] how the heavens and earth were created" (*Abot de-Rabbi Nathan* A, 39). According to Saul Lieberman, this passage refers to an old Jewish doctrine of a divine Demiurge involved in the creation, much like notions developed in Gnostic sources.[57] The passage links knowledge of God's "likeness on high" with the transformative knowledge which comes as a result. To know the figure on the throne (the hypostatic *kabod*) is thus to be initiated into the mysteries of creation. But just what is meant by this knowledge? On the basis of the query in *Sifre Deuteronomy* 355 ("What is the *middat kabod* on high?"), it is not unreasonable to conclude that this was some knowledge of the extraordinary measurements of the heavenly Anthropos. Indeed, the technical formulation of Moses' rejection of the people's request shows that this was considered esoteric information of a most exalted kind—"from the lower heavens you may know [*yode'im*] the *middat kabod* on high"!

The central purpose of the final section of *Sifre Deuteronomy pisqa* 355 is to prevent popular knowledge of God's supernal "likeness," and it is just this which allows us to comprehend the exegesis of Deuteronomy 33:26. Accordingly, I would suggest that, for the sages of our midrashic pericope, the phrase *'ein ka'el yeshurun* ("There is none like God, O Jeshurun!") was further understood to mean: "One [viz., the people] may not [*'ein*] see [*yeshurun*] the likeness of God [*ka-'el*]." That is to say, He who rides the heavens to rescue His people may not be seen *because* His majesty is in the supernal heights (*ga'avato sheḥaqim*). Indeed, this is just the point explicitly made in the *Midrash Ha-Gadol* version cited earlier. After having Moses answer the people's query for knowledge with the words *'ein ka'el yeshurun,* this text adds: "For if one cannot even look [*le-histakel*] at the lower heaven, how much less [could one look] at the measure of His Glory [*middat kevodo*]"! Thus, in contrast to the intimate correspondence between God and Israel found in the opening section of the midrash, the final portion of *pisqa* 355 provides a dogmatic assertion of divine transcendence. At the same time, the negative sense of the withdrawal of God to the *sheḥaqim* ("high vaults") in the second part is revised. God's exalted place is in the heavenly heights, and nothing of the "likes of" Him may be perceived by the earthly eye. In this way the sages make a strong cultural point. While the exoteric domain of the commandments is open to all, and righteous obedience to these precepts brings the transcendent God nigh, supernal splendor may only be inferred from the lower spheres. The people must rest content with that possibility, and with the heavenly gift brought to them by Moses from on high.

One of the recurrent scriptural sources cited by the rabbis in connection with the theme of Moses' heavenly ascent and reception of the Torah is Psalm 68:19: "You ascended to the heights [and] have taken spoils; you have received gifts on account of mankind" (cf. *b. Shabbat* 89a). In fact, in the Targumic paraphrase of this passage, the subject of the ascent is actually glossed as Moses and the spoil identified as the "words of Torah." In the process of this resignification, the Targumist translated the Hebrew verb *laqaḥta* ("you received [gifts]") as "you gave [*yehavta*] gifts"—presumably by exegetically transposing the Hebrew consonants *l-q-ḥ* into *ḥ-l-q*.[58] In any event, it was this reading that influenced the author of Ephesians 4:8, who renders this word in his use of Psalm 68:19 by Greek *edōken*.[59] The same reading is also found in the *Testament of Dan*.[60]

The homily in Ephesians 4 is particularly valuable to the present inquiry. In his citation and interpretation of Psalm 68:19, the teacher (arguably a disciple of Paul) replaces Moses with Christ who, he says, ascends above "all the heavens, in order that he might fill all things" (Ephes. 4:10). Each person, he adds, has been given "grace according to the measure [*metron*] of the gift of Christ" (v. 4). And some individuals have also been graced to perform "works of service in order to build up the body of Christ" (v. 12), "until we all reach unity in the faith and knowledge of the Son of God becoming a perfect man and attaining the measure [*metron*] of [the] stature [*ēlikias*] of the fullness [*plērōmatos*] of Christ" (v. 13). The section concludes with final reflections on the spiritual body of Christ, which the community of faith constitutes and builds up in love (4:15–16).

This midrashic exposition is not easy to comprehend, in part because it derives from a mystical understanding of divinely given graces which collectively constitute the spiritual structure of Christ, and in part because it anticipates a mystical fulfillment whose precise properties are not explicitly indicated. The reading seems to indicate that the perfection of the individual members of the believing community leads to a building-up or perfecting of the spiritual structure of Christ, this being an anthropomorphic configuration. There also seems to be some synonymy between reaching "unity in the faith and knowledge of the Son of God" and "becoming a perfect man and attaining the measure of the stature of the fullness of Christ." That is, reaching the highest faith and knowledge is a perfective achievement through which one fully unites with Christ.

Attaining "the measure of the stature of the fullness of Christ" is thus a profound mystical achievement. Moreover, given that this "stature" is related to the spiritual body of Christ, I would interpret "the *metron* of the stature of Christ" as the teacher's theological and terminological equivalent for the measure (or extent) of the divine Anthropos in Jewish sources—like the *middat kabod* in *Sifre Deuteronomy* 355. On this view, Ephesians 4:7–16 presents Christ as the supernal Anthropos in the image of the invisible God,[61] so that perfected faith in and knowledge of this heavenly figure lead to some sort of mystical relationship witht the divine figure on high.[62]

The portrayal of the mystical body of Christ in Ephesians 4 thus provides more than a technical parallel with our midrash text. It suggests that ancient Jewish speculations on the divine Glory in heaven underlie the teacher's theological transformation in the early church. More precisely, even though certainly the "measure [*metron*] of the gift of Christ" in v.4 interprets Romans 12:3, I would suggest that the theosophical use of the term *metron* in Ephesians 4:13 is rather influenced by the Hebrew term *middah* (or *shi'ur*), in much the same way as certain early Christian uses of the Greek word *morphē* ("form") reflect the prior Hebrew term *tzurah*,[63] or as the Pauline notion of Christ's *sōma tēs doksēs* ("body of glory"; Phil. 3:21) is arguably a reformulation of the Jewish notion of the *guf ha-kabod* ("body of the Glory").[64]

Further support for this line of argument lies in a stunning pun embedded in the Gnostic tract known as *The Gospel According to Philip*. We read there that Christ has two names: "Messiah" and "measure."[65] This apparently unrelated conjunction of nomenclature has recently been shown to derive from a clever play on the Hebrew (or Syriac) stem *m-sh-ḥ*, which yields both words.[66] Even so, we may still wonder what led to such a paronomastic conflation. Our foregoing consideration of the phrase *middat kabod* in old rabbinic thought suggests that the pun in this tract only makes sense in light of an older christological tradition that linked the Messiah to the measure or figure of the divine Glory on high. In turn, that theology is an exegetical transformation of earlier Jewish speculations—a precious witness of origins despite its new form.

5

Midrashic Theologies of Messianic Suffering

The theme of messianic hope is omnipresent in classical Jewish life and literature. It fills the Talmud and Midrash; is repeated in any number of prayers and rituals; dominates the choice of prophetic lections *(haftarot)* for the Sabbaths and festivals; and structures homiletic perorations as well as poetic prayers *(piyyuṭim)* for the liturgical year. Reviewing this vast corpus of material, one is struck by the deep structure of expectation and trust that constitutes Judaism in its many expressions and forms—despite, or perhaps because of, the complete or incomplete realization of prophetic promises of final redemption. Paradoxes therefore abound, especially where the messianic manifestations are based on bold interpretations or theologically daring conceptions. In other cases the paradoxes even extend to the very formulation of standard prayers, as in the midrash that praises Israel for concluding its daily supplication that God redeem His people with the words: "Blessed art Thou, O Lord, who redeems Israel [*go'el yisrael*]"—despite the fact and persistence of their present suffering.[1]

In the midrashic collections, the overall virtues of constancy and hopeful waiting often give way to a voice of insistent immediacy. Some dozens of cases express the urgency of the issue in such pointed questions as: "When will You [God] redeem us?"; "When will King Messiah come?" and so on—*'ematai 'atah go'alenu; 'ematai yavo' melekh ha-mashiaḥ; 'emat 'ati mashiaḥ; 'am'ai la' 'ati melekh ha-mashiaḥ ha-yom; matai 'ati bar nafle?*[2] Following these queries answers are given that encourage or condemn calculations of the end, that set the conditions of human action or attitude, or that discuss the particular merit *(zekhut)* of the

Patriarchs or the Torah that may mitigate or facilitate rewards and protections in the judgment to come. These separate instructions are usually brief, most likely condensing much longer formulations on the subject of messianic expectation.

In certain instances, the midrashic sources preserve condensed apocalyptic schemes and other statements of unexpected value. An ancient teaching of Resh Lakish is exemplary in this regard, for he decodes the primal features of *tohu bohu,* "darkness" and "deep," in Genesis 1:2 in terms of the four evil kingdoms (Babylon, Media, Greece, and Rome), and the "spirit of God" (in the next phrase) in terms of the Messiah who will come in the end.[3] Not only does this sage read eschatology (last things) into a formulation of protology (first things)—thus promising the end at the very beginning—but his interpretation preserves a striking teaching about the Messiah. Just how concretely one should take his identity of the *ruaḥ 'elohim* ("spirit of God") with the *ruḥo shela-mashiaḥ* ("spirit of the Messiah") is not certain, though one cannot exclude the possibility that this midrash preserves an old notion that the historical Messiah will manifest a primordial divine form (either of God or created by Him).

There are other instances that indicate a rich (though largely lost or obscured) mythology of the Messiah. The following two examples may attest to this point and move us closer to our theme of messianic suffering. The first is based on a homily interpreting Daniel's own revelation of the meaning of one of Nebuchadnezzer's dreams. Daniel praises God as He who "reveals deep and hidden things" *(galei' 'amiqata' u-mesatrata')* and concludes that *nehora' 'imeih sherei'* ("light dwells with Him"; Dan. 2:22). Concerning this light, Rabbi Abba Sarungaia said: "This is the King Messiah."[4] Nothing more is stated; but this much says a lot. For in this interpretation the Messiah is identified with the primordial light, whose origin was the subject of much rabbinic speculation. According to one view, the created light derives from an uncreated effulgence covering God like a garment; according to another opinion, mundane light derives from "the place of the Temple," which I take to mean the heavenly Temple that various traditions mention as one of the things created or anticipated by God during the first 6 days of creation.[5] R. Sarungaia's tradition is different. For him the Messiah is the light (perhaps uncreated) that dwells with God on high. A later version of this sage's teaching identifies the *nehora'* ("light") with one of the primordial names of the Messiah. This too is an old notion, but seems to have somewhat neutralized the old myth, perhaps for polemical reasons.

The second example to be adduced here bears on another of the old messianic names preserved in classical rabbinic sources. In the Talmud at *b. Sanhedrin* 98b we read as follows: "And the Rabbis say: His name is *Ḥivra'*, 'The Leper' of the House of Rabbi, as it is said [in Isaiah 53:4] 'surely he has borne our sickness [*ḥolayenu*], our suffering he endured . . ..'" This is a puzzling sequence, since there is no connection between the name and the prooftext drawn from Isaiah 53. Something seems to have gone awry in the text; and this suspicion is confirmed by the reading of this midrash preserved in Raymundo Martini's polemical work, *Pugio Fidei*.[6] In that medieval compendium, after the first name and some explanations, comes the following teaching: "The School of Rabbi says: His name is *Ḥulya'*," and goes on to give the aformentioned biblical citation. The verbal play between the name *Ḥulya'* ("The Afflicted One") and the word *ḥolayenu* in Isaiah 53:4 is just right, and I am therefore inclined to suspect that Martini's citation preserves an authentic Jewish teaching of a suffering Messiah, excised from the Talmudic tradition through internal or other censorship.[7] This deletion may not actually have occurred until sixteenth-century Christian printings of the Talmud, since the name *Ḥulya'* with the prooftext from Isaiah 53:4 is still cited by Don Yitzhak Abravanel (1437–1508) in one of his works on messianic tribulations, the *Yeshu'ot Meshiḥo* (2nd 'Iyyun).[8]

The existence of old rabbinic notions of a suffering Messiah can be further supported by an old liturgical poem by Eleazar be-Rabbi Kallir on the Messiah, entitled "Yinnon" (which also connotes the sense of affliction),[9] written for the afternoon *Musaf* service on *Yom Kippur.*[10] The poet extensively utilizes passages from Isaiah 53:5 and 11 in his teaching that the Messiah will bear the sins of Israel and shall be wounded *(meḥolal)* because of their transgressions, so that the people will be justified before God and "healed through his wound" *(nirpa' lanu ba-ḥavurato)*.[11] As a recitation for *Yom Kippur,* the prayer anticipates a messianic atonement for sins, though there is no mention of death or sacrifice.

Kallir's prayer indicates how deeply authentic the notion of a suffering Messiah was in classical Judaism. Indeed, in a homily found in *Pesiqta Rabbati* 31, the sages even refer to the excessive suffering endured by the Messiah in every generation, according to the sins of that generation.[12] Several chapters later, this same collection preserves a valuable cycle of homilies that shed further light on this theme of the suffering Messiah. Study of this material is not new; in fact the materials in *Pesiqta Rabbati* 34–37 have been ably discussed by Gustav Dalman[13] and Arnold Goldberg,[14] among others. Nor was the importance of these texts lost on earlier generations. For example, the material was excerpted into the *Pirqei Mashiaḥ*[15] and the Apocalypse of Zerubavel,[16] and commented upon in recent centuries by Azzariah dei Rossi[17] and Nahman Krochmal.[18] In what follows, I shall hope to contribute further to this important cycle, and to highlight the interplay between Midrash and myth in the development of Jewish theologies of messianic suffering.

Pesiqta Rabbati 34–37 contains the final homilies in the cycle devoted to the seven weeks of consolation following the fast of *Tisha' Be-'Av.*[19] The text thus runs parallel to the sequence in *Pesiqta de-Rav Kahana.* These homilies draw on prophetic lectionaries *(haftarot)* taken from the later portions of the book of Isaiah, where the overall subject is national consolation, joy, and renewal. However, *Pesiqta Rabbati* 34–37 is distinguished in several ways: first, by the unique occurrence in *Pisqa* 34 and 35 of *haftarot* based on non-Isaianic passages;[20] second, by the very strong emphasis on the theme of suffering and a messianic figure called Ephraim; third, by the special structure of the four homilies, which are of the *ruaḥ ha-qodesh* ("holy spirit") type—thus giving a prophetic and even semi-apocalytic dimension to the various sermons based on words of David, Solomon, Isaiah, and Jeremiah; and finally, by the literary coherence of the chapters considered separately and together, particularly in terms of themes and prooftexts. Particularly notable in this last regard is the recurrent (explicit and implicit) use of verses from Isaiah 53, Zechariah 9, and Psalm 22—all passages of importance in New Testament messianology and in contemporary Christian literature.

The opening section of *pisqa* 34 sets the terms and themes to follow. As is typical of the *ruaḥ ha-qodesh* form, the opening biblical verse addresses a historical entity through the question *keneged mi 'amaro PN la-miqra' ha-zeh,* "With respect to whom did (David or Isaiah, etc.) speak this passage?" The first one, Isaiah 61:9 ("Their offspring shall be known among the nations"), is applied to a group called the *'avelei tzion,* or "mourners of Zion." They are mentioned a few verses earlier as the ones to whom the Lord will bring "comfort" on the day of redemption, providing them with "a turban instead of ashes, a festive ointment instead of mourning, [and] a garment of splendor instead of a battered spirit" (vv. 2–3). This contrast is striking and renews the hope given to the ancients. It was picked up in later centuries, and actually constitutes the polarities of our homiletical cycle—beginning with the themes of mourning and sorrow in *pisqa* 34, and ending with the promised exaltation of the faithful in garments of splendor in *pisqa* 37. This deep structural integration of the homilies is another indication of their (final) compositional coherence.

The "mourners of Zion" seem already to have constituted an identifiable group after the destruction of the first Temple. The prophet does not mention any particular practices of theirs, but we do have evidence from the nearly contemporary Elephantine papyri that after the destruction of the Jewish Temple in Yev the citizens performed such mourning rites as wearing sackcloth and fasting, abstaining from oils and wine, and practicing sexual abstinence.[21] Mourning rites preserved from Tannaitic sources in the first centuries (C.E.) show related developments, and the groups involved may have formed ascetic circles.[22] Whether directly related or not, those specifically designated in *pisqa* 34 as *'avelei tziyon,* "mourners of Zion," are marked by two distinguishing characteristics. The first is their perpetual supplication of divine mercy; the second is their unabated hope in divine salvation.[23] The two behaviors are related; and because of them the group was persecuted by other Jews[24] but protected by God on high. In fact, the Isaianic passage cited earlier, referring to the "offspring" or *zar'am* of the group, is midrashically interpreted so as to give the mourners assurance that God will stay "their hand" *(zero'am)* in times of trouble.

Further, according to this *pisqa,* one of the characteristics of the mourners is that they "arise early every morning to beseech [divine] mercy." The precise character of this vigil is not clear, though there can be little doubt that it must have included rites of sorrow for the destroyed Temple and appeals for divine mercy during the sufferings of exile. But a deeper, more mythic dimension was apparently involved. To appreciate this we need only look further on in the homily, where God declares that He will "Himself" testify on behalf of "the mourners who have sorrowed with Me [*she-nitzṭa'aru 'immi*] for My destroyed Temple and ruined Shrine." The prooftext for this is taken from Isaiah 57:15, where God declares that He will be "with the downtrodden and humble of spirit [*'et dakka' u-shephal ruaḥ*]." But this latter expression of divine comfort for humans says the opposite of what the preacher has just declared—that is, until he indicates that the scriptural passage must be construed midrashically as *'itti dakka' u-shephal ruaḥ*, which I take to mean that God will be "with" those who are "downtrodden with Me [*'itti*]." Such persons, the preacher adds, have humbly accepted derision and all the while have kept silent "and not attached merit to themselves" *(ve-lo' heḥeziqu ṭovah le-'atzmam)*.

This notion of the participation by humans in divine suffering goes well beyond other midrashic expressions on this topic. For example, even the bold rereading elsewhere in *Pesiqta Rabbati* of Isaiah's word of comfort to Israel (*naḥamu, naḥamu 'ammi*, "Comfort ye, comfort ye, My people") to signify God's appeal for consolation from Israel (*naḥamuni, naḥamuni 'ammi*, "Comfort Me, comfort Me, My people") does not speak of humans sharing in divine sorrow.[25] A certain distance still remains between the people and the divine Mourner. What is more, the sufferings that the "mourners of Zion" share with God in our homily invert the standard midrashic topos in which God Himself determines to be with Israel in her travail. In those cases, the prooftext "I [God] shall be with [Israel] in [her] trouble [*'immo 'anoki be-tzarah*]" from Psalm 91:15 is not immediately understood to mean that God will rescue Israel from travail—but rather, first and foremost, that He will participate in the people's bondage or exile.[26] By contrast, the *'avelei tziyon* ritually endured the sorrows of God and derision and persecution by men, an experience that only confirmed their self-understanding as suffering servants. One may sense as much from the use of terminology from Isaiah 53 throughout the *pisqa*.

But I would suggest that more lies behind this persecution than a reaction of mockery at excessive rituals of mourning or expectation of salvation. To be sure, the "mourners" are defined as those who "passionately desired [God's] salvation, evening, morning, and noontime" *(she-ḥamedu ha-yeshu'ah 'erev va-boqer ve-tzohorayim)*. But this alone is not noteworthy. More to the point is the preacher's contrast of the "righteous of the world" *(tzaddiqei 'olam)* with the "mourners" *('aveilim)*. Speaking for God, he criticizes these righteous ones: "Even though words of Torah are necessary for Me [*she-divrei torah tzerikhim hem 'alay*], you loved [*ḥibbiytem*] My Torah but did not love My Kingdom."[27] God then swears that those who truly desired the Kingdom are held in favor, and goes on to single out the "mourners" and their suffering with special regard. The text is opaque, and one may well wonder just what is going on.

This passage can be explained through a version of a midrash on the verse "If I forget thee, O Jerusalem, let My right hand forget its cunning," as taught by Rabbi Eleazer ha-Kappar. It occurs earlier in the homilies of consolation in *Pesiqta Rabbati* and is presented as a word of God (and not the cry of human mourners). The teaching goes as follows.

> My Torah is in your hands, and the End is in Mine, and the two of us need one another [*ve-sheneinu tzerikhim zeh la-zeh*]. If you need Me to bring the End, I need you to observe My Torah in order to hasten [*kedei le-qarev*] the building of My Temple and Jerusalem. And just as it is impossible for Me to forget the End, which is (like having) "My right hand forget," so you have no permission [*reshut*] to forget the Torah written "From His right hand, a fiery law for them" [Deut. 33:2].[28]

It is not necessary to go into the full mythic background presupposed by Rabbi Eleazar to observe that what is at issue in this midrash is a codependency between Israel and God with respect to the end, and the centrality of Torah observance as a necessary catalyst. Indeed, the end is not presented as a divine reward for the merit of obedience, but as somehow dependent upon the human performance of the commandments. This necessary nomism and the word *tzerikhim* ("need") explain the puzzling clause mentioned earlier from *pisqa* 34. There too it would appear that God testifies that "the words of Torah are necessary," while the new issue is the spiritual focus of the worshipper on His messianic Kingdom. Now it is this which distinguishes the "mourners of Zion," and one of the factors which led to their persecution may have been a certain anomistic tendency on their part (along with features of asceticism and social renunciation) that appeared in direct conflict with the world-affirmative character of Torah piety. Imposing laws of mourning upon themselves while the Temple was in ruins would have inevitably resulted in the suspension of many positive commandments. Several sources in rabbinic literature seem to me designed to neutralize just such activities.[29] By contrast, while never denying the Law, *pisqa* 34 is all praise for those who yearn mournfully for salvation. Indeed, the righteous only merit their reward after they respond in tears to God's statement that only "the *'aveilim* merit [the Messiah], because [only] they acknowledged him and did not think of themselves [*ve-lo' ḥeftzam ba-hem*]."

The turn to the figure of the Messiah brings the *pisqa* to its close. Two points deserve special note. The first is that this figure is named *'Oni* (or "Sufferer"; based on a rereading of Zechariah 9:9 as "*'Oni,* who rides on an ass"), because he is persecuted *(nit'aneh)* in jail and reviled by fellow Jews (called *posh'ei Yisrael*). In this, the Messiah is like the "mourners"—or, as the text says, they are "like him" *(domim lo)* and will be exalted with him. This remark deepens our understanding of the structure of suffering and expectation of the *'aveilim.* They not only imitate divine sorrow and participate in it, but they also live messianically in the strict sense. Their behavior and its consequences is a messianic posture that is vindicated by God. By contrast, the Messiah's own suffering vindicates the sinners and nonbelievers. This point is just adumbrated at the close of *pisqa* 34—but it is a salient theme in subsequent homilies.

Before we consider that aspect, it is important to refer to another issue: at the close of the *pisqa,* the Messiah called *'Oni* ("Sufferer") is also designated "Ephraim, My first born [*bekhori hu'*]" (Jeremiah 31:9). This passage leads to the prophetic assertion that "he" *(hu')* will be in the days of the Messiah *and* the world to come, "and [that] there will be none other with him [*ve-'ein 'aḥer 'immo*]." This striking formulation has the ring of a polemical assertion, stating in an unequivocal way that, for the preacher and his circle, there will be only one messianic figure—and that he will be the sufferer called Ephraim. Clearly, any other messianic figure, like David, is excluded; and by saying that Ephraim will be in *both* the days of the Messiah and the world to come, a sequence of figures (one, like Ephraim, who suffers at the messianic advent, and another, like David, who rules in the subsequent age) is also excluded. What is more—and I deem this point crucial—there is no notion here or in the subsequent chapters that the suffering Messiah is called "Ephraim, son of Joseph" (as in other sources), or that he dies in battle before the great End. Indeed, there is no mention whatever of a messianic death, or that death is even part of the messianic scenario. The stress is solely on Ephraim's suffering and its salvific function. As we learn from the sequel in *pisqa* 36, that suffering links the Messiah to God's own suffering. And for this he is exalted on high.

Pisqa 36 expands the messianic scenario to mythic proportions, and it continues but also contradicts features found in *pisqa* 34. The contradiction comes first, by way of a comment on the verse that opens the homily. After citing Psalm 36:10, "With You is the source of life, and in Your light we shall see light," the preacher proceeds to identify the "source of life" with the Torah, through which the worshipper may enjoy God's own light in time to come. Only after this clarification does he go on to depict the pre-mundane nature of that light and its relationship to the Messiah. Thus he exalts obedience to the Law as the means by which one may benefit from the messianic glory—with nothing said about the beatification of messianic mourners. Nevertheless, there is a strong thematic link to earlier motifs through God's naming of the Messiah as "Ephraim, My righteous Messiah [*meshiaḥ tzidqi*]," and the emphasis on the importance of suffering in the days before the End.[30]

Although the preacher says that God "envisioned the Messiah and his deeds" before the creation of the world, we learn that the great commission scene of the Messiah takes place during "the six days of creation." Accordingly, the preacher has utilized or developed a myth that goes considerably beyond the well-known tradition that the "name of the Messiah" was one of the things thought of by God at this primordial time.[31] Indeed, in our version, both the Messiah *and* his name already exist during the first six days.

The dialogue that unfolds between God and the future Messiah at this time is of crucial importance to the messianology (and apocalyptic theology) of the preacher. In it, God warns the Messiah of horrible sufferings that he will endure in the final days because of the sins of the people, and asks him, "Do you willingly accept this?" [*ritzonekha bekhakh*] and adds that if the Messiah is unhappy at this prospect, he is unacceptable. In response, the Messiah says: "With joy and gladness [*be-gilat nafshi uvesimḥat libbi*] I accept all this, so that no one in Israel will be doomed"; and he goes on to add that his salvific actions are not only for the living but also for all those who have died since Adam. This theological notion apparently used to be more widespread in Judaism; it had been cited by Martini from a lost midrash by Rabbi Mosheh Ha-Darshan[32] and had achieved notoriety in the Debates of Tortosa and San Mateo.[33] The Messiah thus joyfully embraces his future suffering, using an old legal phrase indicating willing and unreserved agreement,[34] because this suffering for sins anticipated before the creation will "save" every human that is or ever was.

Before continuing with the homily itself, let me add parenthetically that the notion of a willing acceptance of suffering is not unique to this source. It is in fact a widespread feature of old Jewish legal sources, and includes such terms as "will" and "love."[35] In the light of this, it may be proposed that the well-known rabbinic expression that speaks of the acceptance of suffering "in love [*me-'ahavah*]" means nothing less than the willing and full-hearted acceptance of the travail. Significantly, a notable formulation of this idiom is found in the Talmud, in a detailed interpretation of Isaiah 53:10 preserved by Rabba (*b. Berakhot* 5a). All this provides an intriguing parallel to the ideas articulated in the *pisqa* passage. Nevertheless, it must be emphasized that the type of suffering mentioned in the Talmudic source only benefits the specific individual. It thus stands in sharp contrast to our homily, which speaks of the joyful acceptance by a Messiah designate (at the beginning, in principle, and in the fullness of time, in actuality) of all the punishments due the unborn souls found with him before the creation[36]—and that his joyful endurance of suffering for universal sins would save them all.[37]

But despite the Messiah's good intentions, the *Pesiqta* homily continues, the tribulations of the End are great, and Ephraim cries out in suffering, claiming that he is but a creature of flesh and blood. God then answers him by recalling his agreement in primordial days, and by saying that "now your suffering will be like My own [*'akhshav yehei tza'ar shelekha ke-tza'ar sheli*]." God goes on to describe His suffering since the destruction of the Temple by Nebuchadnezzar, and even boldly applies the passage in the Song of Songs that says "My head is filled with dew" (Songs 5:2) to His own tears. Upon hearing this, the Messiah is consoled, and says, "*nityashevah da'ati; dayo la-'eved she-yehei ke-rabbo;* I am reconciled; it is sufficient that a servant should be like his master." This marks a recurrence of the earlier theme, in which the *'aveilim* suffer God's sorrow, although now this act of human suffering has a world-redemptive effect. In recognition of this, the Patriarchs say to Ephraim (in *piska* 37), "You are greater than us; for though we are your ancestors, you have borne the sins of our descendants [*she-savalta 'avonot baneinu*]."

This last allusion to Isaiah 53,[38] and the preceding reference to the salvation by Ephraim of all sinners who have died since Adam, allow us, I believe, to affirm the authenticity of a remarkable midrash on messianic suffering cited in Martini's *Pugio Fidei*,[39] as follows.

> Rabbi Yosi the Galilean said: You may learn the merit of the King Messiah and the reward of the righteous from Adam, who was given but

> one negative commandment, and having transgressed caused death for his generations and those to come until the end of time. Now which attribute (quality) is greater, Goodness or Punishment? Conclude that Goodness is the greater and Punishment the lesser; for [if] the King Messiah was persecuted and sorrowed for the sinners [*mit'aneh u-mitzṭa'er be'ad ha-poshe'im*], as is said [Isaiah 53:5], "And he was wounded for our sins," how much the more will [this suffering] provide merit for all the generations [*kol ha-dorot kullan*], as it is written [Isaiah 53:6], "And the Lord visited upon him the sin of all of us."

The foregoing teaching has a parallel in the *Sifra de-Bei Rav, Dibbura' de-Ḥovah* (12.10), as Saul Lieberman noted many years ago.[40] In it, Rabbi Yosi teaches the merit of the righteous using the same *a fortiori* argument as in the Martini version. The salient differences are that the *Sifra* passage says nothing about the Messiah, does not quote from Isaiah 53, and instead of referring to messianic suffering speaks of the merit of refraining from the sacrificial sins of *piggul* and *notar,* and of "self-affliction [*mit'aneh*]" on Yom Kippur.[41] For these reasons (and assuming scribal changes), Lieberman concluded that the version in the *Pugio Fidei* is a Christian forgery.[42] But this is not a foregone conclusion. For one thing, the difference between the stress on the merits of the righteous and those of messianic suffering in our two texts is formally no different than the difference between *Seder Eliahu Zuṭṭa* 21 and *Pesiqta Rabbati* 36, where the same two types occur. In both cases, it may be said, we have either parallel versions, with different tendencies, or, more likely, the transformation of texts dealing *inter alia* with the sufferings of the righteous into teachings about messianic suffering.

Beyond this, a far more important consideration in evaluating the Martini midrash is that its key elements regarding suffering for sinners occur in *Pesiqta Rabbati* 34, 36–37. In both cases the suffering goes back to the sin of Adam, on whose account death entered the world; in both cases, the suffering meritoriously saves all sinners; in both cases Isaiah 53 is a central text; and in both cases the suffering of the Messiah is limited to wounds. Nothing is mentioned about an atoning death for sin, and nothing is mentioned about a Davidic ancestry. Accordingly, there seems to be no more reason to assume Christian influence in the midrash gathered for Martini by his Rabbi Rachmon than in our *Pesiqta* cycle.[43]

Undoubtedly, these sources were part of an inner Jewish development of messianic interpretations based on Isaiah 53, the antiquity of which need not be doubted. Already in the second century (C.E.) Justin Martyr has Trypho repeatedly say that the Jews expected a suffering Messiah, though he denied that it was Jesus.[44] In another striking testimony, reported by the author of the *'Avqat Rokhel* (preserved in Hulsius' *Theologia Judaica*), we have a significant variant of a reading found in *Pesiqta Rabbati* 36. In that latter context the Messiah-designate "joyfully" *(be-simḥat libbi)* accepts suffering to atone for the sins of Israel ("so that no Israelite will be lost"), as well as for all those that God has thought to create but are not yet born.[45] In the new instance the primordial scene receives the following formulation:

> The Holy One, blessed be He, took out the soul of the Messiah [from under the heavenly throne?], and said to him: "Do you wish to be created and redeem my children after 6000 years?" He answered, "Yes." [Then] He [God] said to him: "If so, you will bear [*tisbol*] sufferings to annul their sin [!]; as it is written: 'Truly he has borne our sickness' [*'akhen 'et ḥoloyeinu hu' nasa'*].' [And] he said to Him: "I shall bear them joyfully [*'esbol 'otam be-simḥah*]."[46]

Significantly, Isaiah 53:4 is the chief prooftext for this text on messianic suffering, generating a divine warning and a willing human acceptance of the tribulations to come. The cultural importance of this verse, along with its sequel (v. 5), is reaffirmed by way of a precious manuscript first published by Adolph Büchler, in which these two verses serve as the conclusion to a triennial *haftarah* recited for the lectionary *seder* (unit) Genesis 29:1–40:29.[47] It thus dramatically attests to the public nature of this theme in liturgical contexts well before the end of the first millenium—and possibly much earlier. Within this rich exegetical tradition, the uniqueness of the messianic "tractate" in *Pesiqta Rabbati* lies in its exalted theological correlation of human with divine suffering, and of course in the naming of the Messiah Ephraim.

But why Ephraim? This is an old hedge with many thorns. Among the diverse explanations that have been proposed, quite typical are those that elide this person with a messianic figure called Ephraim ben Joseph and, stressing that figure's death, suggest Christian influence.[48] Other scholars have asserted that this figure was developed to separate the Messiah son of David from sufferings in the end of days.[49] But none of these suggestions comport with the imagery of our textual cycle, where Ephraim has no patronymic and does not die. Accordingly, there is room for a more exegetical approach. Given the emphasis on messianic suffering in our *Pesiqta* chapters, the frequent recourse to prooftexts from Isaiah 53, and the reference to Ephraim as God's "firstborn" (Jer. 31:9),[50] one may wonder whether these matters are more intimately linked. On closer inspection just this appears to be the case, for there are several striking connections between Isaiah 53:4, 5, and 14 and Jeremiah 31—specifically, those verses where Ephraim says that "I have been sorely afflicted [*yisartani va-'ivaser*] and "have borne the shame of my youth [*nasa'ti ḥerpat ne'urai*]" (vv. 18–19).[51] The identification of Ephraim with the suffering servant in Isaiah 53 would further result in Ephraim's association with the atoning function of the sufferings described there. As the whole process would proceed at the level of midrashic intuition, there is no explicit proof.

But there may be another reason for the choice of Ephraim, and that would lie elsewhere in this prophecy of Jeremiah, who said that God will restore Ephraim and turn his "mourning into joy [*'evlam le-simḥah*]" (Jer. 31:13). Since the preacher of *Pesiqta Rabbati* 34 was clearly a sympathizer (if not a member) of the mourners of Zion *('avelei tziyyon)*, that phrase would have special significance. Indeed, since its language is poignantly similar to God's promise that the mourners of Zion shall be given "a festive ointment instead of mourning [*shemen sason taḥat 'eivel*]" (Isa. 61:2–3), it would undoubtedly suggest to later listeners that this prophecy would be fulfilled through one named Ephraim. As we have seen, this was just the point made by the preacher in *Pesiqta Rabbati* 34–37 in unequivocal terms.[52] For him and his audience, Ephraim was "he that cometh"—he and no other.

Whether the homilist reasoned in these exegetical terms we shall never know. And how he convinced his audience of the truth of his claims is also unstated. But we must not underestimate the thick patterning of citations in his oratory, and that he claims to deliver teachings revealed by the Holy Spirit to Isaiah, David, Solomon, and Jeremiah, respectively. Not least of the marvels of this cycle is the alignment of the rabbis with the revelation of hidden mysteries. In this respect, the classical remark by Rav Abudimi, that "Since the destruction of the Temple prophecy has been taken from the prophets and given to the sages," has been paradoxically confirmed—though far beyond that sage's wildest imagination.[53]

6

Five Stages of Jewish Myth and Mythmaking

The gods must be happy with their human muses—if the bounty of myths be any measure. For what sights have not been described as divine activities, and what sounds not heard as sacred speech? Some mythmakers say that the stars testify to the valor of ancient deities; others claim that the roiling sea plots a revolt against the lord of heaven. And who knows if the blood-red dawn is the sign of birth or death in the hidden heights? Certainly myth is in the mind of the beholder, and in all the forms (both personal and cultural) through which it finds expression. The life of myth oscillates between these two poles.

Historians of religion have long been enthralled by the origins of myth. The result is a vast library of Babel, filled with works in search of beginnings and some first naiveté. Indeed, the formulations of myth seem to attract the scholarly mind like a siren calling from primordial depths. But the persistence of myths also leaves no doubt that mythmaking is an ongoing creative process, endlessly sprung from the coils of imagination. Fascination with this enduring creativity is also part of the enchantment of myth.

As a student of Judaism I have long been under this double spell, though many have argued that its literatures are protected by the seal of monotheism. The Hebrew Bible is commonly said to have thoroughly broken with pagan polytheism and its mythic impulses.[1] Accordingly, the few myth-like formulations that visibly remain are read as poetic tropes or ancient, frozen forms. In a similar way, these and other figures in rabbinic literature are deemed to be popular images serving homiletic ends—but with no deeper or living sense.[2] The defenders of a pure monotheism thus triumphantly survey the rubble of mythology at the base of Sinai, and presume that only golden calves could be made from these leftovers. Accordingly, when myth arose in the heart of medieval Kabbalah with undeniable vigor, even great scholars could only assume an alien invasion.[3]

This view is puzzling, not least because it assumes that rabbis educated for a millennium in an allegedly nonmythological tradition suddenly decided to eat from this new tree of knowledge—all the while proclaiming it as the deepest truth of Judaism. Indeed, if myth and monotheism were so incompatible, how did the sages of medieval Spain and Germany turn the trick so silently and so successfully? This query begs the question, and invites a reconsideration of rabbinic Midrash and its own biblical sources. The result is quite a different perspective on the life of myth in Judaism, a life that runs parallel to the path of philosophical rationalism charted by Philo, Saadia, and Maimonides. For if these great thinkers strove to refine the divine imagery of Scripture in the fire of allegory, another exegetical trajectory begins with the myths of Scripture and develops new ones of much daring and drama throughout antiquity and the Middle Ages. There are no breaks here, only layers of hermeneutical transformation.[4]

In an effort to make these strata visible, the ensuing discussion will attempt a concise archeology of the mythmaking imagination in biblical, midrashic, and kabbalistic literature. And precisely because the imagination lies at the heart of this historical process, a speculation on the primary forms of myth will serve as an introduction. The concluding stage of poetic myth will, paradoxically, recall these imaginative origins from the opposite end of the spectrum.

As I suggested earlier, a primary factor in the creation of myths is that it arises in the mind of the beholder. No two persons or cultures will necessarily perceive the same sense in the sounds and sights of existence, nor name them alike, nor describe their patterns in the same way. But in this naming and fabulation myth is born and develops.[5] Recurrent shapes are noted and narrated in relation to other shapes, and dramas are perceived in the arc of heaven and the weather on earth. Through these acts and interludes the gods first appear on the stage of myth. Put somewhat differently, we may say that myth is fundamentally the creative representation of existence as divine actions described in human terms. It is thus the work of the imagination, perceiving and positing the world as its own manifestation. Herder had it best, when he said in his own myth of myths: "As all nature sounds; so to Man, creature of sense, nothing would seem more natural than that it lives and speaks and acts . . . The driving storm, the gentle zephyr, the clear fountain and mighty ocean—their whole mythology lies in these treasure troves, in *verbis* and *nominibus* of the ancient languages; and the earliest dictionary was thus a sounding pantheon."[6]

For some, "the voice" of God is the thunderous blast "over the mighty waters"—"shattering the cedars" and "kindling flames of fire" (Psalm 29:3–7); while for others it is a thin timbre after the tenebrous passing of the storm (1 Kings 19:11–12).[7] And what of the earthquake that shatters the earth? For some ancient Greeks this is caused by Poseidon *enosigaios*, who in eerie anger so shakes the earth as to cause the lord of the dead himself to leap from his throne in fear that the terrestrial crust will break and the dark spheres of hell be exposed to the light (*Iliad* 20.57 ff). According to one rabbinic sage, the *zeva'ot* mentioned in the Mishnah are "earthquakes" caused by the tears of God falling into the Great Sea, when He thinks of His people in exile and utters a world-resounding cry of sorrow. Other rabbis proposed that the earth tremors are due to God clapping His hands or squeezing His feet under the Throne of Glory.[8] In the process of transmission, even these mythic views have been acculturated by scriptural proofs. But the reader is not deceived. The myths come first, as dramatic decoding of the "sounding pantheon" of existence.

There is thus an epistemological paradox at the heart of myth: the gods can be seen and heard, but only in human terms. The primordial terrors and fascinations which excite myth (the nameless sights and sounds of existence) are formulated in a subjective space opened up between this *mysterium* and the self-conscious human self. Here emerge the shapes and forms of myth; and to the extent that they seem not merely personal musings but transcending truths about divine life, these fabulations are stabilized and preserved by the culture for recitation and rite. Momentary pronouncements, reflecting first-order formulations of myth by individuals, may come to endure through their valorization as foundational accounts of the origin and nature of things.[9] The myths will then speak with an apparently more objective voice—one that masks their all-too-human origin, so that they might sound like some all-knowing revelation from a time "when the heavens had not yet been named, and the earth had not yet come into being." In this transformation, myth may fulfill the mythmaker's deepest desire.

But far more important is the fact that in this transformation from personal to public expressions, myths become second-order formulations of culture. This is their second stage. Over time, the primary evocations of myth are stylized and reworked into sophisticated composites, harmonized with local temple traditions, or retold in new contexts. Think of the so-called Babylonian Epic of Creation *(Enuma elish)*. Any number of its motifs or episodes can be traced back to earlier Sumerian and Akkadian myths, often with varying plots and divine heroes. In other instances, the duplication of actions or contradictory and uncharacteristic formulations may arguably derive from different smaller myths or revisions.[10] Such reworkings show how key motifs and figures entered different settings and served different needs over many generations. The upshot is the bold reuse of myth, whose vitality undergoes reciprocal transformations. Myth becomes constitutive of tradition.

Cross-cultural and inter-cultural reuses of myth are especially intriguing for appreciating its powers of regeneration and acculturation. The relation between Near Eastern mythology and similar topics in the biblical sources has long constituted a special case—both because the fuller pagan evidence has magnified or helped discern traces of myth in Scripture, and because analysis of similarities and differences between the two culture spheres transcends mere scholarly interests and bears on issues of Western cultural identity. The efforts of comparison and contrast have therefore been a not altogether innocent endeavor. For one thing, methodological interests and judgments have been variously affected by presuppositions about the nature of myth and Israelite monotheism; for another, these inquiries are often guided by all-too-contemporary religious commitments. A common course has thus been to argue that myth is a feature of polytheism whose many gods are largely gendered forces of nature. This position is then contrasted with biblical monotheism, which is characterized by a single God of sovereign will, who transcends nature and is known through acts in history. This comparison is not incorrect, so far as it goes. But as an ideological wedge, it serves the purpose of separating myth from monotheism.

Just this split may be vigorously contended. Indeed, the majesty of myth would be greatly diminished were it defined by only one type of religious phenomenon. We have already suggested that the medieval record attests to complex integrations of mythic images and themes into the most traditional of circles. At this point it may suffice to say that monotheistic myth is not alien to ancient Israelite monotheism. In fact, from the complexes of mythology of second-millennium Mesopotamia and Canaan, diverse "bundles of tradition" were absorbed into biblical culture and nativized in various ways. These bundles are, to be sure, quite far (in the main) from the *numina* of sight and sound that animate first-order mythology. They are rather second-order formulations that remake the old pagan myths in the context of living monotheism.

Psalm 74 provides an initial example. In an extended appeal, a supplicant cries out to God, asking "Why, O Lord, do You forever reject us . . . in anger"?, and requesting that He "Remember the community that You made Yours long ago" (vv. 1–2). The theme is then developed that God's foes have destroyed His shrine, and reviled both Him and His people (vv. 3–9; 18–23). At the center the psalmist repeats this point (v. 10), and poignantly asks: "Why do You hold back Your hand, Your right hand"? (v. 11). There then follows this recitation of divine praise.

> O God, my king from of old,
> Who brings deliverance throughout the land;
> You it was who drove back Sea [*Yam*] with Your might,
> Who smashed the heads of [the] [*Tanninim*] monsters in the waters;
> You it was who crushed the heads of Leviathan,
> Who left them for food for the denizens of the desert;
> You it was who released springs and torrents,
> You made the rivers run dry;
> Yours is the day, and also the night;
> You established the moon and sun;
> You fixed the boundaries of the earth;
> Summer and winter—You made them. (vv. 12–17)

In his invocation, the psalmist clearly alludes to events at the beginning of creation—mentioning first the destruction of the primordial sea-monsters, and then various acts of world-ordering. The poetical depiction is striking, and several of the images and terms recall Genesis 1—so much so, in fact, that one might even suppose that our psalm unit is adapted from that account. But the differences are too fundamental.

Genesis 1 speaks of the creation of the *Tanninim* in the sea, but has no battle references whatever; it shows a strong interest in the creatures and vegetation of the earthly environment; and it presents God's creations as the result of royal decrees. Nothing could be farther from the strife and drama portrayed in Psalm 74. What is more, the battle images of the psalm are not merely poetical tropes. They rather partake of a literary tradition shared with Canaanite mythology. In that corpus the god Baal destroys sea-monsters with exactly the same names and epithets as those found in the biblical text.[11] Accordingly, it would be more accurate to say that the psalmist has produced a monotheistic reworking of an older nature myth and integrated it into an independent synopsis of the strife or origins. Thus this account neither rivals Genesis 1 nor doubles it in figurative terms. More like the prologue to Psalm 89 (vv. 10–13), or the whole of Psalm 104, Psalm 74's mythic images express God's might at the beginning of the world. The canonical priority of Genesis 1 for later tradition implies no inherently privileged position for its version and theology over the other depictions of origins preserved in ancient Israelite culture. Before the canonical ordering and closure of Scripture, there were merely different accounts in different circles—no hierarchy whatever.

This view can still concur with the opinion that the final shape of the Hebrew Bible is not mythic—in the sense that its overall concern is not with pre-mundane or divine events. Indeed, the shift of focus to God's involvement in human history is readily granted; and one will equally note that the battle against primordial monsters in Psalm 74 is also incorporated into a historical framework. But this only underscores the mythic realism preserved in this piece. Speaking from the standpoint of historical crisis, the psalmist repeatedly refers to God in personal terms and recites the old *magnalia dei* in hopes that God will reactivate His ancient powers in the present. One would hardly expect that such a discourse and such a need would produce fictive figures. Why would the psalmist depict a victory he believed never happened if his manifest purpose is to solicit divine help on that very basis? Too much is at stake to assume that the myth invoked is nothing other than a deceptive trope or dead letter. Moreover, the very attempt of modern commentators to split myth off from history when God is involved in both can only reinforce ancient and modern prejudices. I would therefore stress that, for the psalmist, there is no gap between the events *miqedem*, "from of old," and the new ones he prays for. For him, God is a mighty king of power, who revealed His might in the past and can do so yet again. Over time, the enemies may change from water dragons to churlish heathens—but this hardly makes the newer divine battle less mythic. I therefore propose the term "mythistory" for such phenomena—and mean by it an account of mundane events where God or the gods are involved from beginning to end.

The well-known plea in Isaiah 51:9–11 reinforces this point. "Arise, arise, clothe yourself with power, O arm of the Lord," says the prophet, "Arise as in days of old [*miqedem*]." He then goes on to recall to the arm (as a personified entity) its great triumphs against the sea monsters *Tannin* in primordial times and against *Yam* at the time of the Exodus, in the hopes that this arm will be revived and rescue the nation in the present. Ancient and medieval commentators were beset by the stark realism of the invocation, and often read the unit in figurative and allegorical terms. In this way they saved the text—for their own use. But the biblical prophet is hardly in an allegorical mood; and he hardly invents the terms of his prayer. Like the psalmist in Psalm 74, this prophet looks to the Lord's arm as the agent of all divine victories; and again like the psalmist, who repeatedly addresses God as "You" when reciting His deeds, the prophet twice invokes the arm as "you" when recalling its past powers. Speaking from exile, the prophet hopes that human events may again be the sphere of divine involvement so that they will be transfigured mythically.

This reconstruction of the relationship between myth and history in ancient Israel is thus grounded in speech-acts in which a mythic scenario (itself composed of bundles of tradition) is fully integrated into monotheistic theology. Precisely how the psalmist or the prophet understood the reality of Leviathan and the arm eludes us. But it is hard to imagine that on a topic as serious as acts of divine redemption these speakers would juggle with tropes. Many examples confirm this point, and some of them even persuade modern interpreters to acknowledge the theological power that several common ancient Near Eastern myths exert in the Bible. But they stop there, as if the rest of biblical imagery about God were wholly other than myth. This approach cuts a deal with the imagination. It acknowledges the ancient myths, but regards them as essentially alien forms accommodated to Scripture's higher (nonmythic) purposes. This tack is particularly useful when it comes to figures depicting

God riding to Sinai on a storm cloud, or envisaging His appearance in battle spattered in blood—images used to depict acts of Baal and Anat in Canaanite literature.

But one may well wonder whether attempts to regard such biblical imagery as (mere) metaphors of Near Eastern origin are meant to defer to or deny that which is mythically manifest as a native truth. After all, the biblical narrator injects no qualifications into his speech, but speaks forthrightly about real divine manifestations. Surely the matter is complex and requires reflection on the status of certain images of the divine in the Hebrew Bible. That granted, it does not follow that if Scripture proclaims that God cannot be seen by the natural eye, He cannot be conjured by the mythic imagination. Is this not, to the contrary, just how He is made manifest *sub specie textualis?*

I would go further. Just as there is a mythic dimension to the presentation of God's great deeds in time, so does the Bible resort to myth when it comes to portraying the divine personality. While this dimension is not in principle different from the accounts of the lives of the gods in Mesopotamia or Greece, the distinctive feature of the monotheistic myth of ancient Israel is that its God is a unity of traits found separately among the "other gods," and (in its view) is of a higher order of magnitude. Promise and purpose, requital and memory, wrath and mercy—all these are among the vital aspects of the divine Person in relationship to Israel and the world. Indeed, just here is the core of monotheistic myth as it is imagined by narrators and poets and prophets. In the Hebrew Bible the divine person makes a covenant with His people and punishes the offenders; while the human person fears the consequences of sin and wonders whether divine mercy may assuage stern judgment. Is this divine care and involvement not part of the mythic pulse of Scripture? "In anger, remember mercy," cries the prophet, and receives a terrifying vision of God's advent in return (Habakkuk 3:2). It thus takes a certain theological solipsism to contend that the angry dooms of God are mere metaphor in the Bible, while the punishments of Shamash or Nergal are myth elsewhere. Indeed, in chapter 28 of the book of Deuteronomy one section of the curses is exactly the same as another found in an Assyrian vassal treaty, with only changes of divine nomenclature marking the difference.[12] In the same vein, why assume that God's advice to Noah before the flood is a literary figure but that Ea's counsel to Utnapishtim is myth—unless one is concerned to "save Scripture" from its own depictions. Let the theologians and literary exegetes ponder the forms of biblical anthropomorphism as they will; one is still left with its bold psychological and personal realism. Even God does not deny it. For when He says through the prophet Hosea that "I am God and not a man," we should not suppose this to be some revelation of transcendental impersonality. Being a God rather means, as God Himself says, "I will not act on My wrath," for "I have had a change of heart, (and) all My tenderness is stirred" (Hosea 11:8–9). Control of anger is thus a decisive difference between "God and . . . man," and in this divine attribute later psalmists put their trust. I would call these dynamics of the divine personality—described in relation to human beings—"mytheology."

As considered here, biblical myth turns on two poles: the inheritance and monotheistic transformation of mythic bundles from the ancient Near East, and concrete and dramatic features of the divine personality. Both aspects are constitutive. Only by taking the realism of these formulations seriously will it be possible to get behind the rationalistic depletions of myth so characteristic of modern ideological scholarship, not to mention their eighteenth-, thirteenth-, ninth- and even first-century predecessors. What is more, this recovery of Scripture will in turn reveal the "mythistory" and "mytheology" so central to ancient Israelite thought and to the sages of the Midrash. Indeed, ancient rabbinic theology is the direct heir of ancient biblical myth, centering its focus on the divine actions and personality revealed to them through Scripture. To be sure, this theological orientation is no mere repetition of earlier formulations, but routinely takes the more mediated form of exegesis—boldly reinterpreting and recombining the received words and images of Scripture. In this way the older mythic bundles were enlarged and new ones formed. The process and result of this work is a new type of mythmaking, or *mythopoesis*. It begins where the Hebrew Bible closes: with the canon.

The third stage of Jewish mythmaking thus takes the entirety of Scripture into account; and when viewed from that vantage point, the creation account in Genesis 1 clearly has a privileged position. For the sake of literary and theological coherence, all other references to the events of this primordial time had somehow to be coordinated with it. In doing this work, the ancient rabbis established the principle that if Moses' words in Genesis 1 were terse or obscure, they could be explicated through other passages where more details were given.[13] Such passages include references to God's creative acts in Psalm 104, where we read that God robed Himself in light like a garment, or stretched out the heavens like a tent cloth. For the sages, the similes in these passages did not mean that the events so described were any less real. Read superficially, they appear as mere tropes; but to the rabbinic eye mythic fragments of theological significance could be perceived. God did robe Himself in light, and He did stretch out the heavens—even if the account in Genesis 1 omits this depiction or says so in less dramatic terms. By being linked to this master narrative, a variety of other creation images in the Scripture were charged with a mythic valence. Moreover, the reintegration of such mythic fragments into Genesis 1 also gave that text a new mythic content. It was as if some deep mythic substrate emerged from the depths, filling the spaces of Genesis 1 with concrete mythic vitality. In a remarkable manner, what this biblical document had suppressed returns to full view in the Midrash. Indeed, from this point of view, midrashic exegesis exposes an archeology of the cultural mind. Elsewhere, too, the liberated exegetical imagination opens the words of Scripture and finds hoary myth curled at their root.

On first hearing, for instance, God's regal word in Genesis 1:9 would seem far from myth. He says: "Let the waters be gathered *(yiqqavu ha-mayyim)* under the heavens to one place." To be sure, this brief depiction is itself not altogether free of myth; but one will readily admit that the limitation of anthropomorphic features to speech does much to spiritualize the process of creation, and in any case the command does not appear to be addressed to any other divine entity with independent will or personality. Thus, if this evocation be myth in some sense, it is certainly drained of any dramatic elements that would give the account full mythic substance. Accordingly, the figure of God's transcendent will and lordly speech in Genesis 1 may be high theology, but as myth it is flat and boring.

The rabbis do much to change this situation. For example, in an anonymous homily found in Midrash *Genesis Rabba*,[14] the phrase "Let the waters be gathered" is starkly juxtaposed to Psalm 104:7, where the psalmist says to God: "At the blast of Your fury, the [the waters] fled." Nothing more is added, and one would hardly know from this that the image derives from a mythic pattern depicting the rout of the sea by a divine hero. Nevertheless, enough is suggested by the figures of fury and flight to indicate that, for some sages, an undercurrent of mythic drama lay concealed beneath the waters gathered at God's command. For Rabbi Levi, on the other hand, this drama was entirely benign. In his teaching, the sequence of phrases in Psalm 93:3 ("The ocean sounds, O Lord, the ocean sounds its voice, the ocean sounds its pounding [*dokhyam*]") is adduced to show that the waters praised God and obediently accepted His dictate to go to the place designated for them. To make this last point, R. Levi cleverly chose to interpret the obscure Hebrew word *dokhyam* in the last clause as a composite of two—the Aramaic word for "place" *(dokh),* and the Hebrew word for "sea" *(yam).* Other sages also interpret this psalm to refer to the obedience of the primal waters, but interpret the word *dokhyam* as a statement by the waters that they are "suppressed" *(dokhim).* In so doing the old mythic undercurrent has again billowed up to betray a tale of primordial rebellion and defeat.

A passage in *Midrash Tanḥuma* fills in the details.[15] Starting from a query about the meaning of the phrase "He stores up the ocean waters like a mound" (Psalm 33:7), the interpreter proceeds with the following mythic explanation.

> When the Holy One, blessed be He, created the world, he said to the Prince of [the] Sea, "Open your mouth and swallow all the primal waters." He answered: "Master of the Universe, I have enough [water] of my own," and began to cry. [Thereupon] God kicked him to death, as Scripture says, "In his strenghth He battered Sea, and in His cleverness smote Rahab" [Job 26:12]. From this you can see that Prince Sea was called Rahab. What [then] did the Holy One, Blessed be He, do? He crushed [the waters] and trampled them, and thus did the Sea receive them; as it is said, "He [God] trod over the back of the earth." [Amos 4:13]

This remarkable vignette gives concrete testimony, if such were needed, that the sages read Scripture with living myths in mind—transforming older mythic bundles through biblical phrases, and developing new monotheistic composites. Old traditions of combat (and even technical terms thousands of years old, and not found in Scripture) are revised to conform to the master narrative of Genesis 1: the battle takes place in the course of the creation, and it results from the rebellion of a created entity, not a primordial or rival divinity. Taking all the creation images of Scripture as so many dispersed fragments of a shattered myth, the sages (here and elsewhere) reconstruct its pieces into various mosaics, depending of the issue that occasions the specific teaching. In the process, true mythic fragments (like Job's reference to the smiting of Rahab) are removed from their original poetic settings and rehabilitated as new scriptural myths. And at the same time, highly poeticized figures in the Bible (like the psalmist's reference to the gathering of the sea in mounds) are frequently mythicized in their new contexts. Nothing argues more for a living mythic imagination than this reworking and elaboration of the acts of God.

But midrashic mythmaking goes further. Like His representations in Scripture, the rabbinic God not only acts but feels, reacts, and remembers with much pathos.[16] In short, this God also has a personality, and His personality is particularly tied to the fate of Israel. This is only to be expected, since rabbinic mythmaking is intimately linked to the language of Scripture studied and recited on Sabbaths and holidays, when the historical and religious life of the people would be pondered in the light of God's eternal word. Nevertheless, one is still struck by the frequency with which the divine acts and feelings of Scripture—particularly those of judgment and anger—are either intensified or reversed in Midrash. Through such means, the sages invent myths of pathos and consolation for the heirs of Scripture, out of its very language and formulations.

The motif of the arm of the Lord may again serve as an example. We noted earlier that psalmists and prophets believed that the withdrawal of this agent of salvation is a cause of sorrow and longing. A mourner of Zion laments this explicitly, when he cries in despair after the destruction of Judea: "The Lord has swallowed without pity all the pastures of Jacob . . . [He] broke the horn of Israel in fury, [and] withdrew His right arm before the enemy" (Lam. 2:2–3). The elegy goes on in this vein, combining images of divine aggression with others in which God withdraws His protection. The image of the arm exemplifies this loss. But is it myth? The abundance and nature of the other tropes, and the absence of a narrative schema that would fit the images into a more coherent dramatic shape, suggest that the image of God withdrawing His arm (like those of swallowing, breaking, and trampling) are but metaphors of terror, figures of God's horrific fury.

It is therefore a wonder that the sages should have perceived in this trope of the arm not only myth but a hidden expression of divine sympathy. Yet they do. A striking case is a homily from the *Pesiqta de-Rav Kahana* (17.5).[17] According to that account, when Resh Lakish once gave a sermon of consolation, he opened it with the great oath of constancy, "If I forget thee, O Jerusalem, let my right hand forget its cunning" (Psalm 137:5), and immediately correlated it with the just-cited lament that God "withdrew His arm before *(mipnei)* the enemy." In so doing, the sage boldly transformed the trope. For now God is said to have pondered the travail of His people and, recalling His avowed commitments to Israel, as when He swore that "I shall be with him in trouble" (Psalm 91:15), He bound His own arm behind Him in sympathy with Israel for the duration of the exile. To achieve this exegetical *tour de force,* Resh Lakish boldly reinterpreted the old lament, construing the adverb *mipnei* to mean that God would withdraw His arm *because* of what the enemy did to His people—not *in the face* of the advancing horde. Once bitter, the words now pour sweet honey to salve the wounds of suffering. Concretizing the trope, Resh Lakish has God re-enact its details. This results in a new myth, born of metaphor. In a later version preserved in the third Book of Enoch (48 A), that very arm is seen in mystic vision to be weeping tears into the sea of exile, as all about the saints of Israel recite "Arise, arise, clothe yourself in strength, O Arm of the Lord." But the tears keep flowing. The scene of sympathy depicted in the earlier Midrash (in the *Pesiqta*) has thus been combined with the Talmudic trope of God dropping tears of sorrow into the sea (*b. Berakhot* 59a). The result is a composite myth, constructed out of several midrashic myths and biblical verses. As the canonical boundaries expand, rabbinic myth invents itself.

Fundamental to the mythic inventions of Judaism is the role of language as a shaping force of the imagination. Indeed, myth and language are intricately connected; a deep dialectic affects them reciprocally. At its core, myth tries to articulate the sounds and sights of the divine in the natural world. Arguably, the grammar of existence is the first sounding script. In their second-order formulation, whose corpus for our purposes is the Hebrew Bible, the cultural components of language predominate. The myths go native, so to speak, and become the units (or bundles) of tradition in constantly revised literary forms. Now the sounds and sights of the divine include primordial and historical dramas of God's interactions with the world. In time, narrative patterns emerge that provide both sequence and consequence to the dramas. Here the pulse of myth varies with the impulse of the speaker, who now makes bold and now retreats, whose figures are alternatively transcendent and immanent, and who gives greater or lesser access to God's personality. For the emerging Scripture of the Hebrew Bible, the language of myth articulates the cumulative sights and sounds and stories of God in His relationship to Israel and the world.

Rabbinic Midrash reads this language and coordinates its diverse images. In its third-order mythic formulations, the whole of Scripture provides the linguistic signs of God's deeds and personality. The details are there—plain to see, or clarified with the help of exegesis. An obscure point in one place is illumined by a clearer expression elsewhere, and telling gaps are filled by actions told in other settings. The patterns vary, depending upon their literary starting point and the context of the details being considered. Thus the forms of the combat myth differ as they appear in prayers, prophecies, or narratives. Similarly, the myths of creation differ depending on whether they are separate citations in a psalm or diverse images correlated with a master narrative like Genesis 1. In all these ways, exegesis constructs mythic forms new to Scripture.

For the masters of Midrash, the language of Scripture manifests God's historical actions and concerns in mythic terms. Mystical theosophy is different. It builds upon the results of Midrash, but goes much further in its mythic achievements. This brings us to a fourth type of mythic formulation, more radical than the preceding three because it involves Scripture in a different way and gives more play to the exegetical imagination. Judging by such classical works of mysticism as the books of *Bahir* and *Zohar*, from the twelfth and thirteenth centuries, respectively, Scripture is less the intersection of the divine with human history than the revelation of human history as divine life. On this view, Scripture as a whole is myth—the symbolic expressions of God's own Being. But this divine drama is concealed from ordinary sight, and only revealed through the insights of the exegetical imagination. Perceiving the hints of supernal wisdom in Scripture, the exegete constructs mythic fabulations from its words so that the hidden light of God might appear. Indeed, mystical mythmaking refashions Scripture into verbal prisms in the hope that primordial wisdom might be refracted through them into the heart of the seeker. So viewed, the mythic imagination is a tool of the spiritual quest, and mythmaking a ritual of divine disclosure.

In the *Zohar*, the self-manifestation of God is imagined through various conceptual schemata. One of these is as the structure of a Personality, patterned in three archetypal triads and a final tenth gradation. These elements interact in complex ways—both within each triad and in sets of combinations. The uppermost triad is the most recondite, and comprises such unknowable levels of mind as Thought, Wisdom, and Understanding; the second triad has more emotional valences, and includes the values of Judgment, Mercy, and their synthesis called Splendor; the third triad, below these two, manifests the forms of divine constancy or continuity called Eternity, Majesty, and Foundation; and the final gradation integrates these potencies as God's Kingdom. These attributes take on dramatic mythic form as they are arranged in the shape of a primordial Anthropos. From this perspective, the upper triad corresponds to features of the mind and heart; the second triad to the left and right arms (or sides) and the mediating spinal column; the third triad embraces the two legs and the active male principle of generation; and the final gradation is the receptive and fecund female principle.

In the relationship of the two upper triads (especially) to the lowest gradation there is thus a gender differentiation of male and female, which gives images of integration and union powerful erotic valences. This differentiation of gender becomes even more complex insofar as these supernal gradations are identified with various biblical personalities. In this way the relations between the potencies of the Godhead take on the dyadic configurations of father-mother/ brother-brother/ sister-sister/ and husband-wife relationships. To read Scripture properly (theosophically) is therefore to perceive in the life history of its human characters symbols of the inner drama of the divine Personality. This is myth in every sense—but of the most esoteric and mysterious kind.

From the mystical perspective, the diverse biblical narratives and laws conceal instructive truths about the divine Personality—about its deep structures and the ways they may combine, balance, rupture, or be repaired. For example, the sin of Adam reveals the way the essentially interactive unity of Divinity may be disrupted through human emphasis on one element to the exclusion of the whole; the interpersonal relationship of Abraham and Isaac in the episode of Isaac's near-sacrifice reveals something of the complex ways that mercy and judgment or love and limits must always be interrelated; Joseph's ability to overcome sexual temptation and rise to power as a provider in Egypt dramatizes the inner structure that links restraint with giving and ascetic withdrawal with grace; and the expressions of desire between the beloved maiden and King Solomon in the Song of Songs symbolize the deep longing for harmony that pulses in the recesses of Being. Each biblical phrase teaches such truths of the Godhead *le-fum 'orḥeih,* each "according to its manner," each in accordance with its particular language or literary features. Such divine teachings are the nuclear myths that comprise the megamyth of Divinity.

The complexity of Zoharic myth is further compounded by the fact that many of its vital symbols are impersonal in nature. The configuration of triads may therefore give way to the structure of a tree rooted in a garden, or to a pattern of streams flowing into a sea, or to a cluster of wells with reviving water—all depending upon the biblical narrative at hand and its own pattern of imagery. The four streams of Eden and its two trees with mysterious fruit all have cosmic symbolism, as does the sequence of cisterns in the desert, or the structure of the Tabernacle and its sacral objects. However, it is important to stress that these impersonal symbols are never a subject of inquiry in and for themselves. They are rather natural symbols used to convey more of the allusive richness of the divine Personality. Thus to explore these impersonal symbols in their positive or negative forms—as open or blocked wells, or as flowering or withered trees—is to consider the constructive or disruptive relations within the Personality of the Godhead. Exegetical mythmaking teaches these truths in vibrant and innumerable ways.

Despite some stereotyped repetition of certain intra-divine patterns, the teachings of the *Zohar* retain a remarkable vitality. Indeed, the spiritual profundity revealed in any number of exegetical constructions, as well as the prolific variety of myths that appear on every page, suggest a still-fresh spirit of creativity, although the mystics themselves believed that they were in touch with a fixed structure of wisdom. Perhaps it was the very diversity of scriptural language that kept the teachers alive and seeking; for each sentence of Scripture is different, and this meant that the truths of Divinity could not be summarized or reduced to any one pattern. One may further suppose that it was this very linguistic vitality that prevented mythmaking from becoming idolatrous. The exegete's sense of touching the mysteries of God with words was outrun at every step by each new verse or pattern of verses, and by the mystic's perception that no myth was the ultimate or final formulation of truth.

Scripture for the kabbalists is thus a vast Myth of myths of God's Personality; and the reconstruction and revelation of this Myth of Divine Being through the language of Scripture is at the center of fourth-order mythic formulations in Judaism. As we have suggested, exegesis and mystical search are one here. Singly and together, the mystic companions of the *Zohar* seek to "open" verbal passages into Divinity through their interpretations of Scripture; and insofar as their mythmaking is true, to construct imaginative realities that are somehow homologous with God's Being. In this way, mythmaking attempts to reveal God through God's own scriptural traces. Indeed, in the reconfiguration of letters and language which this order of myth achieves, divinity (as exegetically imaginable) is activated out of Divinity (the Scriptures). This is myth on the way to Myth.[18]

If the creative energy of earlier centuries was bound to the mythmaking imagination, its vitality has been depleted over the generations. Especially in modernity, myth takes a fateful turn and fades into metaphor. Of course there are many earlier points where myths seem to have faded into literary tropes, or so we think, as we compare these figures with living mythologies. May one not perceive something of the weak pulse of myth behind such biblical figures as God swallowing up death (Isaiah 25:8), the floating of the earth upon the waters (Psalm 24:2), or God's advent to earth on the wings of the wind (Psalm 18:11)? Surely, as I suggested at the outset, myth is in the mind of the beholder and one person's metaphor may be another one's myth. Nevertheless, even if one grants some mythic vitality to these or other biblical images, it must be conceded that they are at best stenographic signs of a lost or dispersed mythology. For in their new settings, these mythic images (if such as they be) are cut loose from a more encompassing mythic plot or framework. At best, they function as the ciphers or citations of a fuller narrative, and depend upon that known or implied context for their mythic power. When that setting fades or is forgotten, the older allusions appear as metaphors.

The shifting of narrative ground is fundamental to this process. As certain images no longer cohere or describe the nature of things, however figuratively, the figures fade into subjective *poesis*. The poet is the word-maker here, not the mythographer, and his temperament is the spring of his aesthetic achievement. Indeed, the modern poet's inner nature and personality are crucial to his creativity; and his poetry is wrought from his own subjective history, despite its capacity to speak to other persons who may share his sensibilities. The exteriorization of images in poetry may thus have myth-like qualities, but not the aura of realism which characterizes true myth—whether it is a myth of the natural or supernatural world, or whether its authority comes from the texture of Being or the text of Scripture.

The modernist turn to private images is part of the subjectivization of truth and its re-grounding in the human personality. This often imbues the images with an illusional quality. Only rarely will a strong poet release images that appear to arise from the very ground of being. In such cases we are on the brink of myth, and may cross over to that realm insofar as the images cohere in some narrative sense. I would even say that the poet becomes a mythmaker when his images (or myth-like metaphors) bring a new dramatic vitality to the sights and sounds of the world, for himself and for his readers. In the process, the poet may utilize and transform images from earlier tradition; and such a process may even give the new myth an unexpected exegetical freshness. Nevertheless, the new moment is not exegesis per se but a return through subjectivity to the sights and sounds of existence. This renewed attempt to produce a "sounding pantheon" despite the hobbling inflections of self-consciousness is a kind of second naiveté. It mirrors the first stage of mythmaking suggested at the beginning, but darkly, for it is the modern soul that looks through the new glass.

One must therefore be thankful for great poets like Ḥayim Naḥman Bialik. His vision of a winter day—"harder than flint . . . like a single piece of hammered work"—recovers the mythic texture of things and provides a hint of the nascent fifth stage of Jewish mythmaking. In verse entitled "From the Winter Songs," the poet's muse fills him with the pounding of that spectral season, and creates through him a vision of "the air" where "there still hang gleaming / drops from the breath of God, from / the vapour of His mouth."[19] Can you hear in the "gleaming drops" *(tzaḥtzuḥei ha-ziv)* resonances of mystic images used by the old synagogue poets and visionaries; or sense in the ice-forming "breath of God" *(nishmat 'eloah)* and the "vapor" *('eid)* of His mouth allusions to the books of Job and Genesis? In this arresting formulation, the poet's metaphors create a personal mythology of the reborn world, and even boldly mythicize the Bible's earthly "vapor" as the very "breath of God."

And what of the other vapors of the village? Bialik intones how "the smoke from the chimneys, like/ the beard of the Ancient of Days, curls/ majestically, and rises to the heights." How far we are from similar anthropomorphic images of God in the older books of Daniel and the *Zohar*,[20] and yet how mysteriously near. How near we are to the throne of heaven upon which this God sits—as close, it seems, as the earthy similes of Bialik's imagination. For now the ice sits upon the roofs "like alabaster helmets" *(qob'ei ha-shayish)*, in an image so reminiscent of Rabbi Akiba's ancient warning of a *trompe l'oeil* that may mislead mystics in the sixth heaven.[21] But no visionary will be deceived by this trope. Indeed, Bialik's whole purpose is to put us into a new mythic mind here below. In his view there is no need to ascend on high for this vision of wintry alabaster; one only needs a natural eye capable of seeing the divine sights of this world.

Just this is the gift of the poet's mythwork. His images revive our vision and let us see anew. Through his purified words we may attain (if only for the space of the poem) a renewed sense of the sights and sounds of existence, in *verbis* and in *nominibus*. How near we are to myth in Bialik's re-creation of the world—and yet how far, how very far.

7

The Book of *Zohar* and Exegetical Spirituality

The book of *Zohar* is the masterpiece of Jewish mysticism. Ostensibly a commentary on the Torah, it pulses with the desire for God on every page. One may even say that the commentary is carried by this desire, and that its protean creativity is primarily motivated by a longing to experience the divine realities uncovered by mystical interpretation.[1] Towards this end the full range of tradition is activated, from late antiquity to the thirteenth century, when the book of *Zohar* appeared in Castile.[2] Recovering theosophical truths in the teachings of Torah, the mystics ascend exegetically into God.[3] This process invites attention.

According to the teaching of the *Zohar*, the spiritual powers of All-Being descend from the highest realms in diverse patterns of appearance. Torah is one such manifestation. Not merely law and lore and religious expression, the mystics proclaim its inner essence to be the vitality and wisdom of God Himself. Scripture may therefore be many things to its readers—folly and fable to the scoffer, secret and source to the wise of heart.[4] Those of plain sense are content with the straightforward context, while the religious seeker looks more deeply for hints of heavenly illuminations. "How splendid are the ways and paths of the Torah," says Rabbi Pinḥas ben Yair in a Zoharic homily—"for in each and every word there are so many thoughts and good things for humankind, so many pearls shining light on every side." And then, comparing the Torah to a tree with roots, bark, pith, branches, leaves, flowers, and fruit, the sage exults: "so the words of the Torah have plain-sense, exegetical derivations [legal and homiletical], speculative allusions, numerical tallies, hidden mysteries, impenetrable mysteries, one above the other, [and laws dealing with] unfit and fit, unclean and clean, forbidden and permitted."[5]

In this catalogue of exegetical bounty, the language of Scripture contains transcendental meanings that far exceed the concerns of normative rabbinic piety. A quick glance at *Song of Songs Rabba* is instructive. Near the beginning of this midrash we read how the divine words of the Decalogue came to the people at Sinai, and each and every word appraised the listeners of the vast system of law that would stem from these roots. "Do you accept this word upon yourself?" says each word. "There are such and so many rules in it, such and so many penalties in it, such and so many decrees in it, and such are the religious duties in it, and such are the lenient and stringent features of it, and such and so are the rewards in it."[6] For Rabbi Pinḥas, even this vast potentiality may be superseded. The Torah conceals infinite truth, as befits a word of God.

In great textual cultures like Judaism, the process of thought is always exegetical—be it simply the reformulation of older tradition or the detailed derivation of new scriptural sense.[7] This is profoundly true of the *Zohar* as well. No summary is therefore adequate to its content or pertinent to its character. Rather, the mystical theology of this work unfolds word by word, in the thickness of semantic solutions. Inspired by a bold exegetical impulse, the teachings of the *Zohar* combine imagination with explanation in unexpected ways. This is as true for the primary circle of teachers (the mystical fellowship in the text) as for the widening circle of disciples who retrieve the original teachings and transform them through study.

Exegetical spirituality is thus grounded in the hermeneutical process. As a result, the interpretative imagination is linked to the concrete language and images of Scripture, and is sustained by their syntax and intertextual relations. To this extent the exegetical spirituality of the *Zohar* is a species of the midrashic imagination. What distinguishes Zoharic exegesis is its search for esoteric layers within Scripture—esoteric layers of the Godhead, of Torah, and of the self. This concern affects its peculiar dynamism. For while midrashic exegesis activates the letters and words of Scripture along a horizontal plane, Zoharic exegesis adds a vertical axis—through its belief that the grammar of Scripture conceals traces of a hidden, supernal truth.[8] The verbal dynamics of biblical sentences are thus expressions of esoteric processes deep within the Godhead. This being so, mystical exegesis rings true when this divine reality is revealed to consciousness.

Throughout the book of *Zohar* the disciples meet and meditate on the words of Scripture, hoping to achieve spiritual and theosophical instruction through exegetical means. Overall, three types of instruction are exemplary. The first takes Torah itself as its subject, and seeks to reveal the benefits of Torah study for humans as well as the theurgical effects of such exegetical piety upon God. The second type focuses on more personal matters, and provides spiritual counsel for the worshipper as well as an elucidation of dangers on this path of piety. Such piety is particularly concerned with the perfection of the human self, sought through a rejection of negative instincts that diminish its worth. This endeavor leads to an enhancement of one's divine soul and a neutralization of the demonic forces that assault it from within and without. The third type of Zoharic exegesis has a different goal, which is an understanding of the nature and dynamism of the Godhead. Theosophical truth thus flashes forth from the words of Scripture, as exegetical inspiration penetrates its arcane essence. The ritualization of these divine truths in personal prayer is a significant but derivative aspect of their exegetical recovery.

To appreciate the vastness of Zoharic exegesis and its spiritual dimensions, each of these types will be taken up in turn. A striking example of the first type, in which Torah and its study are the subject of hermeneutical reflection, is a cycle of teachings by Rabbi Pinḥas ben Yair.[9] His comparison of the mystery of the Torah to a tree is in that cycle. His choice of that image—an archetypal one that recurs throughout the *Zohar*—was not accidental. In fact, the analogy was directly conditioned by the biblical verse that was taken up for discussion, Deuteronomy 20:19—a rule prohibiting the destruction of trees during a prolonged military siege. In his spiritual exegesis, R. Pinḥas converts each textual element to new theological ends. Gradually its symbolic meaning unfolds. The discourse proceeds as follows.

> "When you besiege a city many days in order to capture it, you must not destroy its trees [*'etzah*],[10] by wielding an ax against them. For you eat of them, (therefore) you may not cut them down. Are trees of the field human against which you would lay siege?" [Deut. 20:19] . . . This verse has a literal meaning and a homiletical meaning. And it also

has supernal wisdom to instruct whoever needs it.[11] Happy is the portion of those continually preoccupied with Torah. What does the Torah say of one so preoccupied? "For his delight is in the Torah of the Lord, and in His Torah he meditates day and night. He will be like a tree [Psalm 1:2-3]."[12]

As the homily develops in classical midrashic form, a connection between these two biblical verses is established. At the outset they are simply linked by their common rhetorical identification of a person with a tree. But such a comparison is static, and not yet transformed by dynamic exegesis. This process begins when the teacher turns to the simile in Psalm 1. Starting with this comparison, in which a Torah scholar is likened to a productive and well-rooted tree, R. Pinḥas adds a deeper dimension. In his figuration the student of Scripture will become a tree of wisdom, deeply rooted in the wide-branching areas of Torah. It follows that such a sage will also benefit his city in times of danger. The point brings the homily back to the biblical law, which is now read in an entirely new way. No longer just an order addressed to soldiers during a siege (the plain sense), the command is now allegorically revised and interpreted as conditions imposed by God upon His angel of destruction (the homiletical sense).[13] He tells this angel that only the sinners of a city may be destroyed—not "its trees" *('etzah),* which symbolize the scholars of Torah, "the tree of life" of the community.[14]

At one level, then, the teacher interprets the biblical rule in terms of the prophylactic power of study for the individual; but he quickly adds a social dimension through the trope of the tree. Adding a verbal play to his symbolic reading of *'etzah* ("its trees"), the homilist says that the scholars will be saved because they provide the people with spiritual "counsel" *('etzah)* for their collective salvation. In this respect ben Yair's interpretation parallels a reading of Deuteronomy 20:19 found in the Babylonian Talmud. In that context Rabbi Zeira teaches that the Torah compares a person to a tree from which one may eat, implying that "if a scholar is a worthy man, one may eat [learn] from him"—but if not, one may not learn from him and he should be cut down.[15]

In our homily, R. Pinḥas goes further. Not content to linger on the worldly benefits of Torah study, he immediately shifts to a mystical plane. From this perspective the boon of exegesis transcends earthly needs, and feeds "the mighty Rock, from whom emerge all the holy and powerful spirits." This figure in the *Zohar* alludes to the lower feminine gradation in the divine hierarchy called *Shekhinah,* the matrix of all the powers that vitalize Divinity in its ontological manifestations.[16] Accordingly, the Torah scholar is at once a tree of Torah in this world and a source of sustenance to the *Shekhinah* on high.

This mystical interpretation itself is deepened later in the passage. We are told that since the destruction of the Temple, God on high has been nourished solely by the words of Torah that the scholar renews "in his mouth." The particular divine cognomen used here is "the Holy One, blessed be He," a denomination for the masculine gradation of Divinity (called *Tiferet*), which is the heavenly consort of the *Shekhinah.* This gradation is also called the Tree of Life, a symbolic archetype for the all-inclusive Torah in the divine realm. Accordingly, through the tree of Torah that he embodies in study, the Torah scholar serves as a spiritual conduit to the heavenly powers. In this capacity he provides a bipolar role "above and below"—nourishing the supernal sources of his creativity from below, and transmitting their powers downward to the people. As a symbolic "tree of the field," the scholar is nothing less than a mystical consort of the *Shekhinah* (symbolically known as the heavenly "field"), and serves as the earthly counterpart of *Tiferet* in the heights of heaven.

Through this higher service, as it were, the "advice" of scholars is also transformed. At the level of midrashic truth, the spiritual counsel of sages was valued for its capacity to induce the repentance of sinners and thus save them from divine punishment. The mystical effect of their actions is greater. As heavenly mediators imbued with saving powers, Torah scholars may also bring the repentant sinners to that most narrow of heavenly realms where complete forgiveness is granted—a realm symbolically designated as the place of "siege" *(matzor)* in the biblical text.[17] In this transformed sense we may read the first part of Deuteronomy 20:19 in terms of the saving role of God's agent on earth (the sage), going beyond the reading of it as a condition imposed upon His heavenly angel of destruction. The biblical verse thus serves as a complex symbolic prism for Rabbi Pinḥas, refracting different mystical meanings simultaneously. Correspondingly, the Torah encodes several aspects of a myth of salvation: scholars are to be saved from divine doom so that they may restore sinners to absolute atonement in heaven.

It should be added as well that the symbolic sphere of *matzor* also refers to the "mighty Rock" above—this in turn being a symbol for the most exalted Mother of the highest gradations (*Binah* or Understanding). Like her lower feminine counterpart, the *Shekhinah*, this divine "Rock" is also nourished by the scholar, though now through the very sinners who are restored by him to her womb. Heeding the "counsel" of the sages, which are the words of Torah used for social benefit, the wayward return to their most supernal source.[18]

Rabbi Pinḥas ben Yair began his exegesis of Deuteronomy 20:19 with the exhortation that "[t]his verse has a literal meaning and a homiletical meaning. And it also has supernal wisdom to instruct whoever needs it." His interpretations trace this multiple trajectory, moving successively from a reading of the words as a military rule to the personal and communal benefits of Torah study, and ultimately to a perception of the human role in the sustenance of the Godhead. In the process, the rhetorical thrust of the central metaphor (linking men to trees) is transformed. At the initial level of practical action, the earthly warrior needs to be told not to destroy the trees of the field during a siege—for "are trees . . . human [literally, a man] against which you would lay siege?" Surely not; the rhetorical question reinforces the prohibition of the rule. But this correlation changes at the midrashic or homiletical level, and with it the rhetorical purpose of the comparison. Read as an independent phrase after the opening admonition, the Hebrew words *ki ha-'adam 'etz ha-śadeh la-bo' 'aleykha be-matzor* lend themselves to an entirely positive assertion: "Man is a tree of the field who goes on your behalf in the siege." On this reading the Torah scholar is the archetypal man, a human mediator who serves his community in travail.

The mystical meaning builds on the literal dimension of this reading, even as it simultaneously interprets the images symbolically. Through such a characteristic interfusion of hermeneutical registers (the literal and the symbolic), a mythic dimension emerges from Scripture. In this case the scholar assimilates the properties of the Torah he studies and becomes a tree—a cosmic tree, in fact, that links the earthly and divine realms into one divine whole. So viewed, scriptural study is an act that virtually transforms the practitioner into a symbolic configuration of divine powers.

The spiritual transformation of the exegete *through exegesis* is the profound truth repeatedly dramatized in the *Zohar.* This is so principally because Scripture is a configuration of Divinity; accordingly, the interpreter is affected by the transcendental features which he penetrates in the course of study. In other respects, the *Zohar* reveals religious ideals and values that the adept must attend to. Once again, these deeper truths are not mere surface instructions, but deep wisdom recovered through exegesis.

An instructive example is the *Zohar*'s concern with the purification of the inner self. This usually takes expression through homilies or exegeses warning the seeker of the dangers of impurity and natural desire. In fact, just these two dangers are the subject of an exhortation delivered by Rabbi Shim'on bar Yoḥai, in a teaching launched by the textual conjunction of two apparently unrelated topics. The first of these is the negative commandment, "You shall not make molten gods for yourself [*lakh*]"; while the second is the positive injunction, "You shall keep the feast of unleavened bread [*matzot*]" (Exodus 34:17 and 18).[19] "What has the one [rule] to do with the other?" the master asks, and then answers his own rhetorical question by reference to an old exegetical solution that said that "One who eats leaven [*ḥametz*] on Passover is like an idol-worshipper."

This pithy admonition arises from an old homiletical technique for interpreting sequential verses. It recalls the nearly similar Talmudic teaching of Rabbi Eleazar ben Azariah, who reportedly said (based on the same sequence) that "Whoever despises the festival times is like an idol-worshipper."[20] Rabbi Shim'on develops this point here, and adds to it a new mythic dimension.[21] He says that when Israel left Egypt, they left the "other domain," called *ḥametz* ("leaven bread"), belonging to the demonic Other Side.[22] In so doing they went from the realm of idolatry to that of pure worship, unencumbered by alien forces. But this action is not a one-time achievement, since the domain of *ḥametz* can also be manifest through *śe'or*—this being another term for leaven (in Exodus 12:15) and an old rabbinic metaphor for the evil inclination.[23] Indeed, the Other Side uses this *śe'or* as an agent to penetrate the human will, insinuating itself as an alien force that "little by little" overwhelms its host and perverts him away from piety. According to the teacher, this false presence is nothing less than a "molten god" or idol made within the "self" (Exodus 34:18)—a recurrent eruption of the "other domain" in the human heart. Hence one must "keep the feast of unleavened bread" (Exodus 34:19), to guard perpetually against this danger.

At this point Rabbi Yehudah offers a different approach to the conjunction of Exodus 34:18 and 19, and takes his homiletical starting point at a different verse, "Desist from man, who has [but] breath in his nostrils, for by what is he to be [highly] accounted?" (Isaiah 2:22).[24] At first glance this blast against human pretense has little to do with our theme. But the sage deftly exploits the prophetic passage in order to mediate between the two verses in Exodus. In so doing, he provides another instruction about self-made idols. The teaching begins with the first clause, "Desist from man," and proceeds incrementally through the several clauses of the verse until his point is established. The exegetical process takes him from social rules to a theosophy of the soul, and finally to the spiritual effects of one's inner psychological state.

Starting with the obvious, R. Yehudah wonders just what the injunction to desist from man could mean, since it is hard to suppose that its purpose is to counsel people to cease from human company altogether. He therefore initially proffers an explanation that reads the verse as advice to worshippers not to greet their fellows before praying to God. This instruction alludes to a teaching of Rav found in the Talmud: "Whoever greets his fellow before he prays is as if he made him [the neighbor] into a place of idolatry [*bamah*]; as is said, 'Desist from man, who has breath in his nostrils, for by what [*ba-meh*] is he to be accounted?' [Isaiah 2:22]. [Hence] do not read *ba-meh* but *bamah* [that is, desist from one who regards another as a idol, greeting him before God]."[25] But this bold interpretation is passed over without comment, since it does not explain the middle clause dealing with the breath of one's nostrils.[26] As the homilist explicates this section, the exegesis deepens and Rav's explanation returns with unexpected force.

Rabbi Yehudah's discourse on the middle phrase, "who has breath in his nostrils [*neshamah be-'apo*]," is a *tour de force*. He begins by giving the verse a spiritual turn, so that the interdiction serves as a warning to keep away from people who have strayed towards evil and defiled their divine soul (*neshamah*). Having raised this issue, the teacher then begins a more esoteric interpretation. It is based on the belief that each human being is created in the image of the divine hierarchy, such that he receives "in his nostrils" a holy spirit comprised of three divine elements—*nefesh* (soul), *ruaḥ* (spirit), and *neshamah* (super-soul).[27] Ideally, this triadic soul structure is unified on the model of the supernal structure of divine gradations,[28] and constitutes the person as a "whole" and "faithful servant" of God. One may associate with such a person, says R. Yehudah, "and become his companion in order to learn his ways." But one must keep away from someone who clearly defiles this unity, and thereby brings his *neshamah* into ruin.

At first glance this interpretation of the phrase is puzzling. One can hardly suppose that the sage wished to instruct his fellows to desist from those who have a "soul" in their nostrils—for this manifestly contradicts his intention. On the other hand, how does he find a negative treatment of the *neshamah* in this passage? The answer lies in a powerful pun. In speaking of a person who destroys his soul, the sage says that he succumbs to the force of "his anger" *(rugzeih)*. By this (Aramaic) turn of phrase, it is clear that the (Hebrew) word *'apo* in Isaiah 2:22 has been reinterpreted. In the preacher's mind the term no longer refers to the "nostrils" of all mortals but to the "anger" of the emotionally unbalanced. This metaphorical extension of the noun for "nose" or "nostrils" is common enough in biblical usage, but its exegetical employment here transforms Isaiah's instruction altogether. No longer giving a word to the wise to desist from relying on mere humans (a widespread biblical theme), R. Yehudah offers new spiritual counsel. He advises the true worshipper to desist from those who corrupt their divine souls through anger, by allowing this force to enter them like "an idol." Such persons are no longer servants of their divine Master but idolators, and one must steer clear of them.

With this last assertion, the homily arrives at its main point. Significantly, R. Yehudah does not adduce the old rabbinic dictum that "One who is angry is like an idol-worshipper."[29] He rather makes his argument from Scripture, taking the exegetical comment of Rav (cited earlier in the homily) and giving it a new twist. As will be recalled, this sage interpreted the interrogative *ba-meh* ("by what"?) in Isaiah 2:22 as *bamah,* a site of idolatry. His interpretation was concerned with the case of a person who greets humans before prayer. Now, in light of the focus on one's divine soul and the corrupting power of anger, R. Yehudah makes a new observation. The pious must desist from all association with those who uproot their divine souls so that alien spirits can grow in their place. Such a person is himself "accounted a *bamah,*" an idolatrous object of defilement against which a servant of God must stand guard. In R. Yehudah's understanding, this was precisely the reason that Scripture juxtaposed the warning not to make molten idols "for oneself" with the injunction to "keep the feast of unleavened bread." Exegetically recovered, the sequence of commands in Exodus 34:18 and 19 serves as an exhortation to the worshipper to "preserve the power of holiness and not exchange it for the Other Side."

With this explanation, R. Yehudah adds a new peril to R. Shim'on's initial warning. More dangerous than the insidious quality of the evil inclination, which grows like leaven in one's nature, anger destroys the divine harmony of one's soul and replaces it with an alien spirit. Both R. Yehudah and R. Shim'on present these dangers in mythic terms, as demonic powers that may invade the worshipper whose mind or emotions stray. Spiritual constancy and watchfulness are thus absolutely necessary, lest a man be transformed into an idol. Our homily serves these hortatory ends through an exposition of the dangers to the self and a warning to take care. Notably, both the danger and the antidote are revealed through textual exegesis—a way of truth on the way to truth.

The foregoing examples of Zoharic interpretation develop through the exegetical transformation of biblical passages—using the dynamics of the Bible's surface sequence to ascend in spiritual wisdom. Indeed, the verbal dynamics of the Torah and its changing images were repeatedly converted into possibilities of spiritual instruction. At the highest end of the spectrum, these insights focus on the mystery of the Godhead—its primordial and sempiternal truths. A profound example of this is an esoteric exegesis of a verse in the book of Genesis. Earlier, we explored its mythic possibilities; the ensuing shows its mystical transformation. The teaching unfolds in stages.

> "And God said: Let the waters be gathered," etc. [Genesis 1:9]—by way of a line [*qav*], in order that it should be by a straight path; for all emerged, while still hidden, from the mystery of the primal point, until it reached and gathered in the supernal Palace. From there it emerged in a straight line to the remaining gradations, until it reached that "one place" which gathered all together into the totality of male and female. And what is this? The "Life of the Worlds." "The waters"—that emerged from above, from the upper [first] letter *he* [of the Tetragram]. "Under the heavens"—[is symbolized by] the small *vav*, which explains [the spelling of] the letter *vav* [of the Tetragram. The word *vav* is spelled with the letter *vav* twice.]: one [*vav*] is the heavens, the other [smaller one] is [the region] "under the heavens." [After this occurs,]

> then: "let the dry land appear"—this is the lower [final] letter *he* [of the Tetragram]. This [one] is revealed, and all the other [letters are] concealed; and from this final [element] one may perceive [the wisdom] that is concealed. "To one place"—since here is the bond of unity of the upper world.[30]

The mystical exegesis of this passage is a meditation on Genesis 1:9—overtly about one act of divine creation, it is now revealed as an esoteric process that traces the emergence of Divinity from the most supernal and hidden of mysteries to all the successive gradations of divine Being. This is figuratively described in the *Zohar* as the extension of the primal point into a straight line, the gradual and dynamic transformation of undifferentiated unity into "the totality of male and female." Esoteric concealment marks this entire process until the manifestation of the lowest gradation, through which alone the upper realities may be perceived. The beginning of the divine emanation is encoded in the scriptural words "And God said: Let the waters be gathered"—which express the divine will that Being flow toward its cumulative reservoir in "the one place"; while the end of the sequence is found in the phrase "and let the dry land appear"—which expresses God's desire that the concluding gradation become manifest, to reflect all the higher processes on its plane.

In developing his interpretation, the mystic draws on esoteric and exoteric traditions. For example, he can rely on his hearers' knowing that the primal point is Supernal Wisdom *(Hokhmah)* and that the appellation God (Elohim) is the gradation of Understanding *(Binah),* the heavenly Palace. Further, the "heavens" stand for the gradation called Splendor *(Tiferet),* the male "line" *(qav)* that connects the upper feminine gradation of *Binah* with the lower feminine one called here "the dry land"—this being the *Shekhinah.* This line spans six gradations, hence *Tiferet* is symbolized by the letter *vav* which is the sixth letter of the alphabet. Spelled with two *vavs,* the letter *vav* thus symbolizes both *Tiferet* (the first and extensive *vav*) and the gradation called Foundation *(Yesod),* this being the principle of masculine virility that is symbolized by the second and (so-called) smaller *vav.* It is structurally found below *Tiferet* (the "heavens"), and hence referred to in Gen. 1:9 as the area "under the heavens."

We thus see that our biblical verse is a sequence of symbolic clusters encoding the mysterious flow of Divinity out of primal hiddenness and into revealment. A similar truth depicting the emergence of divine Being from the primal point of *Hokhmah*, and thence *Binah*, is revealed by the *Zohar* pages earlier, in connection with the opening words of Scripture: "In the beginning, God created." In that case the teaching is simply asserted, without clarification or justification. Similarly, the *Zohar* also spoke there of how the primal spark "measured out a measure" *(medid meshiḥa')*[31]—but without elaboration. By contrast, in our case, this mythic assertion is exegetically justified by the verb *yiqavu* ("be gathered"), which is understood as implying the extension of a "line" or "measure" *(qav)* from the upper spheres of Wisdom to the gradation (called Foundation) marked in Scripture as "one place." This interpretation of the verb is derived from an ancient rabbinic comment on the divine delimitation of the primal waters at the creation of this world.[32] It is now applied to a process within Divinity. Hence the teaching provides a mystical reinterpretation of a midrashic observation, and widens the mythic opening provided by that tradition.

But the esoterism of Genesis 1:9 is even more complexly configured. As the *Zohar's* interpretation unfolds, it is clear that the line is only one theosophical coordinate of the phrase; the other is the holy divine Name (the Tetragram) Y-H-V-H, which is coordinated with the symbolic language of the verse. Thus the straight line descends from "the waters" of the well of Understanding, this being the first letter *H(e)* of the Name, to the "place" known as "the life of the worlds"—the divine gradation called Foundation *(Yesod)*, symbolized by the small letter *V(av)*.[33] After this happens, "the dry land" can appear: the revealed manifestation of divine Kingdom *(Malkhut)*, symbolized by the second letter *H(e)* of the Name. Accordingly, the biblical phrase encodes the supernal structure of Divinity as symbolized by the letters H-V-H of the divine Name. Although the initial Y *(Yod)* is not mentioned explicitly in this exposition, it is always implied in kabbalistic parlance by the primal point of origination, the source of the line.[34]

This way of studying Scripture produces both a revelation of esoteric knowledge and a contemplation of the eternal process of divine creativity.[35] And since all of Scripture is one truth, other passages may deepen the discussion. This is precisely what happens in the present case, where one can virtually observe the teacher associate from one phrase to another. Thinking about the gathering of the waters into "one place" brings to mind the words of the prophet Zechariah, "YHVH is one, and His Name one" (Zech. 14:9).[36] Why the doubling of the creed here? What does the second assertion add to the first, and how does this relate to Genesis 1:9? The teaching explains.

> "YHVH is one and His Name one." There are two unities here—one is the upper world [of the supernal structure], which is unified in its gradations; and one is the lower world [of the divine structure], which is unified in its gradations. The bond of unity of the upper world extends until the [gradation called] "Life of the Worlds," where the upper world is established and unified in its unity;[37] and it is therefore called "one place," [for] all the gradations and extensions gather there and become one, with no division whatever. And this is the only gradation where there is such a unification, where all the gradations are concealed in a hidden manner with one desire.[38]

This interpretation of Zechariah's words allows the exegete to go further in his exposition of Genesis 1:9, and to identify the "one place" of that verse with the first of two supernal unities. The first, as we learn, is the ingathering of all the higher gradations in a bond of concealment; or, as the text immediately adds, in a gradation that "unifies the world of revealment in the world of concealment." It is here (in the gradation of *Yesod*) that the upper powers are balanced in a hidden way, yet with a desire to be disseminated into the final divine gradation (*Malkhut* or *Shekhinah*), where they become manifest to humans. Accordingly, this bond is also called the "Life of the Worlds," since it receives the gradations in the higher world and channels them to the one below. It is in this lower sphere that the second unity occurs, in the image of the first. This is the mystery of the appearance of the dry land.

The "dry land" is thus the symbolic locus of mystical vision, and the place where the upper unity gathered in the gradation of *Yesod* may be perceived. To mark this truth the exegete cites several texts in which the verb *ra'ah* ("see"), used in Genesis 1:9 to denote the appearance of the dry land, is also used for the visualization of the divine Glory in the final gradation and for the appearance of the rainbow *(qeshet)* in the cloud—this being the manifestation of the upper unity in the lower one.[39] The teaching adds that the three colors of the rainbow (white, red, and green) show the radiance of the semblance of the divine Glory,[40] united in their manifestation below as they are in their concealment on high.[41] What is more, this configuration of color is said to be "an illumination concealed in the rotation of the closed eye."[42] It is thus not restricted to the mystical vision of the few.[43] Rather, a rolling of the eyes may result in a manifestation of colors for the practitioner—an illumination whose esoteric truth is the dynamic unity of God. The mystery of the appearance of the dry land in Scripture thus includes the potential visualization of the divine Glory by the inner eye of contemplation. Exegesis and spiritual practice serve the same ends and confirm their reciprocal truth.

The teacher goes further. The idea of the triune colors in the upper and lower unities leads him to another expression of this truth found in the credal formula "Hear, O Israel, YHVH is our God, YHVH is one" (Deut. 6:4). Struck by the triune assertion of Divinity made here (reading: "YHVH-Eloheinu [our God]-YHVH is one"), he says:

> *YHVH Eloheinu YHVH* ["The Lord our God the Lord"]. [These words refer to] the hidden colors that are not visible and bound to [the gradation of] "one place," [forming] one unity above.[44] The [three] colors of the rainbow below unite . . . just like the hidden colors [on high]. And these constitute another unity [and are the] secret of [the words] "and His Name is one" [Zech. 14:9]. [Further:] "Blessed be the name of His glorious kingdom forever" is the lower unity; [whereas] "Hear, O Israel, YHVH our God YHVH is one" is the upper unity: one parallel to the other, here six words [*Barukh shem kevod malkhuto le-'olam va-'ed,* "Blessed be, etc."] and there six words [*Shema' yisrael YHVH Eloheinu YHWH 'eḥad,* "Hear, O Israel, etc."]. [Just so is the secret of] "Let [the waters] be gathered [*yiqavu*]"—[this is] the measurement [*medidu*] of the line [*qav*] and a measure [*mishḥeta'*]. Here six words, and there six words. The measure [*mishḥeta'*] is the [mystery of] the hardened spark, as it is written, "Who has measured [*madad*] the waters in the hollow of His hand?" [Isaiah 40:12]. And this is [the mystery of what Scripture means by] "Let the waters be gathered." This is the measurement [*shi'ura'*] of the Creator of Worlds, *Yod He' Va'v He'* [*Y-H-V-H*].[45]

This passage provides a further glimpse into the exegetical theology of the *Zohar.* The hermeneutical pivot is the word *'eḥad,* "one," first found in Genesis 1:9. Through a correlation of it with Zechariah 14:9 and the phrase "YHVH is *'eḥad* [one]" in Deuteronomy 6:4, the verse in Genesis is said to refer to the upper of two supernal unities. Balancing these passages is the lower unity—designated in Genesis 1:9 by the word "dry land," and by the phrase "and His name is *'eḥad* [one]" in Zechariah 14:9.

A third reference to this lower divine unity is said to be found in the formula "Blessed be His glorious kingdom for ever," which is normally recited *sotto voce* after the declaration of the upper divine unity by means of Deuteronomy 6:4.[46] The identification of this formula with the lower unity is presumably based on the phrase God's "kingdom," since that term symbolizes for the Jewish mystic the final divine gradation called Kingdom *(Malkhut)*. In light of the previous discussion, it is even possible that the reference to God's "glorious kingdom" (*kebod malkhuto;* literally, "the glory of His kingship") was understood to designate the mystical appearance of the divine Glory *(kabod)* within the gradation of Kingdom, as part of the complex unity below.

This striking correlation between liturgy and theosophy is even more precisely indicated though the correlation made between the six (Hebrew) words in each of the two formulas "Hear, O Israel" and "Blessed be His glorious kingdom" and the six upper and lower divine gradations, respectively. At first glance this link appears to be merely numerological; but on second view it appears to be a mystical reinterpretation of an ancient rabbinic practice. According to a report preserved in the Babylonian Talmud, in the context of determining the proper intention for reciting the *Shema'* prayer ("Hear, O Israel," etc.), the following exchange took place: "Rabbi Yirmiyah was once sitting before Rabbi Zeira, and the latter saw that he was prolonging the word *'eḥad* ["one," in the formula "Hear, O Israel . . . the Lord is *'eḥad*"] excessively. He said to him: 'Once you have made Him king [*'amlikhteih*] above and below and the four quarters of the heaven, no more is required.'"[47]

This admonition is puzzling as well as intriguing. It is puzzling, since there was already an established tradition that explained why the *Shema'* heads the paragraphs that follow: because by its recitation the worshipper would "receive upon himself the yoke of the Kingdom *(Malkhut)* of Heaven."[48] What is the relationship between this liturgical acceptance of divine kingship and its ritual establishment? Presumably, Rabbi Zeira's words hint at some mental or gestural enactment of the encompassing reality of God.[49] This may be deduced from an intriguing Talmudic reference to the practice of waving the offerings as well as the palm fronds (on the feast of Tabernacles) in six directions—above and below, and in the four compass directions.[50] This suggests the possibility of a parallel practice in connection with the daily recitation of divine kingship, performed by bodily gestures or mental intentions.

Further confirmation of just such a ritual enactment of divine kingship comes from its formal legitimation in the important twelfth-century halakhic codification, *Sefer Ha-'Eshkol*, by Rabbi Avraham ben Yitzḥak of Narbonne (the Rabi Abad). He cites the ritualization of the *Shema'* formula transmitted by Rabbi Yehuda ben Barzillai al-Barceloni, and explains that "one must enthrone [God]" during the recitation of the final two letters of the word *'ehad* through head movements (nodding up and down while enunciating the second letter *ḥet*, and in the four compass directions while prolonging the final letter *dalet*).[51] These movements were presumably accompanied by meditative intentions as well—and the whole matter, I would suggest, serves as the background of our Zoharic passage. In this case, building on a theosophical metaphysics, the worshipper is told that recitation of the six words of the *Shema'* formula will establish the unity of the upper divine realm, even as the recitation of the six words of the "Blessed be His glorious kingdom" formula will do the same in the lower realm. The *Zohar* further links these contemplative intentions to Genesis 1:9, and specifically indicates that this double unification is found in the Hebrew phrase *yiqavu*, "Let [the waters] be gathered."

What is confusing is that there are not two series of six words here. Indeed, the meaning of the assertion "Here six words, and there six words" is opaque even for this esoteric passage. The solution may lie in the fact that the word *yiqavu* is explained to be "the measurement of the line *(qav)* and a measure." Accordingly, one may suppose that the author was struck by the fact that the word *yiqavu* is spelled *y-q-v-v;* that is, with two *vavs* (the first to mark the consonant, the second to mark the vowel). And since for him every jot and tittle in Scripture has significance, it is possible that the word *(yi-qav-vu)* was interpreted as containing a mystical hint of the upper and lower realms. In that case, the element *qav* would indicate the "line" that descends through six upper gradations from *Binah* (Wisdom) to *Yesod* (Foundation; the "one place"), and the final letter *vav* (which is numerically 6), alluding to the measure that includes the entire expanse of the "hardened spark"[52]—a metaphor for the impulse of will that arises in the hidden recesses of Divinity and gives rise to all the gradations of divine Being, from the highest Crown *(Keter)* in Nothing *('Ayin)* to the lowest one *('Atarah)* in the Kingdom *(Malkhut)*.

The totality of Divinity marked by the verb *yiqavu*—"the measurement of the line and the measure"—thus includes the manifestation of the six upper gradations in the lower realm of the supernal hierarchy. It is called here a *shi'ura'* ("measurement"), a fairly undisguised allusion to the Shi'ur *Qomah* or infinite stature of God.[53] Accordingly, when the *Zohar* instructs the worshipper to contemplate the divine gradations in prayer, the entirety of the Godhead is intended—above and below, in all the forms imagined by kabbalistic interpretation. In this respect, scriptural exegesis and spiritual practice are complementary; what the one discovers, the other enacts.[54]

The exegetical spirituality made manifest in the *Zohar* is thus a complex fusion of myth and ritual. First and most important, the seeker's quest for divine truth is bound up with the myths of God imagined through the work of exegesis—an achievement that puts him in mind of the hidden mysteries, and in connection with them. In turn, these esoteric myths are enacted in liturgical recitation and mystical contemplation—for the sake of God and man. The circularity of this spirituality is as paradoxical as it is profound: a search for certainty through the theological myths of the exegetical imagination.

"Blessed are those who study the Torah in order to know the wisdom of their Master, and who know and understand the supernal mysteries." But how can a person learn to "know his body . . . and how [it] is arranged; or "understand the secrets of his super-soul [*neshamah*], [and] the soul [*nefesh*] that is in him"; or even "the world in which he lives, and upon what it is based; and after this, the supernal mysteries of the world above, in order that he might recognize his master"?[55] The lesson of the *Zohar* is that everything depends on the integrity of tradition and the authenticity of exegesis. Of the two the first is primary, and establishes a connection between the spiritual fellowship of Rabbi Shim'on's circle and all earlier seekers from whom they derive trust and direction on their path. Together they form a chain of tradition, which is the very meaning of the word *kabbalah*. But the desire to penetrate the mysteries of Scripture goes beyond tradition by its innovative nature. Accordingly, everything depends on the capacity and character of the interpreter, on his spiritual composure and imaginative powers. This adds a paradoxical dimension to our subject, for it reveals that the whole project of exegetical spirituality repeatedly risks failure—both the failure of exegetical nerve, and the perversion of exegetical desire.

In the book of *Zohar* the test of truthfulness lies, therefore, with the fellowship of the faithful. Only they can determine, through intuition and their evolving tradition, whether any act of exegesis is an authentic creation or the bluster of human vanity.[56] Accordingly, one of the signs of successful exegesis in this book is the cry of joy among the disciples, when they sense that they have heard a "portion" of divine truth from their fellows. Another sign is when an interpretation is sealed by a kiss among friends, whose mutual love inspires them on their exegetical way to God.[57] The *Zohar* is the great product of this love, and the gift of tradition to all who would follow on this path.

8

Substitutes for Sacrifice in Judaism

Sacrifice is a primary ritual. Whether in thanks or penitence, alone or with family, in purity or to mark the end of defilement, worshippers offer their cattle and crops—and sometimes themselves—to insure the continuity of life and divine care.[1] Naturally, every sacrificial system has its own duration and diversity; and those who would understand the nature of piety in any culture in which sacrifices were performed would do well to examine the meanings attached to that system.

In the following, I wish to cast an eye on Judaism, and in particular on the transfiguration of sacrifice in Jewish thought and practice. The subject, of course, is enormous—first, given the continuity (with one brief gap) of ancient Temple sacrifice for a full millennium (from the founding of the Solomonic Temple at the beginning of the first millennium B.C.E., to the destruction of the Second Temple near the end of the first century C.E.); and second, given the exegetical and theological discussions on every conceivable and inconceivable aspect of these rites ever since. Nevertheless, certain fundamental shifts may be discerned, so that a consideration of the substitutes for sacrifice in Judaism will bring into focus certain transformations of rabbinic religiosity—and its mediation through scriptural interpretation.

The ensuing exploration is therefore less concerned with the broad question of how ancient Judaism reinvented itself after the loss of the Temple service and its fundamental rituals of atonement, expiation, and communion, than with the specific issue of how the sages recast these efficacious acts of divine-human reparation into new acts and concepts. In this regard we shall see how, through a series of substitutions, the rabbis reinterpreted and reenacted the old Temple sacrifices as instances of ritual piety for personal benefit, and then, continuing our inquiry into the Middle Ages, how these rabbinic rituals were themselves redefined as priestly gestures in the service of Divinity itself. In this double process, rabbinic Judaism became a religion with sacral mysteries of supernal significance.

To put matters into perspective, the first focus must be on the Hebrew Bible, the foundation and sustaining document of rabbinic Judaism. For despite pointed critiques of sacrifice and its value in the prophetic, liturgical, and wisdom traditions of Scripture, the overall system of sacrifice and its importance were never totally undermined or denied, and the tradition was always a basic component of acts or visions of national restoration. This holds true for the prophet Isaiah and the psalmist, as well as the post-exilic Temple vision of Ezekiel and the foundation rites of Ezra. Indeed, contentions over practice and privilege notwithstanding, the communities of ancient Israel and their rabbinic or sectarian inheritors believed that the sacrificial cult performed regulative obligations in service to God, with provisions for His cultic servants, and provided forms of reparation for national or individual faults committed against the civil and sacral rules of covenantal obligation.

The ongoing independence of this covenantal pattern in ancient Judaism (what is called the halakhic way), as well as the emergence of prayers independent of the sacrifices, did not gainsay the centrality of the Temple in people's religious consciousness. Two old rabbinic dicta are indicative. The first asserts that "As long as the Temple existed, the world was blessed for its inhabitants and rains fell in their season";[2] the second makes an equally powerful claim: "No person who lodged in Jerusalem for a full day could stay possessed of sin . . . [for] the daily morning offering made expiation for transgressions committed in the nighttime, and the eventide offering made expiation for transgressions committed during the day."[3] Thus despite—or perhaps precisely because—of their ideal formulations, we can sense that the forms of cultic practice were clearly vested with powers of cosmic and human maintenance.[4]

To be sure, such mediations of blessing, fertility, and ritual reparation through the Temple service were not matters to be taken lightly—and certainly not after the destruction of the Temple in 70 C.E. Daily, Sabbath, and festival prayers make repeated reference to hopes for the restoration of the Temple and the return of the divine Presence, and the special *Musaf* or additional service for the New Moon, Sabbath, festivals, and high Holy Days make precise and poignant references to the sacrificial obligations due on those occasions, and express hope in the speedy renewal of this service. Given these anticipations of Temple restoration, it is quite likely that the Mishnah itself, with its excessive emphasis on civil and sacrificial matters long out of practice, was an attempt to produce an ideal blueprint for a restored national judiciary and cult. Other Jews could not rest on such utopian formulations, and rallied or revolted in the hope that the Temple would be built in their day. The hope pinned on the pagan Roman Emperor Julian is just one of many examples of overwrought expectations.[5]

The centrality of sacrifice in ancient Judaism explains the acts of ascetic renunciation adopted by early and later "mourners of Zion," as well as the rabbinic effort to institute concrete acts in "remembrance (of the destruction of the Temple in) Jerusalem" *(zekher li-yerushalayim)*.[6] It also helps explain patterns of ritual substitution that developed among the sages and are expressed in various prayers and exegetical comments preserved in the Talmud and Midrash. While these sources are not numerous, the new attitude they convey deserves attention. Indeed, they evoke a sense of equivalence between the curtailed sacrifices and their ritual substitutes.

With this shift, mimesis becomes basic to the religious imagination; vicarious forms function "as" the real thing. Given the powerful mediations effected by sacrifice—particularly the reparation of divine-humam relations ruptured by sin—the rhetoric in which the substitutes are couched in the old sources should not be unilaterally dismissed as mere hyperbole. The needs served by sacrifice were too basic for recommended substitutes to be without efficacy. Moreover, it was as concrete expressions of piety that these formulations were received by centuries of legal codifiers and mystics, and integrated into practice and theology all out of proportion to their meager representation in the earlier sources. In this way their features became constitutive of Jewish religious reality.

To provide a sense of the spectrum of comments, the ancient teachings shall be presented under several headings and in the forms of expression—largely hermeneutical—by which they shaped Jewish consciousness. The first of these categories deals with the atoning function of *concrete acts* of the body. Of singular significance is the following prayer of Rav Sheshet (a Babylonian Amora from the late third century C.E.). It is reported that when he kept a fast, he used to add the following prayer:

> Sovereign of all the Universe, it is revealed and known to you that in the time when the Temple was standing, if a person sinned he would bring a sacrifice, and although all that was offered of it was its fat and blood, he received atonement therewith *(u-mitkapper lo)*. And now, I have kept a fast and my fat and blood have diminished. May it be Thy will to account my fat and blood which have been diminished as if *(ke'ilu)* I had offered them to Thee upon the altar, and do Thou favor me.[7]

For all the formulaic language of this personal entreaty, its structure and technical terms confirm the new reality I wish to explore. Note first the temporal polarity, which contrasts the past ("when the Temple was standing") and the ritual present ("now")—the time of Rav Sheshet. The sage employs both the cultic vocabulary used for a sin offering in Scripture (including references to fat and blood) and the technical terms for atonement and favor (Leviticus 4:27-35).[8] But the striking point here is that a new personal ritual is offered as substitute for an older divine norm (presently inoperative). It is presented as a formal equivalent for the old (because of the fleshly substance consumed), along with the request that this similarity be regarded "as if" *(ke'ilu)* the original sacrifice had been performed. The anxiety and urgency of the prayer make it unlikely that Rav Sheshet is merely projecting a rhetorical trope—for his whole concern is to be simultaneously the officiant, the offering, and the beneficiary of his bodily sacrifice. Indeed, the absence of the Temple gives rise to a paradoxical situation in which the ancient substitution of an animal for the sinner (whose link to the animal is marked by a ritual leaning of his hand upon it) is reversed, and the sinner sacrifices himself—*ke'ilu*, "as if." His own diminishment seeks to mediate heavenly favor.

There is no way to know whether Rav Sheshet's practice was widespread in Jewish antiquity; but certainly his attitude towards sacrifice was not unique, given the repeated (and stylized) use of the term *ke'ilu* ("as if") in other contexts concerned with the reframing of ritual. To explore this point, a second category of examples may be noted—cases involving acts of *ethics and piety.* Here an exegetical dimension is added, so that the projection of an "as if" substitution is rhetorically justified by scriptural proof. Thus, in one instance, Rabbi Yehoshua b. Levi (a Palestian Amora of the early third century C.E.) taught:

> Come and see how great are the lowly of spirit in the esteem of the Holy One, blessed be He, since when the Temple stood a man brought the burnt-offering and received the reward of a burnt-offering, a meal-offering and received the reward of a meal-offering; but as for him whose mind is lowly [*she-da'ato shefelah*], Scripture ascribes it to him as if [*ke'ilu*] he had offered every one of the sacrifices; as it is said, "The sacrifices of God are a broken spirit" [Psalm 51:19)] More than that, his prayer is not despised, as [the verse] continues, "A broken and contrite heart, O God, Thou willt not despise."[9]

This teaching concludes a little anthology of logia decrying haughtiness. Like Rav Sheshet's prayer, Rabbi Yehoshua b. Levi's homily looks back to the time when the Temple was still standing and reads the biblical trope ("the sacrifices of God are a broken spirit") concretely, in order to deduce from the correlation of "sacrifices" (in the plural) with humility that the latter is like a comprehensive sacrifice, and also to assure listeners of the acceptance of contrite prayer. In making his points the sage chose his scriptural proof strategically, since Psalm 51:19 is part of a larger critique of sacrifices, in the course of which the worshipper requests God to open his mouth in prayer because He does not "want" sacrifices (v. 17).[10] But this elevation of prayer over sacrifice may be more than the psalmist's preference; it may be an assertion due to necessity. One suspects as much, given the conclusion to the Psalm, in which the rebuilding of Zion is anticipated and with it the offering of acceptable sacrifices. Since this coda goes against the whole thrust of the preceding prayer, it is likely that it was added in the exile, after the destruction of the First Temple and the temporary disruption of sacrifices. However this may be, both the valorization of prayer as a humble offering and the anticipation of the renewal of sacrifices in God's good time served Rabbi Yehoshua's purposes after the destruction of the Second Temple. The sage's teaching is clearly geared to a generation bereft of sacrifices and consoles them with a scripturally justified proclamation of the high value of a lowly spirit. In his mouth the "as if" formula functions to reinforce the rhetorical exhortation of humility and penitence in order to stress the *vicarious efficacy* of a sacrificial spirit. Diverse passages dealing with substitutions for physical sacrifices support this sense, and it is mentioned in particular cases where the focus is on liturgical rites.

The use of rhetorical strategies to confirm the ritual efficacy of actions other than sacrifice is more developed in another homiletic exegesis, formulated by the generation after Rav Sheshet; in it, divine anger is fully assuaged and transformed into love for the penitent. The teaching, reported in the name of Rabbah b. Mari (a Babylonian Amora from the fourth century C.E.), is an interpretation of Hosea 14:3, "Take with you words and return unto the Lord; say to Him, 'Forgive every sin, and accept that which is good, so we shall render for bullocks the offerings of our lips.'" Going considerably beyond a reading of this passage as an expression of the power of repentance and verbal confession, the sage shows how the worshipper may not merely pacify God but gain positive benefits as well. Through deft exegesis the prophetic teaching is now revealed to state that even if one sins in secret, God is not only assuaged by his "words" of entreaty but actually "accounts this to him as a good deed [*ṭovah*]"; and, what is more, that "Scripture even accounts it to him as if [*ke'ilu*] he had offered up bullocks."[11]

Although he leans on Scripture, the preacher clearly goes beyond Scripture's statement that the penitent's words are "like" the payment of bulls. In addition to the primary replacement of confession for sacrifices and an assertion of their rhetorical equivalence, he incorporates two significant extensions: the pacification of divine anger, and the conversion of the original iniquity into a positive good deed.

The rhetorical dimension of this teaching is obvious, but so is its authoritative aura, by virtue of the presentation of the teaching as a scriptural truth. In this case the "as if" formula has a compelling effect. Playing off the substitution of words for bulls implied by Scripture, and presenting the injunction as a ritual formula given by God Himself to the penitent (that is, "Take with you words and . . . say to Him: 'Forgive every sin,'" etc.), the homily strongly suggests divine authority for its assertions. In a world without sacrifice, God appears to say that repentance has vicarious power. Hermeneutics mediates the replacement.

A third teaching leaves even less room for a rhetorical interpretation, and that is the celebrated rejoinder of Rabbi Yoḥanan ben Zakkai to Rabbi Yehoshua (ben Ḥananiah)'s lament that "the place where the sins of Israel are atoned for" is destroyed.[12] In it Rabbi Yoḥanan (a Palestinian Tanna of the first century C.E.) consoled his younger colleague with the strong assertion that "we have an atonement equivalent to it, and that is acts of lovingkindness; as Scripture says, 'For I (God) desire lovingkindness, not sacrifice'" (Hosea 6:6). The boldness of this assertion is powerful enough as is, without any qualification of *ke'ilu*. But the full force of Rabbi Yoḥanan's consolation emerges from the larger homiletical context in which it is now embedded. The teaching introduces the dialogue between R. Yoḥanan and R. Yehoshua by citing Rabbi Sim'on the Just's proclamation that "lovingkindness" is one of the three pillars upon which the world stands, for which he finds scriptural support in the phrase "the world is founded upon lovingkindness" (Psalm 89:3). In this manner, tradition extends and deepens Rabbi Yoḥanan's consolation. Far from lamenting the loss of sacrifices as being a liability in achieving atonement, the worshipper has gained recognition of the world-creating power of lovingkindness. Lovingkindness is deemed no mere replacement for sacrifices, but a return to primordial powers and the true act of divine favor. One may even wonder whether this teaching contains a silent rebuttal of old myths in which the foundational act of cosmogony is a sacrifice.[13]

Thus far, several categories of substitutive actions in ancient Judaism have been invoked—including acts of concrete physical mortification, as well as acts of mental contrition and ethical service. As a result, the old sacrificial rites are reactualized through new acts of sacral efficacy—performed by laymen acting voluntarily in the world. They thus stand in sharp contrast to rituals performed by priests in the sacred shrine. This said, one more category of the resignification of sacrifice in rabbinic antiquity may be added—one that is even more typical of the sages and their belief in the *sacral powers of study* and of written Scripture as a substitute for divine speech. What I have in mind are the uses to which the very scriptural record of sacrifices is put in an era after their actual performance. This goes beyond the mere assertion that Torah study is superior to sacrifice, as the following teaching in the *Abot de-Rabbi Nathan* makes clear. Continuing an exposition of the verse "For I desire mercy and not sacrifice, and the knowledge of God rather than burnt offerings" (Hosea 6:6), we are told that

> Torah study is dearer to God than burnt-offerings. For if one studies Torah he comes to know the will of God, as Scripture states, "Then shalt thou understand the fear of the Lord, and find the will of God" [Prov. 2:5]. Hence, when a sage sits and expounds to the congregation, Scripture accounts it to him as if [*ke'ilu*] he had sacrificed fat and blood upon the altar.[14]

This teaching is pertinent to our inquiry, but also puzzling, since it is not clear from the scriptural verse cited why Torah study is like a sin-offering. One might conclude that the phrase "Then shalt thou understand the fear of the Lord" implies something of the self-sacrifice of the sage to a life of godly knowledge through study. Without denying this possibility, the conclusion suggests the stronger assertion that Torah study *is itself* a priestly act that effects atonement. In fact this passage seems to offer a new mode of Temple service—one purified and spiritualized of all materiality, yet having transformative powers. A comprehensive examination of the entire passage reinforces this suggestion, for the homily is built upon a significant hierarchy of ritual actions: at the lower rung are bloody sacrifices, not all parts of which are consumed on the altar; then come burnt-offerings, which are wholly consumed; and at the apex is Torah study, which is the consummate and most immaterial of devotions, transcending burnt-offerings in the same measure that acts of lovingkindness are superior to sacrifices of flesh. In the new spiritual order of this post-destruction teaching, the sage is the new priest, and scriptural exposition a sacral gift of the highest and most favorable sort.

Related teachings are even more explicit concerning the sacrificial power of Torah study. The collection of teaching preserved at the end of the Talmudic tractate of *b. Menaḥot* (110a) is most instructive in this regard. Each one invokes the expression *ke'ilu* ("as if") to note the functional equivalence of Torah study and Temple service. The first two are fairly general: "scholars who devote themselves to the study of Torah wherever they are," or "at night," are treated "as if" they "burnt and presented offerings" to God or "were occupied with the Temple service." The third more closely specifies that "scholars who are occupied with the laws of the Temple" are considered "as if the Temple was built in their days." But it is the fourth and fifth interpretations that connect the performative benefits of study with the transformative effects of sacrifices in a detailed way. The whole unit is most important for understanding the reformulation of the role of sacrifices in classical rabbinic Judaism, and deserves full citation.

> Resh Laqish said: "What is the significance of the verse 'This is the law for the burnt-offering, for the meal-offering, for the sin-offering, and for the guilt-offering' [Leviticus 7:37]? It teaches that whoever is occupied [*ha-'oseq*] with [study of] the Torah is as if [*ke'ilu*] he were offering a burnt-offering, a meal-offering, a sin-offering, and a guilt-offering." Rabba asked, "Why then does the verse say '*for* the burnt-offering, *for* the meal-offering'? It should rather have [simply] said, 'a burnt-offering, a meal-offering'!" "Rather," said Rabba, "[this formulation] means that whoever is occupied with the [study of] the Torah needs neither burnt-offering nor meal-offering nor sin-offering nor guilt-offering." Rabbi Yitzḥak said, "What is the significance of the verses 'This is the instruction [Torah] of the sin-offering' [Leviticus 6:18] and 'This is the instruction [Torah] of the guilt-offering' [7:1]? They teach that whoever is occupied with the laws of the sin-offering is as if [*ke'ilu*] he were offering a sin-offering, and whoever is occupied with the laws of guilt-offering is as if [*ke'ilu*] he were offering a guilt-offering."

The rhetorical cast of these interpretations should not obscure their exhortatory force or the expiatory function of study for Jews who lived after the destruction of the Temple. The interpretations give remarkable and unusual insight into the rabbis' perception of their own priestly powers, not to mention the powers latent in Scripture and their activation through study. Indeed, the concern here is to establish substitutes for sacrifices without sacrificing their benefits. In the intermediate time between the lost Temple and its (human or divine) restoration, Torah study (as verbal recitation and as exposition) provides vicarious acts of atonement and cultic benefit. Now the tent of Torah (as the sages called it) is a new Temple, and the recitation of Scripture adds a component that never existed in the silent service of the ancient Shrine.[15]

The religious importance of the concerns regarding sacrifice, along with their presentation as scriptural teachings, give good reason to suggest that the substitutes proposed were believed to be efficacious in the important matter of atonement and expiation. At all events, the midrashic teachings considered so far suggest the beginning of a new attitude towards defunct but crucial cultic praxes. The process continued into the Middle Ages. Particularly in Spain, in such great collections as the *Zohar* and *Zohar Hadash*, from the thirteenth and fourteenth centuries, there is ample evidence to testify to a transformative intensification of earlier expressions of piety. The result is a further revaluation of sacrifices in Jewish spirituality.

The overall conception of biblical sacrifices in the medieval Jewish mystical tradition differs sharply from the near-contemporary philosophical exposition articulated by Moses Maimonides, who regarded the sacrifices as limited but lamentable concessions made by the divine legislator to pagan habits of mind developed by the ancient Israelites during their long bondage in Egypt. The institution of bloody sacrifices was thus a necessary evil, in his view, and a necessary compromise of the ideals of a pure and refined monotheism.[16]

By contrast, the mystics of the Zoharic corpus conceive of the ancient sacrifice ritual (subject of extensive commentaries) in terms of maintaining, purifying, and rebalancing the supernal divine spheres—thrown into disrepair, pollution, and imbalance by human sin.[17] Sacrifice also allows the human being to realign himself, through the offerings, their officiants, and their consumption in fire, to the great chain of divine Being. Within this mystical system, sacrifices have vast theurgical and magical powers—and this holds true both for those sacrificial actions not affected by the destruction of the Temple (like circumcision and martyrdom) and for substitutions discussed earlier (such as fasting, humility, and Torah study). A review of these latter reveals the mythic world of mystical praxis, as well as the exegetical dimension that shapes these imaginative constructions of cultic processes.

Rav Sheshet's prayer at the conclusion of a fast requested that the diminishment of his fat and blood be regarded as a sacrifice. This topic is powerfully reconfigured in the *Zohar*, in a complex exegesis of the biblical verse, "My beloved is mine and I am his, who feeds among the roses" (Song of Songs 2:16). For the interpreter, the rose is of course the mystic rose, whose scent sustains the world, and whose red color turns white when heated, without losing its fragrance. This pattern of colors (red-white) symbolizes the divine attributes of Judgment and Mercy respectively, as well as the corresponding human states of sin and repentance. What is more, says the teacher, red and white are always offered together in the sacrificial cult, and their world-sustaining scent rise from them both, when in proper proportion or combination. This applies to the fragrance produced by the incense-offering of frankincense, which is white, and myrrh, which is red, as well as to the fleshly sacrifices of fat and blood, which are white and red respectively. To correspond with the duty to offer God "the fat and the blood," as Ezekiel says, the human worshipper may correspondingly offer his own fat and blood through fasting; and in the same way that "it is fire alone that is used to turn a rose, that can be both red and white, into something entirely white, . . . [and] turn a sacrifice into something entirely white, [so] similarly, a man who fasts, and offers both his fat and his blood, turns white [or pale] because of the fire [namely, the fever caused by his weakened condition]."

In this reduced and sacrificial state, says Rabbi Yehudah, the body may become "an altar of atonement." For example, Rabbi, when he fasted, used to pray, "It is evident to You, O Lord my God and God of my fathers, that I have offered to you my fat and my blood, and I have broiled them in the heat of my body's weakness. May it be Your will that the breath that rise from my mouth at this time may be as the scent that rises from the sacrifice on the altar-fire, and may you look kindly upon me." The passage concludes by referring to this breath (the equivalent to the sweet savor of the sacrifices) as an altar of atonement.[18]

In this remarkable teaching, the human act of fasting is configured within the complex symbolism of red and white characterizing the relationship between the supernal gradations of Judgment and Mercy. Moreover, within this system of correspondences, leading from the human body to the sacrificial animal and incense to the heavenly realm, fasting has the theurgical purpose of turning divine judgment into mercy, even as the breath of the person fasting (the odor of the breath) is like the scent that perfumes the powers of judgment. This purified exhalation, as well as the words of prayer that may be spoken, are the substitutes of sacrifice, said Rabbi Abba in conclusion, "provided that [the one who prays] has in mind the purpose we have described."

The powerful role of fasting in a state of pure intention and devotion, as well as its effect upon the Divine Corpus itself, are clarified by a related teaching attributed to Rabbi Neḥuniah ben Haqanah, that only when one fasts and offers to God his heart and his will, does he bring a "perfect sacrifice"; for it is only through this act of penitent renunciation that one may become an altar of atonement for oneself and the entire cosmic structure. In other words, the supernal realms may be repaired by virtue of the nourishment activated in the brain and heart of the divine Anthropos, and carried to all the heavenly powers by means of a perfectly humbled human mind and heart in service to God.

Equally powerful is the second-order substitution of the fragrance of sacrifices by the study or recitation of the paragraphs dealing with the incense offered on the inner altar, which are recorded in the Mishnah and found at the beginning of the daily and Sabbath services (as well as after the Sabbath morning *Musaf* service, for example). According to Rabbi Shim'on,

> If one only knew how exalted (the section dealing with) the incense-offering was in the eyes of the Holy One, blessed be He, they would take each single word and make of it an ornament for their heads, like a crown of gold. And whoever wishes to study it should examine it in every detail. And if he concentrates upon it every day, he will have a share both in this world and the world to come. Pestilence will disappear from him and from the world, and he will be delivered from all the (evil) judgments of this world, from evil powers, from the Judgment of Gehinnom and the Judgment of the alien kingdom.[19]

The teaching goes on to explain how, in addition to its apotropaic functions, the recitation of the incense section "in concentration and delight" purifies, repairs, and forges links in the heavenly hierarchy through a reparation of the letters of the divine Name, whose combination both is and symbolizes the hidden bond of all Being. In this way, the person who recites activates the powers of the ancient incense-offering. This, in the smoke of its fragrance, conceals secret letters of the Holy Name, which the priest in his holiness could see wafting heavenward—creating links and unities in every realm, and joy to God through its sweet savor. It is thus that the proper articulation of the rabbinic recipe of incense is an incantation of supernal power, whereby the lay worshipper performs a priestly function on behalf of God and the world through the breath of his body. What is more, in this mysterious way, the self is converted into a sacrificial entity, uniting the office, its officiant, and its substance into a spiritualized offering for the sake of God. One can hardly imagine a more grandiose understanding or a more awesome assumption of human powers. For the sages in the book of *Zohar,* and for its reciters through the centuries, the rupture of the Temple's destruction was in this way effectively overcome.

The same benefit is gained when the recitation is not a rabbinic text (like the incense-offering) but the Torah itself. Not just the study of the biblical laws of sacrifices brings atonement, but Torah study generally. Building upon the notion mentioned earlier, that when the Temple was standing in Jerusalem no one was bereft of atonement, one teaching succintly explains: "Come and see. When Israel were in the Holy Land they were without sin, as they have explained,[20] because the daily sacrifices that they offered gained atonement for them. Now that Israel have been exiled from the land, and there is no one to gain atonement for them, the study of Torah gains atonement for them, and worthy deeds."[21]In this exalted spiritualization of sacrifice, the student of Torah is transformed into a priest, and study itself into an act of atonement. The daily offerings are now transmuted into the perpetual service of study.

Here some mystics were prone to add a further distinction, exalting the esoteric study of Scripture over the texts of the rabbinic curriculum, and the performance of good deeds as the purest offering of all. Indeed, on this view, offering the secrets of the Torah back to God is deemed a sacrificial conversion of the words of Scripture into the purest of substances, a type of fine flour that is to nourish the realms on high.[22] At this level of spiritual service, there is no mere "remembrance of [the Temple in] Jerusalem"; for the devoted sage serves in a mystical temple, far beyond and despite the rubble of history and the realm of "as if." In purest piety, the written Torah now becomes an oral offering, a gift of God to God.

9

Contemplation of Death in Jewish Piety

Two ideals have guided the love of God in Judaism. The first is the quest for spiritual perfection, whereby the worshipper turns wholly to God and longs to cleave to the divine reality with such intensity as to die to his mundane self and this world; the second is the act of martyrdom, whereby the faithful desires or is prepared to commit his life in witness to the wholehearted love of God in his soul.[1] These ideals recur over the millennia in ever new forms and are typified by two scriptural sources. Their ostensive and exegetical meanings have shaped the beliefs and practices by which these spiritual ideals have been realized. The desire for spiritual perfection is classically expressed by the exhortation "to love the Lord your God, to walk in His ways, and to cleave to Him" (Deut. 11:22), and may be distinguished from the injunction to "love the Lord your God with all your heart and with all your soul" (Deut. 6:5)—in which the total commitment of one's soul may mean a martyr's death, as an influential rabbinic interpretation enjoins (*Mishnah Berakhot* IX.5). Clearly two types of behavior are involved. To engage in a spiritual quest of the first kind involves daily praxis and mental focus; while the realization of the second involves a singular, one-time commitment of will. It is therefore of considerable interest to observe how these distinct types were correlated and became mutually reinforcing.

An early example of the integration of the two ideals is found in the midrashic collection of *Sifre Deuteronomy*.[2] Like the mishnaic comment which precedes it, the biblical command to love the Lord "with all your soul" is understood to mark the limits of spiritual devotion—meaning "even if He takes your soul." And as if to reinforce this point, the *Sifre* passage supplements the Mishnah's laconic remark with a quotation from Psalm 44:23: "For Your sake are we killed all day long [and regarded as sheep for the slaughter]."[3] Clearly, the manifest purpose of this citation is to correlate individual and collective ideals. The shift to the common plural "we" underscores this point; and the affect of the phrase "for Your sake are we killed" reinforces the reason for the self-sacrifice. From this perspective, the biblical reference to being killed "all day long" is a poignant image dramatizing repeated and murderous persecution.[4]

But despite this apparent meaning, Rabbi Shim'on ben Menasia took the words "all day long" literally, and provocatively asked: "Now is it really possible for a person to die *all day long?*"[5] Put this way, the interjection seems at once contentious and bizarre. This was not, however, the purpose of the sage; the question is a rhetorical ploy to introduce a spiritual transformation of the content. To it R. Shim'on gives this qualification: "[Accordingly, the phrase "killed all day long"] can only mean that the Holy One, blessed be He, accounts it for the righteous as if [*ke'ilu*] they are killed every day." At first glance, this explanation seems merely to replace one conundrum with another. For how does it explicate the first half of the verse, where the psalmist says that the people are "killed all day long"? The first clue towards an answer lies in the phrase "we are regarded [*neḥshavnu*] as sheep for the slaughter." From his explanation, it is clear that R. Shim'on has introduced three midrashic moves into the Psalm passage. First, he transfers the focus of the verb "regarded." What is meant in Scripture is that the people are regarded as sheep by their enemies; but on the basis of the midrash, it is now God who takes the people into account. This shift introduces the theological dimension of divine providence and its rewards into the teaching. Second, R. Shim'on reinterprets the particle "as" so that it does not mark a simile but a hypothetical comparison ("as if"). And finally, he applies both of these exegetical revisions (in the second phrase) to the opening clause. The result is a thorough transformation of the martyrological ideal, in which the psalmist's words are now taken to teach that the righteous are meritoriously regarded by God as if they died daily. From a cry of abandonment, the verse now asserts providential care.

But what is the connection of righteous behavior with dying? Given the spiritual shift in focus, it would appear that R. Shim'on is drawing upon a number of rabbinic teachings in which the task of the pious is to "conquer his [evil] *yetzer*"—that is, the inclination to follow natural instinct rather than God's word. In one notable dictum, the struggle would seem to require the actual death of desire; for after teaching that "the righteous are ruled by their good inclination," Rabbi Yosi the Galilean adduces a verse from Psalm 109:22, "For I am poor and needy, and my heart is slain [*ḥalal*] within me." Like the other prooftexts found in this passage, this one is also used to portray an aspect of religious psychology. In comparison with the average and the evil persons, the righteous individual is one who can overcome his baser self and kill his evil heart in order to become a true servant of God. Psychological strife thus provides the drama of personal perfection, and slaying the evil inclination "all day long" is the perpetual combat whereby the devotee may offer "all" his soul to God.[6]

Viewed in this light, what is striking in Rabbi Shim'on's teaching is that he does not simply reiterate rabbinic injunctions about slaying worldly desire. His innovation is rather to say that such self-sacrifice is a ritual substitute for martyrdom—indeed, that such absolute devotion is "accounted" by God to be "like" death "all day long." From an exegetical point of view, the psalmist's hyperbole is transformed into a new spiritual teaching, offered as a normative monotheistic ideal. Notably, it is not the special person or circumstance that is being addressed here. Rather, this is a teaching for all Jews who would truly fulfill their duty to love God in life. In a cultural context where martyrological devotion had become the standard of perfection, the association of such an act with normative piety transfigures self-restraint and gives it special sanctity. Moreover, in presenting his view, R. Shim'on goes so far as to say that God Himself regards the righteous "as if" they die daily for His sake. His words thus push homiletical rhetoric to the edge, and exchange divine presence for the language of despair.

Turning death into a devotional act effectively transforms martyrdom into a daily practice and brings a spiritual substitute into the heart of Judaism. From the perspective of the early centuries, such a shift in religious consciousness is not unique. To the contrary—in the preceding chapter we observed at length how vicarious behaviors were deemed as efficacious "as if" the original rite was performed. Indeed, sages like Resh Laqish taught that the study and recitation of the pentateuchal laws of sacrifice could take the place of the ancient and defunct offerings for atonement; this was sufficient to attest to their ritual efficacy.[7] Indeed, one could hardly imagine that with respect to such fundamental matters as spiritual expiation the sages would merely voice rhetorical tropes. In a parallel tradition preserved in *b. Megillah* 31b, this teaching is even mythicized and presented as a divine pronouncement. At the end of a dialogue between God and Abraham, Abraham asks how Israel can be protected from punishments due to sin in the absence of Temple service, and he is told: "I [God] have already established for them 'an order of sacrifices,' [so that] whenever they read from them I account it [for Israel] as if [*ke'ilu*] they make a sacrifice before Me—and I forgive all their sins!" Such a dictum provides a general assurance that despite the absence of the Temple, the Jewish people are not without divine guidance regarding their atonement. Rabbi Shim'on shows the effect of this mentality in the sphere of private devotion. In both cases, Judaism is spiritualized through exegetical inventions.

By the high Middle Ages the performance of ritual substitutes had entered into the fixed order of prayers and was canonized in codes prescribing liturgical practice—a sure sign that even if the old Talmudic dicta promoting "as if" behavior once had a hyperbolic aura, they had long since been understood and actualized as efficacious acts in the daily service of God. For example, in one of the earliest works on halakhic practice—the *Sefer ha-Manhig* of Rabbi Abraham ben Natan Hayarḥi of Lunel (ca. 1155–1215)—the author first refers to the obligation to recite the biblical rules of daily sacrifices *(parashat temidin)* every day and then adds: "and these are regarded [*neḥshavin*] before God in place of an offering; as it is stated: 'We shall pay the fruit [*peri*] of our lips.'"[8] One cannot ignore here the application and reformulation of R. Shim'on's midrash; in particular, the word "regarded" *(neḥeshav)* has been taken over from the prooftext and inserted into the halakhic explanation, and the term *ke'ilu* ("as if") has been deleted. R. Abraham's phrasing thus speaks eloquently for the cultural processes we are describing. What began as midrash has become a ritual norm.

Continuing this Sefardic tradition, Rabbi David ben Yoseph Abudarham (fourteenth century) states in his liturgical commentary that the rabbis ruled regarding the recitation of "the sacrifices more than other topics, since whoever recites these with intention [*kavanat ha-lev*], it is as if [*ke'ilu*] he offered them [in sacrifice]."[9] But the same practice was also well established in the Ashkenazic rite. Rabbi Zedekiah b. Abraham Ha-Rofe (thirteenth century, Italy) refers to the daily morning recitation of the *tamid*-sacrifice in his *Shibbolei ha-Leqeṭ* as something "required" (*ve-tzarikh . . . liqrot*);[10] and the saintly Rabbi Eleazar b. R. Yehudah of Worms (ca. 1165–1230) comments on the words "to sacrifice to Me" in the biblical prescription of the *tamid*-sacrifice, saying: "The *tamid* should always be performed; and if one should object and say that it is [now] annulled [because of the Temple's destruction], one may answer this [with the biblical verse:] 'Instead of bulls we shall pay [the offering of] our lips' [Hos. 14:3] and [with the rabbinical dictum:] 'Prayer has been established in place of sacrifices.'"[11]

Gradually, statements that stressed the substitution of verbal recitation for sacrifices were incorporated into the prayer book and became explicit petitions interleaved among the paragraphs recounting the rules of sacrifices. Thus by the sixteenth century, Rabbi Moshe ibn Makhir of Safed notes that after reciting the *tamid*-sacrifice in the morning service, the worshipper should say, "May the words of our lips be deemed worthy and acceptable as if [*ke'ilu*] we offered the *tamid*-sacrifice at its appointed time." Similarly, his contemporary Rabbi Yosef Karo (1488–1575) ruled that after reciting the ancient sacrificial prescriptions (concluding with the section dealing with the *'olah*-[holocaust] offering) the worshipper should add: "May it be your will that this be deemed worthy and acceptable as if [*ke'ilu*] I offered the *'olah*-sacrifice."[12] Similar phrases are found in the Ashkenazic rite.

The preceding materials indicate the importance of ritual substitutes in Jewish practice throughout the high and later Middle Ages. The use of the term *ke'ilu* in the texts underscores the paradox at hand—for this expression is both a self-conscious indicator of the difference between the rabbinic recitations and the original sacrificial performance, and a deliberate defense of their efficacy. Given the sacramental nature of sacrifice, such replacements are nothing short of remarkable. Words now replace deeds, with all their power of cultic transformation. No mere imitation of action, the recitations serve as new actions and new offerings in their own right. In due course, this process was extended to include martyrdom as well—thus effectively reversing the teaching of Rabbi Shim'on ben Manasiah. For while that sage had replaced the martyr's death with acts of righteous devotion to divine service, later generations returned to the former ideal of perfect love but sought to ritualize it through study. In its various patterns, such a development introduces the ritual imagination of death into Judaism.

Contemporary with the canonization of the liturgical recitation of the order of sacrifices for the daily atonement of sins, various prescriptions instruct the worshipper in deeper modes of reciting the *Shema'*—the central proclamation of faith and devotion (Deut. 6:4–6). The comments made by Rabbi Moshe de Leon (ca. 1240–1305) in *Sefer ha-Rimmon,* his thirteenth-century commentary on the commandments, are of singular importance in this regard. Concerned to inculcate the proper mental and spiritual intentions in the worshipper, de Leon first refers to the traditional mishnaic and midrashic interpretation of the duty to love the Lord "even if He takes your soul." He then adds the following counsel:

> Every person who loves his Creator, whenever he reaches the verse "and you shall love [the Lord, Your God, with all your heart, and with all your soul, and with all your might]" in the recitation of the *Shema'*, should direct his mind and thoughts towards the love of his Maker, as if [*ke'ilu*] he were giving up his soul for His sake in love, with absolute sincerity, and accepting death upon himself. And it is obligatory upon each person to resolve [literally, determine; *ligmor be-nafsho*] this matter daily. And this is like what [the sages meant when] they said, "For Your sake are we killed all day long, and regarded as sheep for the slaughter." And how splendid if he employs this intention daily in the love of his Maker, and to devote his soul for His sake, as we have said; and He, may He be blessed, wants intention [in worship].[13]

This remarkable passage on martyrological devotion expresses a spiritual intention during prayer centuries before the supposed shift to the spiritual enactment of martyrdom in the sixteenth to eighteenth centuries.[14] What is more, this document already employs the word *ke'ilu* to mark the meditative act. Distinct from contemporary and later uses of the "as if" formula to indicate inner visualizations of the divine Name (and other matters),[15] de Leon's is a mental focusing of intent—a projection of will, as it were, performed daily. The goal is thus to enact the determination to die as an expression of absolute devotion to God. Indeed, the proper attitude during the daily recitation of the *Shema'* is as much a preparation for saintly death as an expression of the living love of God. By his wholehearted intention, the true devotee is already in life a spiritual martyr.

Other, more explicit uses of the *Shema‘* recitation as a preparation and substitute for martyrological death are found throughout the Middle Ages. Particularly influential was the annotation of the celebrated sixteenth-century talmudist, Rabbi Yoel Sirkis, to Rabbi Ya‘akov ben Asher's monumental legal code, the *'Arba‘ah Ṭurim*. "When one recites the *Shema‘* one should have the intention to accept upon oneself the yoke of the Kingdom of Heaven, to be slain for the sanctification of the Name . . . This is what is meant by [the phrase] 'with all your soul'—even if He takes your soul . . . With this intention one will recite it with fear and trembling.[16]

This issue is also articulated in more spiritual works of this period. For example, Rabbi Eleazar Azikri (1533–1600) counsels in his spiritual guidebook, *Sefer Ḥaredim*, that one should resolutely intend to die a martyr while reciting the *Shema‘*, so that if the event should come to pass, he would be ready to devote himself to God "in joy"—and this prayerful resolution "would be accounted *(neḥeshav)* to him as if *(ke'ilu)* he devoted himself in fact."[17] Such a point found notable formulation with the eighteenth-century kabbalist and moralist Rabbi Moshe Ḥayyim Luzzatto (1707–1746). In his work, *Derekh ha-Shem*, he taught:

> One of the conditions associated with this commandment [of recitation of the *Shema‘*] is that each person mentally resolve [*gomer beda‘ato*] to devote his soul for the sake of God's Unity and willingly undergo all manner of sufferings and types of death for the sanctification of his Name—and [the result is that such a resolve] will be accounted [*neḥeshav*] as if [*ke'ilu*] he did the deed in fact, and was [actually] slain for the sanctification of the Name. Moreover, [such a resolve] has great consequences for the benefit of the creation and the more general [mystical] rectification. (IV.4.iv)

Several matters are intertwined here. Beginning with the traditional emphasis on the meritorious benefits accruing to the individual worshipper who accepts a martyr's death while reciting the *Shema‘*, the passage ends with a reference to the resulting boon for all creation and the overall redemption. The meditative act not only produces a ritual exchange (thought for divine merit), but has a theurgical effect on the fragments of fallen existence awaiting rectification. Put differently, but in the linguistic spirit of Luzzatto's formulation, an intense resolve to sacrifice oneself for divine Unity actually influences the restorative unification of all Being. Self-sacrifice thus stands in the center of world-restorative actions, actually replacing the ancient Temple as the site of ritual atonement. Indeed, Luzzatto says that the mental resolve to suffer and die for the sanctification of God's Name is not only like the real enactment of such deeds, but it activates cosmic dimensions as well. Verbal proclamation and mental resolve thus combine as two sides of a performative utterance—with world-restorative results.

In making a mental commitment to die a martyr while reciting the *Shema'*, each worshipper could imitate Rabbi Akiva's martyrological death (during the Hadrianic persecutions, ca. 135 C.E.), which had long been paradigmatic. According to one Talmudic tradition, Akiva joyously announced to his dismayed disciples that he could die fulfilled since he was now able to realize the full meaning of the command to love God "with all your soul"—that being *with his life*.[18] This act became a meditative model for the pious resolve required of all Jews when reciting this phrase during daily worship. But in the later Middle Ages another ritual displacement was added to this act of mental substitution—an act that paradoxically retrieved the older rabbinic forms of substitution, in which the study and recitation of the prescribed rules of sacrifice was deemed sufficient. Just this remarkable turn is found in the ritual manual known as the *Yosef 'Ometz*, produced by Rabbi Yosef Yuzpa Hahn Noyrlingen (1570–1635).

The discussion begins with a citation of a passage from "Rabbi Yosselman Rosheim, the great Court Jew" (d. 1554), in which the rules of martyrology are mentioned along with a stirring exhortation to fulfill this ultimate religious commandment.[19] Rabbi Hahn goes on to urge his readers to learn the halakhic rules well, so that there would be no danger of dying unnecessarily—for an unnecessary death would be suicide and not a sanctification of God's Name in love.[20] This warning is not idle theory but practical counsel borne of necessity. For the likelihood of a martyrological commitment was always present in medieval Europe—Hahn himself witnessed the Fettmilch massacres—and it was thus vital that all adults know the limits and regulations regarding such actions. But however compelling his formulation, Hahn's concern is not new:

it continues in the pattern of cautions raised by ancient and medieval commentators.[21] What is new is rather the justification that Hahn provides for the careful study of these laws. He says:

> In addition to this [aforementioned] reason [for learning the rules of martyrdom], there is, in my opinion, a greater one: that a person should learn those laws upon which the foundation of our faith depends; for their very name proves this, since they are called "[the laws for the] sanctification of the [divine] Name." Accordingly, whoever studies them in all their details, and decides that if, God forbid, an unholy event (as mentioned) should befall him, he will sacrifice [lit., devote; *yimsor*] himself in love for the sanctification of His great Name, then this recollection [of the laws] and acceptance [of martyrdom *in mentis*] will be accounted on his behalf [*yeḥashev lo*] as something done in fact, in accordance with what our sages or blessed memory have said concerning "Whoever is occupied with the [biblical] portion of sacrifices." And the kabbalists have taught likewise . . . And [the sages] similarly expounded in [Midrash] *Sifre* the [biblical verse] "For Your sake are we killed all day long" [as follows:]—And is it possible to to be killed all day long?—Rather [understand the passage to mean that] if one accepts upon himself every day to sanctify His great Name [this commitment] will be accounted [*neḥshav*] as [if he were] "a sheep [brought] to the slaughter" [see *Sefer Ḥaredim,* p. 17]; and [that explanation] is [also] cited there [in *Sefer Ḥaredim*] in the name of the *Zohar,* that everyone should accept upon himself the [readiness] for self-sacrifice [lit., the devotion of his soul; *mesirut nafsho*] for the sanctification of the Name when elongating the [pronounciation of the final letter] *dalet* of the word *'eḥad* ["One," in the first verse of the *Shema'*], and also when he recites [the subsequent injunction to love the Lord] "with all your heart and all your soul."[22]

This important text bears the weight of a millennium and one-half of exegetical invention, and redirects this tradition to a new end. Several arguments are combined. The first invokes the old Talmudic assertion found in *b. Menaḥot* 110b, which states that whoever is occupied with the laws of sacrifice is "as if" he actually performed them and received their benefits.[23] This old teaching is now applied to the study of the rules of martyrdom, with the specific caveat that this performance must be done with a focused and deliberate spiritual intention. Thus it is not solely the detailed study of the laws in question but also the accompanying attitude of determination to die for God in loving devotion that guarantee the efficacy of recitation as a substitute for physical death. In this way Rabbi Hahn gives us to understand that the decisive issue is not actual death but the absolute mental commitment to martyrdom. Religious action has thus been interiorized and made a matter of will. Significantly, the old term *ke'ilu* ("as if") is not used in this formulation. A perfect intention in the service of God is cultivated here as an ultimate ideal; and this attitude substitutes for the real thing until the opportunity to fulfill the commandment becomes actual—*nolens volens.*

A second argument in Hahn's text also builds on this discussion, but invokes the old midrashic teaching of Rabbi Shim'on ben Menasiah in the *Sifre* to make its point. That sage had proposed a spiritual reinterpretation of Psalm 44:23 which claimed that God regards the righteous "as if" they are killed every day. The ambiguities of that resolution were noted earlier, but they are effectively dispelled by R. Hahn's assumption that that teaching refers to the daily resolve of the righteous to die as a martyr. Once again the comparative term *ke'ilu* has been dropped from the older source. Without qualification, the reader is now told that "if" he accept daily the commitment to sanctify the divine Name, *then* he "is regarded" as a sheep led to slaughter.

Rabbi Hahn derives his interpretation, as he notes, from Rabbi Eleazar Azikri's manual, published a century earlier.[24] But Azikri's language retains the rhetorical character of the original and thus sheds instructive light on Hahn's more categorical formulation. After a brief introduction regarding the positive duty to sanctify God's Name, and when it is in force, Azikri adds:

> And let him think [*ve-yaḥashov*] about this [duty of sanctification] when he recites the *Shema'*, at the phrase "and with all your soul [*nafshekha*]" [as well as] the phrase "and with all your soul [*nafshekhem*]."[25] And let him resolve utterly that if he is put to the test he will be resolute and joyously devote his life [lit., his soul; *moser nafsho*] and wealth [to God],[26] like Rabbi Akiva and the sons of Hannah; and [that resolve] shall be considered for him [*ve-neḥeshav lo*] as if [*ke'ilu*] he devoted [it] in actual fact. And that is what is written, "For Your sake are we killed all day long, and regarded [*neḥeshavnu*] as sheep [brought] to slaughter" [Ps. 44:23]—and is it possible for one to be killed every day?; rather, [the meaning is] that the Holy One, blessed be He accounts it [for the merit] of the righteous as if [*ke'ilu*] they were killed

> every day, *when they bring this to mind in this manner.*" Just so is it cited in *Sifre* [*Deuteronomy*]. And in the *Zohar*, in the portion of *Balak* it says that one must also think this thought while prolonging the [letter] *dalet* of [the word] *'eḥad*, and this is its language: "[One must] consider himself among those that devote their lives [literally, souls; *demasri nafshayhu*] for the sanctification of His Name, that is, during the unification [of God] of the *Shema' Yisrael* [recitation]; for every one who puts his mind thus at this passage will be considered [*yitḥashev leih*] as if [*ke'ilu*] he devoted his life for the sanctification of His Name."[27]

This exegetical proof turns on the verb *ḥashav*, in its various uses of "think," "regard," "consider." The homonymous terms allow for the theological link between human meditation and divine merit—a daring midrashic exchange of like for like. The proper thought of the worshipper results in a correspondingly favorable divine regard. Significantly, the old *Sifre* passage is cited *together with* Azikri's interpretative gloss, so that the reader has the impression that the ancient sages taught this very notion. Moreover, the Zoharic passage (III. 185b) is presented as an abstract norm beginning "[One must] consider"—whereas in fact these opening words are uprooted from their context presenting four classes of persons with whom King David identified, which in turn serve as models of proper behavior for the dutiful worshipper. None of that is presented to the reader. Accordingly, Azikri's entire passage is an inventive chain of exegetical constructions, reworked and integrated so as to establish a new norm. The deep structure here is myth and ritual: Rabbi Akiva's martyrdom serves as the most perfect realization of the *Shema'* recitation—a mythic paradigm of absolute devotion. On this basis, Rabbi Yosef Yuzpa Hahn normalizes that act as a ritual intention, and finds support for it in midrashic antiquity. The effect is that life imitates exegesis.

What are the theological reasons for this remarkable development? Granted, the mythic model of Akiva stands tall—but this does not explain the halakhic inducement to develop this exegetical norm. Rabbi Hahn provides the explanation in the portion of the *Yosef 'Ometz* passage omitted above. After he comments that one who studies the laws of sanctification of the Name has the merit of one who has actually performed the commandment, he adds: "And the wise of the kabbalists taught likewise." This is in fact the prelude to the following consideration:

> [And the wise of the kabbalists taught likewise] in response to a problem raised in connection with the transmigration of souls. For they [the

> kabbalists] said that a person could not acquire perfection without fulfilling [all of] the 613 commandments; and were he to omit even one of the commandments of God his supernal garment would be wanting, and he would have to return to the round of rebirth until he had performed all 613 commandments [to perfection]. [Against this] it was objected: "Now surely there are a number of commandments that a person might never have the opportunity to perform." And they [the kabbalists] answered: "If one were to study such laws, and determine to fulfill them if the occasion should arise, or that if one has the opportunity to enable others to perform them he shall do so, [then] this acceptance [of the commandment *in mentis*] would be accounted [for him by God] as a deed in fact."[28]

This text transports us into the world of Jewish mystical metempsychosis—the transmigration of souls—in which one must perform perfectly all the commandments of tradition in order to be released from the cycle of rebirth. According to this kabbalistic notion, found at various points in the *Zohar* (but of greater antiquity),[29] each completed commandment adds a piece to the supernal garment that a person weaves upon his astral body.[30] Failure to clothe one's heavenly alter ego completely returns the embodied soul to the travails of rebirth. It was therefore necessary for those who accepted this kabbalistic tradition to find a means for performing *all* the commandments. For the great *mitzvah* of sanctification of God's Name, the solution provided was ritual study of the rules of martyrdom and proper martyrological resolutions during prayer. In a similar way, one could fulfill many other commandments which time or circumstance made impossible through study of their laws and the determination to fulfill them if possible, and to enable others to do so where feasible. Here again mental commitment becomes an interior act and a true fulfillment of the commandment—though now enabling the worshipper to achieve a perfected service before God and a release from the cycle of rebirth.

The kabbalistic theosophy underpinning this concern for ritual perfection was even more forcefully articulated by Hahn's contemporary, Rabbi Yeshaiah Horowitz of Prague and Safed (ca. 1570–1626). In his masterwork, the *Shnei Luḥot ha-Berit,* Horowitz adduced the mystical tradition that each of the 613 commandments of Jewish observance is related to a different part of the divine Anthropos—a spiritual structure in the supernal realms that is also the archetype for the human being on earth.

Accordingly, one of the mysteries of the commandments as performed by mortals is the capacity of these acts to repair (and rebuild) this heavenly form while simultaneously perfecting the earthly self.[31] Individual and cosmic eschatology are thus at once interdependent and absolutely dependent upon every man's performance of every divine law—even those that one is physically precluded from performing because of spatial setting, historical occasion, or social circumstance.[32] By developing an older solution to this problem, Rabbi Horowitz offered a profound reinterpretation. He combined the ancient idea that the study of the sacrifice was like their performance with another type of substitute: "spiritual preparation" *(hakhanah)*.[33] This has two historical aspects: the period of the patriarchs and that of Sinai.

The first historical aspect of *hakhanah* concerns the question of how the patriarchs achieved spiritual perfection, insofar as they lived before Sinai and thus did not have the concrete commandments to perform. Horowitz's answer is that they realized the commandments in a wholly interior way, through "the power of their preparation [*hakhanatam*]; that is, they were absolutely attached [*devukim be-takhlit ha-devekut*] to the Creator, may He be blessed, and were joyfully prepared [*mukhanim*] to fulfill His will in whatever He might command them . . . And this preparation [*hakhanah*] was *like* the actual deed [*ke-ma'aseh be-fo'al*]." What is more, through the strength of their "absolute preparation" [*takhlit ha-hakhanah*], the commandments the patriarchs did perform covered the entirety of 613 commandments—since the totality was "included" [*kelulim*] in each and every *mitzvah*. After Sinai (the second phase), when the 613 commandments were revealed, pious people practiced what they could do in fact [be-fo'al] and remained prepared to fulfill all of the commandments joyously—so that "what one cannot fulfill [in fact] is [accounted] as if [*ke'ilu*] he [actually] fulfilled [it], since he is prepared [to do so]" through study of the Torah for its own sake. "Thus even though one may not fulfill [a commandment] because it is unavailable to him to do so, but he is [nevertheless] prepared [*mukhan*] to fulfill it, [the commandment] is accounted to such a one as if [*ke'ilu*] he fulfilled it—because he brought the deed to actuality through the power of this preparation [*hakhanah*]."

For Rabbi Horowitz, the capacity of the individual to fulfill the commandments through mental preparation is "a very great mystery" [*rav hu sod ha-hakhanah*], and he goes on to invoke the ancient rabbinic dictum that "whoever studies the [biblical] portion of sacrifices is [accounted] as if [*ke'ilu*] he offered the sacrifices [themselves]" (*b. Menaḥot* 110a]. But the notion of preparation or readiness conceptualizes the deeper precondition. The idea of interior service has thus been raised to a spiritual concept and directly related to human and even divine perfection. It is a triumph of mind over necessity, a service of God through a poised readiness. Before Sinai this ritual service was realized through a spiritual attachment to God and His guiding will. After the revelation this attachment is mediated by the commandments. To be ready to fulfill the Law becomes the ideal state of focused attention.

This readiness can also become the challenge to attain higher states of inner perfection and may lead to spiritual practices of uncompromising intensity. In a remarkable text from a subsequent generation, meditations on martyrdom bring the notion of readiness into fateful fusion with mental substitutions for sacrifice. The text reveals a febrile intensity to serve the Lord and turn interior space into a theater of death-defying rituals. The document is a sheaf of advice known as the *Tzetl Qoṭon,* by the great eighteenth-century Hasidic master, the holy Tzaddik Rabbi Elimelekh of Lyzhansk (1717–1787).[34] Following common Hasidic custom, which has its roots in the medieval moral literature, the Master provides a list of spiritual practices which his disciples are urged to study and practice. The first two items are directly pertinent to our present discussion.

1. Whenever a person is not engaged in Torah study, and particularly when alone in his room or unable to sleep at night, let him think of the positive duty of "and I shall be sanctified among the people of Israel" [Lev. 22:32]. And let him imagine in his soul and visualize in his mind "as if" [*ke'ilu*] a great and awesome fire burned before him up to the heart of heaven; and that he, for the sake of the sanctification of the Name, will overcome his nature and throw himself into the fire for the sanctification of the Name. And the Holy One, blessed be He, converts a good thought into deeds [in his sight], so that the worshipper need not sit idly but may [even at such times] fulfill positive commands of the Torah.
2. A person should also think of the foregoing [meditation of death] during the first verse of the *Shema'* and the first blessing of the *'Amidah*.[35] And he should also intend the following: [that] even if the gentile nations persecute him terribly, and rake his flesh to force him to deny

> God's Unity—heaven forbid!—he will endure these torments and never cower before them. And he will visualize in his mind "as if" [*ke'ilu*] they were doing the foregoing to him, and in that way [he will] properly fulfill the recitation of the *Shema'* and *'Amidah* prayers.

The work advises us to have similar thoughts and intentions while eating, or engaged in sexual intercourse, or during any other physical pleasure.

With this regimen, the imagination of death will have absorbed the totality of the worshipper's life—filling the spaces of solitude, insuring the validity of prayer, and even neutralizing essential acts of human satisfaction. For Rabbi Elimelekh, the old martyrological ideal is transformed: God is not simply or only "sanctified among [*be-tokh*] the children of Israel," but "*within*" their very being. A purified inwardness thus supplements public resistance as the way to sanctify the Name. In a remarkable counterpoint to the meditative practice recommended by Maimonides near the close of his *Guide for the Perplexed* (III. 51), in which the philosopher tells his disciples to meditate on the *Shema'* and the perfection of God when they are in bed and alone, the mystic substitutes an awesome martyrological visualization for rational contemplation. This vision of sacrificial death plays such a central role that the worshipper seeks to annihilate his human will in the fire of his imagination. In this way the intention to die (the "good thought") becomes a deed in fact. Fear of persecution is thus transmuted into a sublime readiness to die—a readiness that is meant to purify the heart and glorify God. Visualizing the death of the self-as-martyr utterly transforms that sacrifice: for now the spiritual training is to be a witness to one's own death. In a bitter revenge against cruel history, the perfected soul becomes a substitute for itself.

10

Joy and Jewish Spirituality

Comprehensive religions give direction to the behavior and inner life of their adherents, marking off proper and improper actions and emotions. Judaism is such a religion, and a vast number of its instructions attempt to guide and even regulate states of delight or sorrow for religious practice and celebration. In the process, various ideals and dangers are formulated. There is thus no purely natural state for humankind in Judaism, or any other religious culture for that matter, since the natural self is transformed from birth into a cultural self—heir through training and tradition to the wisdom and practices of the past. In a tradition as complex as Judaism, the whole range of accumulated values is constantly sifted and reformulated by its teachers in each generation. This is particularly the case with respect to the emotion of joy and its transformations. Over time, some of the deepest dialectics of Judaism are called into play.

An old collection of lists in the ethical tractate of *Abot de-Rabbi Nathan* gives the following catalogue of 10 types of joy *(simḥah)*: gladness, joy, rejoicing, singing, dancing, jubilation, delight, cheerfulness, glory, exultation.[1] In the Hebrew Bible, where they first appear, these terms cover a wide range of psychological states. On the one hand they give expression to such spontaneous feelings as the joy of marriage (Songs 3:11), childbirth (Psalm 113:9), harvest (Isaiah 9:2), or wine (Psalm 104:15); on the other, they appear as general exhortations of proper religious service (Psalm 100:2), or as specific directions regarding the worshipper's attitude when bringing sacrifices and donations to the shrine (Deut. 12:7, 18; 14:26; 16:11, 14–5; 26:12). Indeed, the state of joy is a particular feature of the religious psychology advocated in the book of Deuteronomy: whole-hearted and willing service.[2] So much is this the case that the dire curses at the end of the book are not only for disobedience, as one might expect (Deut. 28:46), but also because the people "did not serve the Lord . . . with joy [*simḥah*] and gladness [*ṭuv levav*] over the abundance of everything" (v. 47).[3] The failure to express open-hearted, unstinting gratitude is thus condemned along with outright disobedience.

In addition to its being an esteemed quality of divine service, two other aspects of joy as religious experience are indicated in biblical sources and suggest deeper levels of spirituality. The first is found in Psalm 19, "the commandments of the Lord are upright, making the heart rejoice" (v. 9). This joyful attitude towards the Law is stressed in various ways in this prayer, and it becomes a virtual leitmotif in Psalm 119. Together, these psalms show a developing link between the study and observance of Torah and spiritual experience.[4] In the present instance, joy is a function of covenantal piety. By contrast, in another aspect of the experience, spiritual joy is the very culmination of personal piety. This ideal finds a striking formulation in Psalm 16, where the speaker moves through several spiritual states. He opens his appeal for divine protection with a statement of spiritual surrender ("I trust in You," v. 1) and a confession ("You are my Lord, I have no good but in You," v. 2). He then goes on to affirm God as his lot and destiny (v. 5), and resolves to be "ever mindful of the Lord's presence" (v. 8). At this spiritual level the psalmist's efforts at divine mindfulness give him a sense of well-being and confidence: "My heart rejoices *(yismaḥ)*, my whole being exults, and my body rests secure." Speaking of this exalted state, the psalmist rhapsodically concludes: "In Your presence is the fullness of joy *(sova' semaḥot)*, pleasantness for evermore in Your right hand" (Psalm 16:9, 10). Moving through a succession of spiritual states, the psalmist proceeds from spiritual surrender to divine mindfulness to a sense of heavenly joy. No higher spiritual level is expressed in the Hebrew Bible; and the ladder of ascension expressed here became a Jewish ideal with many religious and mystical permutations.[5]

The literary sources of classical Judaism continue the earlier biblical traditions about joy—but do so in a distinctive manner. For while many of the key texts are repeated in subsequent rabbinic sources, they are exegetically inflected in light of the sages' concerns with the commandments, religious sobriety, and the study of Torah. This process of exegetical acculturation gave the earlier topics of joy the forms in which they were characterized and transformed in medieval and later thought. From brief, diffuse, and even contradictory statements in numerous biblical sources, a type of spiritual *paideia* developed, in which the topics were clarified, developed, or subjected to didactic nuance and refinement.

Several trajectories characterize ancient rabbinic teachings about joy and set the pattern for later spiritual developments. One of these reflects an overall nomistic concern. It is concisely indicated by the way the biblical command "you shall rejoice on your festival [*be-ḥagekha*]" (Deut. 15:14) was understood by the ancient sages to specify the offering of a special sacrifice (called *ḥagigah*) on the festival.[6] The general divine command to celebrate "*on* your festival" was thus transformed into the specific rabbinic rule to rejoice on the holiday "*by means of* your festival [-offering]." In this way, the biblical command was no longer a general exhortation to rejoice in the bounty of the harvest blessed by God (v. 15), but a halakhically channeled prescription enjoining the worshipper to express joy through a cultic gift of celebration. Other specifications of this verse move in comparable directions.[7]

This overall nomistic transmutation of the expression of religious joy is nowhere more powerfully indicated than in a rabbinic interpretation of the phrase *sova' semaḥot* (Psalm 16:11). In striking contrast to its original sense, which reflected the near-mystic ideal of attaining the "fullness of joy" through God's eternal presence, one line of tradition exegetically re-read the words as *sheva' semaḥot,* and thus understood Scripture as alluding to the "seven [*sheva'*]" required "commandments of the festival of Tabernacles."[8] On this reading, the collective noun *semaḥot* does not connote natural or spiritual "joy" so much as the seven halakhic requirements for proper festival celebration. For the exegetical tradition, the perception of ritual duties in a phrase whose overt sense is manifestly spiritual joy would be a self-confirmation of the point that all proper emotions are conveyed through rabbinic regulations and norms.

Quite another exegetical trajectory differentiates between the emotional state of joy and other religious emotions, and shows how they are related. A striking anthology of opinions is found in the *Midrash on*

Psalms; it contains several solutions to the apparently contradictory relationship between joy and fear in worship, collected and presented as a composite instruction.

> "Serve the Lord with joy" [Psalm 100:2]. Another passage states "Serve the Lord with fear" [Psalm 2:11]. If [one is to serve] "with joy" [*be-simḥah*], how [then could one also serve] "with fear" [*be-yir'ah*]? Rabbi Aibo said: When you are in this world be joyful in prayer and fearful of the Holy One, Blessed be He. Another teaching. [If one serves] "with joy" it is possible that [one will] not [also serve] "with fear." Therefore Scripture [specifically] says: "with fear." Rabbi Aḥa said: "Serve the Lord with fear" in this world ["and rejoice in trembling"] so that you will arrive at the world-to-come "with joy" and behold in the future to come the "trembling" that will seize the scoffers. You will [then] exceedingly rejoice at the trembling that I [the Lord] have brought upon the nations of the world.[9]

In this passage the contradictory commands of divine service found in the book of Psalms are variously resolved. According to Rabbi Aibo, one must integrate joy and fear while in prayer—although just how the doubling of religious emotions is to be realized is not clear. An anonymous opinion extends the ideal of coexisting emotions to the full range of divine service. Again, it would be hard to say just how this affects the valence of joy. Presumably, joyful worship is always affected to some degree by the fear of judgment, and just this constitutes its unique spiritual character. By contrast, Rabbi Aḥa applies the two emotions to different spiritual stages: religious fear is deemed the ideal state for this world, and such piety will be rewarded by bliss in the world to come. This resolution of the contradiction is less intriguing than the complex religious psychology proposed by the other voice in this anthology—and defers the state of joy entirely to a higher (otherworldly) plane of spiritual existence.

There is another contradiction in biblical sources that bears on our theme and had a lasting effect on Jewish religious psychology. The issue in this case is not the difference between the emotions of religous joy and fear, but between two types of joy. That contradiction occurs in the book of Ecclesiastes, where the preacher not only speaks positively about joy, saying "I praised joy (*simḥah*)" (Eccles. 8:15), but also denigrates its futility, with the remark "Of joy [*simḥah*], what good is that?" (2:2).

According to a rabbinic tradition reported in *b. Shabbat* 30b, this is one of several examples where Ecclesiastes contradicts himself, leading some sages to attempt to remove the scroll from circulation.[10] The resolution that saved the book for the canon did not delete the obvious differences in the passages, but rather identified them with entirely different types of emotions. Praiseworthy joy was deemed to be the "joyous [performance] of a religious commandment" *(simḥah shel mitzvah)*, while its opposite was identified with merriment and unconnected to any religious duty. In this way the sages introduced a distinction between natural emotions of happiness, which were not of value, and the joyous performance of the divine commandments, which was behavior deserving the highest praise. As an affective state, the positive quality of joy was at once the willing performance of the commandments and a manifestation of joy in the service of God.

This resolution completed, the rabbinic discussion continues in a striking way. Apparently extrapolating from the previous point, the anonymous voice of the pericope adds:

> [The differentiation between positive and negative joy comes] to teach you that the *Shekhinah* does not dwell amidst sadness [*'atzvut*], or laziness, or folly, or lightheadedness, or [idle] conversation, or worthless matters—but [rather dwells] amidst a joyous matter [connected to the] performance of a commandment [*devar simḥah shel mitzvah*], as is said: "'And now, then, get me a musician.' And behold, as the musician played the hand of the Lord came upon him." (2 Kings 3:15)

On first view, this passage extends the previous teaching. Not only is the first unit (which differentiates between religious joy and merriment) linked to the second (which differentiates between joy and sadness) by the explicatory formula *le-lamedekha* ("to teach you"), but there is also the repetition of the key phrase *simḥah shel mitzvah*, connoting the joyous performance of the commandments. In this reading, the import of the deduction is that joyous obedience evokes the inspiring presence of the *Shekhinah* (or divine Presence),[11] whereas the emotions of sadness or folly (not necessarily in the performance of divine duties) do not. But if following the commandments joyfully brings down the *Shekhinah*, what does the prooftext from 2 Kings 3:15 add, since that passage refers to a mantic act unconnected with divine duties?[12] Moreover, how is one to explain that the *Shekhinah* descends during acts of joyous obedience in the second half of the passage, but nothing is said about observance in the first part dealing with the states of sadness and folly? And finally, one may also note the perplexing and prolix use of the noun *davar* ("matter") before the fixed phrase *simḥah shel mitzvah.*

These considerations suggest that the unit following the formula "to teach you" was originally an independent teaching concerning the contrast between the states of sadness, folly, and the like, when the *Shekhinah* would not descend, and a joyous state, which was a precondition for divine inspiration.[13] On this understanding the prooftext makes excellent sense; for the prophet Elisha had been angry with King Jehoshaphat of Judah (see 2 Kings 3:14), and only when he requests a musician to change his mood to joy does the divine spirit descend and inspire him (v. 15). This suggests that the words *shel mitzvah* ("of a commandment") were added to the phrase *devar simḥah* ("a joyous matter") at a later time, under the impact of the teaching about the two types of joy in Ecclesiastes. With the valorization of the notion of *simḥah shel mitzvah* (the joyous performance of the commandments) in that teaching, the second teaching about joy *(davar simḥah)* was appended to it and transformed from a general teaching about the mantic effect of joy to the divine powers that may descend upon one who performs the commandments with joy. Remarkably, the words *shel mitzvah* in the current edition of the Talmud are not found in the Talmudic manuscripts or in earlier editions;[14] and they are apparently absent as well from the Talmudic text used by the great eleventh-century commentator, Rabbeinu Ḥananel.

Quite dramatically, the textual evidence confirms our analytical conclusion that two distinct ideas have been joined in this Talmudic pericope: the first is a teaching that differentiates between *simḥah shel mitzvah* ("joy connected with [the performance of] a commandment") and *simḥah she'einah shel mitzvah* ("joy unconnected with [the performance of] a commandment"), on the basis of the contradiction between Ecclesiastes 2:2 and 8:15; the second is the connection made between divine inspiration and performing the commandments in a state of joy, with a prooftext drawn from 2 Kings 3:15. The result of the conflation in *b. Shabbat* 30b is the altogether new notion that performing the commandments in joy can lead to divine inspiration.[15] As an independent dictum, the notion that the *Shekhinah* is present only when an individual is in a state of joy was presumably more than a moral exhortation,[16] and may have been originally addressed to ecstatics or mystical adepts.[17] But in its present redactional setting this notion has been nomicized, valorizing the idea that divine inspiration comes only during halakhic actions joyously performed. The teaching thus implicitly rejects anomic ecstasy, while formulating a case for mystical experience within the Law. Such an idea had an enormous impact on mystical teachings in the Middle Ages.

Viewed together, all these teachings on religious joy in ancient Judaism are in one way or another exegetical constructions or clarifications derived from the possibilities or complexities of Scripture. Each dictum or anthology articulates different dimensions of religious psychology valued by the sages, and establishes their relation to normative rabbinic action. The teachings are thus born of the exegetical imagination and enter the curriculum of study as units of cultural *paideia*. In these forms they had an ongoing impact on subsequent stages of Jewish spiritual history.

Ancient rabbinic ideas about joy entered the Middle Ages through diverse legal, homiletical, philosophical, and mystical channels. Particularly instructive and influential in this regard are the concluding portions of Maimonides' legal code dealing with the rules governing the festival of Tabernacles.[18] Biblical, Mishnaic, Talmudic, and Midrashic teachings are integrated here, along with a comprehensive statement on the nature of religious joy. As we have observed, the biblical exhortation in Deuteronomy 16:14 is general and unspecific. The legislator says "You shall be joyful on your holiday"—but no more. Even the *Mishnah* is vague on this point, merely noting that there is a requirement of "joy" *(simḥah)* for the first seven days of the festival and on the concluding eighth day of solemn assembly.[19] All we know about the joyous celebrations on the holiday is that "Pious men and men of deeds" danced before the priest with torches and recited "songs and praises" during the lighting of the lamps on the eve of the first day;[20] and that flutes were played on the fifth and sixth days of the festival during the ritual of Beit ha-Sho'evah.[21] The *Tosefta* adds little more to this picture.[22]

Given these sketchy formulations, and the near absence of specificity regarding joyous activities in the Talmud, Maimonides' construction of a comprehensive celebration—including dancing, singing, and music-making throughout the festival—is remarkable. These prescriptions are formulated in general terms, and, given his citation of the biblical exhortation "You shall rejoice on your festival," one gets the impression that the joy is meant for all worshippers. The apodictic statment that "It is a *mitzvah* to exceed in this joy" only reinforces this impression. Consequently, it is altogether unexpected to hear immediately thereafter that such joyous activies are restricted to sages and scholars—that is, to those whose sobriety and comportment could be trusted. The rest of the nation shall merely "come to see and to hear."

Following this surprising conclusion, Maimonides adds a paragraph on the larger subject of joy, which all persons should express in the course of their religious duties: "The joy [*simḥah*] which a person expresses in doing a *mitzvah*, and in the love of God that He commanded through them, is a great act of worship. And whoever restrains himself from this joy is deserving of punishment from God, as is said: '[You will be punished] because you did not serve the Lord your God with joy and gladness'" (Deut. 28:47).[23]

In this important paragraph, Maimonides makes clear that the joyful performance of the commandments is an exalted form of worship and an expression of the love of God. He even appropriates the doom language of Deuteronomy 28:47 in his address to each individual, implying that the biblical condition remains valid for later times. He goes on to stress that such joy should not be for self-exaltation or aggrandizement; rather, the commandments should be performed as acts of selflessness and humility "before God."[24] In this way, the wholly natural emotion of joy is spiritualized through loving acts of divine service. This halakhic ideal is reinforced by medieval commentators on the passage, who invoke the older Talmudic epigrams that inform Maimonides' teaching. The remark of the *Maggid Mishneh* is indicative:

> [These matters concerning joy] are clarified in several places in the Talmud and in the chapter *bameh madliqin* [*b. Shabbat* 30b], where the sages explained [the verse] "And I praised joy" as referring to the performance of the commandments in joy [*simḥah shel mitzvah*]. And the principle point here is that a person should not perform the commandments because they are required of him and he is forced and constrained to do them, but he should perform them joyfully and thus do what is good because it is good and what is true because it is true; and he should regard their burden as light in his eyes and understand

> that he was created thus to serve his Creator . . . [For indeed] the joyful performance of the commandments and the study of Torah and Wisdom is the true joy.[25]

Roughly contemporary with Maimonides' ideal of joyous performance of the commandments are various passages in the book of *Zohar* which point in the same direction. For example, in a teaching ascribed to Rabbi Yitzḥak, the verse in Psalms enjoining worshippers to "serve the Lord with fear, and rejoice with trembling" (Psalm 2:11), is understood as a series of instructions. A person wishing to "serve his Master" must "fear Him first," and then "he will be able to fulfill the commandments of the Torah with joy." The second half of the verse explicates this passage to mean that one should limit the pleasures of this world through trembling (with fear of God), so that in the end one may serve the Lord with pure joy. "It is forbidden for one to rejoice too much in this world, in connection with earthly things; but with regard to matters of the Torah and the commandments of the Torah, it is permitted to rejoice [*ba'ei le-meḥdi*]. Subsequently, one will find that he can fulfill the commands of the Torah with joy, as is written 'Serve the Lord with joy'" (Psalm 100:2).[26] Thus various biblical passages are expounded to present a guide to spiritual development. At the base level there is the fear of God, which moves one to attempt to delimit earthly pleasure. Subsequently, a person's desire to serve God joyfully, while remaining conscious of the need to withdraw from earthly pleasure, will succeed; then the inner spirit will be refined so that one may serve God with pure joy. This brings an elevation of religious consciousness, and a purification of divine service. In constructing this sequence, Rabbi Yitzḥak formulates a spiritual ideal.

Rabbeinu Baḥye ben Asher, a member of the spiritual circle that produced parts of the *Zohar*,[27] makes a similar point—but in an exegetically more audacious way. For him the famous biblical injunction to "be exceptionally [*'akh*) joyous" on the festival of Tabernacles (Deut. 16:15) was taken as a hint "to delimit the joy of this world,"[28] on the basis of just such an exegetical understanding of the particle *'akh* since the days of Hillel.[29] The result was to invert the biblical teaching and use it as support for a modified ascetic demeanor in this world. In explicating the matter, Rabbeinu Baḥye stated that one should take a middle path with respect to worldly joy, and a complex tack with regard to the commandments. In these actions one should "rejoice and tremble" simultaneously, for there is no pure joy in this world where the evil urge affects everyone—even the righteous.[30] Hence a moderate ascetic rigor is enjoined upon the faithful, in the hope of realizing perfect bliss in heaven.[31] In this respect, Rabbeinu Baḥye falls short of Rabbi Yitzḥak's counsel that spiritual joy may be realized even in this world.

In articulating his ascetic ideal, Baḥye goes so far as to say that "It is impossible for a person to experience the [true] joy of the soul [*she-yismaḥ be-simḥat ha-nefesh*] until he afflicts [*ya'atziv;* literally, causes sorrow to] his body."[32] This extreme position goes beyond merely limiting one's joy in this world. Indeed, it directly contradicts the Talmudic dictum examined earlier, which explicitly states that the *Shekhinah* will not descend to one who is in a state of sadness (*'atzvut*), but only to one in a state of joy (*b. Shabbat* 30b). Even more do Baḥye's words contradict a revision of this passage in the *Zohar,* where Rabbi Yossi teaches that "The *Shekhinah* only dwells in a complete [or perfected] place—never in a place of lack, or defect, or sadness [*'atziv*]; [and] only in an upright place, a place of joy. For that reason, during all the years that Joseph was separated from his father, and Jacob was sad [*'atziv*], the *Shekhinah* did not dwell within him."[33] Sadness is thus deemed a fundamental spiritual wound, a psycho-spiritual defect that prevents the indwelling of divinity in this world. Far from regarding a life of sorrows as the way to heavenly joy, Rabbi Yossi stresses here that it is only through earthly joy that one may become a vessel for God's holy spirit. His words have all the signs of a contemporary polemic.

But this forceful rejection of sadness as incompatible with spiritual life overlooks the legitimate place of sadness in penitence and repentance. Just this point is considered in another Zoharic passage dealing with Psalm 100:2–3. Going beyond earlier treatments of this text, the three key phrases of this passage ("Serve the Lord with joy; Come before Him with jubilation; Know that the Lord is God") are reinterpreted as distinct spiritual instructions for personal and divine benefit.[34] They undoubtedly reflect an accumulated wisdom on the subject of joy in Jewish religious thought.

The discussion opens with the plain sense of the passage. Clearly, the exhortation to worship the Lord in joy is the proper and complete mode of service. The problem arises in the course of repentance, where the worshipper has "a broken heart and a sorrowful spirit" *(ruaḥ 'atziva')*. How can this emotional state comport with the duty to rejoice? The answer in antiquity was nuanced: the penitent worshipper would bring his sacrifice to the shrine in a state of sorrow, and this would be offered before the Lord by the priests and Levites, who respectively embody the principles of joy (grace) and jubilation (song). Hence the meaning of the first two phrases of the Psalm passage ("Worship the Lord in joy" and "Come before Him in jubilation") is that both the priests and Levites must serve together so that the offering of the individual will be done in joy. And because the priests and Levites also embody the divine attributes of mercy and power (or judgment), respectively, their conjunction during the offering unifies these two aspects of God on high. This then is the deeper meaning of the third phrase of the passage. To "Know that the Lord is God" is no less than to effect the unification of Divinity through the attributes of mercy and power, traditionally symbolized by the names Lord (YHWH) and God *(Elohim)*.

But how may the sorrowful soul serve the Lord in joy "[n]owadays, when there are no sacrificial offerings"; how may one who returns to God in penitence, "with a bitter soul, with sorrow [*'atzivu*], with weeping, and with a broken spirit" worship in joy? The answer is to undertake a sacramentalization of the self, in which the worshipper takes on the tasks of the priests and Levites through "the praises offered to his Master, the joy of the Torah, and jubilant singing of the Torah." These actions, we are told, "constitute" the "joy and jubilation" required for divine worship. The penitent individual must thus rise to this level in his daily service, and bring his repentant self as a joyous offering to God through the medium of the synagogue service, private devotionals, and sacred study. Then will his worship be complete.

But even "nowadays" a higher service is possible, teaches Rabbi Yehudah in the conclusion of his teaching. For just as in ancient times the priests unified the divine attributes through mystical intentions during the sacrificial service, latter-day worshippers may also supplement their joyous practice with mystical intentions. Two are stated explicitly. In the first one, the initiate is guided by an esoteric reading of Psalm 24:9, in which David says "Lift up your heads, O gates, and be lifted up you everlasting doors, and the King of Glory will come in." The everlasting doors mentioned here are explained to be the two divine gradations of Mercy *(Ḥesed)* and Fear *(Paḥad)*, symbolizing Joy and Fear in the supernal realm. The worshipper is advised to ascend through these "doors" as he concentrates in prayer on the yet higher divine gradation of Understanding *(Binah)*, which is also known as the Holy of Holies and symbolized by the Tetragrammaton.[35] Like a priest of old, then, the worshipper may deepen his own joyous prayer by mystically concentrating on the Holy Presence of God that dwells above the supernal gradation of joy. Combining religious with supernal joy, his worship serves the Lord in the proper way.

The second mystical understanding focuses on the three phrases of Psalm 100:2–3, and adds a deeper spiritual component. On this interpretation, to "Serve the Lord in joy" means to serve Him *with* the supernal gradation known as *Joy (simḥah)*, also called the Assembly of Israel—His divine consort, also known as the *Shekhinah*. Thus the worshipper must pray with an intention to unify the supernal realm of divinity known as the Lord (the central masculine gradation known as *Tiferet*) with His Bride (the lower feminine gradation known as Joy and the Assembly of Israel). In effecting this mystical union, through his own joyous worship, the worshipper also "Come[s] before Him" with "jubilant song," which symbolizes the divine gradation known as Foundation *(Yesod)*.[36] Accordingly, the imperatives of the Psalm are not only addressed to human religious emotions, but to divine gradations only approached through mystical concentration. Indeed, on this understanding Psalm 100:2 maps out a scale of mystical concentrations which serve the unity of the Godhead itself.

But this mystical service is not the end of the matter, for the worshipper is also told to "Know that the Lord is God" (v. 3). At this level of realization, the religious subject joyously knows that the higher divine gradation called Mercy, symbolized by the divine Name Lord (YHWH), *is* one with the divine gradation called Might (or Judgment), symbolized by the divine Name God *(Elohim)*. Mystical awareness of this theological truth is achieved through the unification of these divine attributes in consciousness by means of meditative intention. The worshipper thus combines the two divine Names in an act of concentration that is the climax of the religious service exhorted in this Psalm. It is in fact a second (and higher) mystical unification, realized only after one has served the Lord *with* Joy. At such moments the worshipper achieves the exalted level of service attained by the Temple priests of old. Integrating supernal Joy into his religious life, the mystic may ascend to a truly transcendental consciousness—beyond the duality of the divine attributes of Mercy and Might (Judgment). Joy is thus the gate to mystical gnosis, to the knowledge that "the Lord is God" in truth.

The exegetical elaborations on the theme of joy from classical antiquity through the Middle Ages emphasize the worshipper's inner dichotomy between *'atzvut* (sorrow) and *simḥah* (joy), and stress the importance of *simḥah* for banishing, deferring, or overcoming the powers of *'atzvut*. The positive effect bears directly upon the individual. Within mystical traditions, personal spirituality also has a divine effect and purpose—to wit, the notable power of joy to rectify the divine Name or integrate the divine potencies in the supernal realms. In these contexts and in the earlier midrashic cases, the elaborations are topical and text-based. That is, the discussions are linked to specific passages and the themes elicited by them are in the unfolding tradition. Mini-groupings of teachings are collected or integrated on specific points; but these do not constitute a broad spiritual instruction in any sense.

By contrast, the religious sources from the sixteenth century show a marked shift of emphasis and genre. A remarkable range of works take up the issue of joy in divine worship and focus on its important and transforming effects—particularly as against older ascetical practices and ideals. Continuing older trends in topical exegesis, Rabbi Moshe Alsheikh went so far as to comment that *simḥah* is "*ha-middah ha-yoter retzuyah,* "the most desirable of [religious] traits."[37] He was not alone in sharing this sentiment. Most texts of this period are concerned to integrate joy into broader discussions of spiritual purpose and action. Particularly notable are assorted discussions in such well-known religious compendia as Rabbi Hayim Vital's *Sha'arei Qedushah,* and Rabbi Eleazar Azikri's *Sefer Ḥaredim.*[38] But pride of place goes to Cordovero's student, Rabbi Elijah de Vidas, and his massive spiritual-moral compendium, *Reshith Ḥokhmah.* Not only is his discussion of *simḥah* the most comprehensive, but his gathering of innumerable biblical, rabbinic, and Zoharic dicta (not to mention comments of his great contemporaries, like Rabbi Yitzḥaq Luria) is organized in a striking theological-spiritual manner. This stunning conspectus of sources arranges these teachings on several registers, and constructs a spiritual agenda and guidebook for the adept.

The core of de Vidas's discussion on religious joy is found in Part Two of *Reshith Ḥokhmah,* in the section entitled "Sha'ar ha-'Ahavah" (The

Gate of Love), chap. 10; but substantive points are also made in chaps. 11 and 12.[39] While there is no formal breakdown into thematic units, it is possible to discern an overall progression from the divine to the human realms, although the two are never totally separated and are in fact mystically correlated throughout. This is apparent from the beginning of chap. 10, where the opening discussion is on the effect of human states of *'atzvut* or *simḥah* upon the divine realm. Indeed, de Vidas's very editorial decision to place a discussion of joy (in chap. 10) after a consideration of acts necessary for the mystical-spiritual repair *(tiqqun)* of the heavenly *Shekhinah,* is stated with explicit programmatic intent: "all the aforementioned acts, which a person should do for the repair of the *Shekhinah,* must be done in joy."[40] De Vidas reinforces this point by adducing two of the most prominent biblical prooftexts used in earlier commentaries on joy. The first is Deuteronomy 28:47 (which, as noted earlier, argues that Israel will suffer "because you do not serve the Lord, your God, with joy"); while the other is Psalm 100:2 (which exhorts the people to "serve the Lord with joy"). In his discussion, the plain sense of these texts are transformed. The concern is not with Israel's failure to perform the commandments joyously, but the effect of this performance (and especially its opposite) upon the divine realm. De Vidas closes his opening paragraph with a citation of the *Zohar*'s reuse of *b. Shabbat* 30b, discussed earlier. By this means he indicates a double dynamic of religious joy: it not only serves to repair the *Shekhinah* in the divine world, but draws her earthward and *into* the celebrant. By providing the proper spiritual energy of religious praxis, joy may repair the divine realm and produce a state of mystical infusion in the worshipper. *Simḥah* is thus an act in the natural world with supernatural consequences.

With this prologue, as it were, the author sets the wide parameters of his discussion. He first turns his attention to awakening the requisite religious consciousness in the reader, so that the redemptive results might be realized.[41] He advises contemplation of God's cosmic goodness, expressed through the harmony of the heavenly hosts. Such a meditative state will not only generate a desire to imitate these divine beings in their joyous service of God, but to reflect upon the song of the heavenly spheres.[42] Psalm 148 provides crucial instruction in this regard. Ostensibly, this hymn merely invokes a hierarchy of halleluiahs—in which all creation is bidden to praise God, from the heavens above to the earth below. But in the mystical sense, the psalm is nothing less than the song of praise of the supernal divine gradations or potencies. That is, each element mentioned in the biblical hymn (the heavens, the earth, the angels, etc.) is decoded as a potency or gradation of the Godhead, such that the span of song that begins with the high heavens and descends through the angelic spheres to the earth below symbolizes the full extent of the Godhead, envisaged as a supernal Anthropos.[43] Accordingly, the mystical secret of the psalm is that the entire divine structure is a concordance of joyful song. This is the hidden truth of its inner dynamic and unity; it is what the worshipper must contemplate in order to activate a similar structure of harmony in his own being. The result for the worshipper is the transfiguration of the self for the joyful service of God. Its reciprocal effect is to repair the *Shekhinah,* and thereby strengthen the supernal songs above.

The awakening of joy through contemplation is thus the first step of a revived religious consciousness. But it must be sustained—particularly against the sorrows of sin, and the depressive diminishments this sadness breeds. Accordingly, de Vidas turns in the next sequence of passages to those sacral actions that may keep joy alive.[44] He begins with the priestly and Levitical powers of joyous Torah study *(simḥat ha-Torah)* and song, respectively[45]; and then considers the prayers of the synagogue (and their effects on the heavenly hosts) and the joyful fulfillment of the daily commandments (which draw the *Shekhinah* to earth). In these various ways the celebrant is infused with radiance and joy, and kindles the upper face(t)s of the divine Being. Holy light then streams downward to the worshipper and illumines him with a supernatural aura.

De Vidas notes that this heavenly mystery is also enacted through the joyful reception of "everyone"—especially one's teacher or a "sage," as well as the poor who come to one's table as "guests" on the feast of Tabernacles.[46] The ethics of everyday life may thus provide sacramental situations of supernal significance. In a striking integration of the mystical effects of this instruction, de Vidas suggests that the word "every" *(kol)* of "everyone" alludes to the fullness of the supernal Crown at the height of the Godhead; that the reference to the "sage" symbolizes the *Shekhinah* at the lowest sphere of the divine hierarchy; and that the (seven) "guests" who must be cared for during the festival week constitute the seven middle gradations of Divinity. Accordingly, if one fulfills these humble duties of kindness in joy, spiritual light is generated in the gradations of Divinity and these irradiate the world below with heavenly grace.

De Vidas's discussion of the feast of Tabernacles (the festival of joy *par excellence*) and the other festival days concludes with reference to the supernal conjunctions effected by joy—symbolized by the unification of the letters of the divine Name.[47] This discussion provides an effective transition to another means of activating joy in the worshipper: contemplation of the Name and greatness of God in isolation *(hitboddedut)*.[48] When properly performed, such meditations may induce a "wondrous radiance, which is [true] joy" that can vitalize the body to a supernatural degree. For indeed the concordance between the divine Anthropos and its human image means not only that every enactment of the commandments by the worshipper (in joy) produces pleasure and harmony in the Godhead, but that every mystical activation of harmony within the Godhead stimulates a simultaneous transfer of its supernatural effects to the human self on earth. Such is the mysterious circuit of joy.

In the remainder of Chapter 10 de Vidas harks back to earlier themes. First he equates Torah with song, so that both its study and the recitation of praises constitute positive expressions of joy and lead to spiritual cleaving to God.[49] This leads to a long warning on the misuse of song and joy, and cautions against frivolity and earthly temptations.[50] The final sections return to the positive expressions of joy (like blessing, prayer, and fulfillment of the commandments), and reemphasize that "love and joy are one thing."[51] The duty to love God and to arouse this sentiment through joyful worship brings the chapter to its climax and links it to a similar emphasis at the outset.[52] As a final caveat, de Vidas stresses the need to conquer despair and sadness—which darken the divine facets on high.[53] By banning sorrow (and also worldly joy), the seeker prepares an inner basis for the influx of God's spirit into his soul. The author concludes his chapter by alluding to the beginning; for here also sadness restrains the descent of the *Shekhinah* while joy induces its indwelling in the human heart.

The deep psycho-spiritual effects of joy thus pervade this part of *Reshith Ḥokhmah* from start to finish—for the sake of the self, and for the sake of the *Shekhinah*. The complex correlation between these two harmonies dominates the discussion. In the chapters that follow, de Vidas turns his focus more directly on the inner life of the person, as his prose rises to ecstatic descriptions illumined by the goals of spiritual perfection. Thus in the context of celebrating the purifications of ritual immersion, the author reminds the adept that it is through joy in the commandments that one may cleave to God, be bound to transcendent Life, and achieve perfection of the soul.[54] These three effects are in fact one, and arise from the depths of faith and trust in God.[55] The flame of love kindled on this altar rises through joyful performance of the commandments into a luminescent transfiguration of the self in God's fire. The highest expression of this devotion is the acceptance in joy of everything that befalls one in this world. In this way, one's wholly natural being is transformed; for to be joyful in one's lot is not a matter of stoic resignation, but of radiant trust in divine truth.[56] The depths of such joy transcend the fruits of this world, and enrich the believer with a divine inheritance. De Vidas finds this spiritual wisdom confirmed by Psalm 97:11: "Light is sown for the righteous *(tzaddiq)*, and joy to the upright in heart." As he interprets the passage, the righteous one, who justifies *(yatzdiq)* God's ways, is sown with the sustenance of heavenly light, even as the hearts of those who resolutely accept their portions of providence are irradiated by joy. The human soul is then "enlightened by the light of [divine] life" (Job 33:30), and expands in holy splendor into the sanctuary of God's Truth. In this Holy of Holies the soul sparkles in silent joy, transformed into an angel of God's presence.[57] Upon this ultimate transfiguration of the self, the exegetical imagination must stand aside. All is joyous radiance, nothing more.

The fundamental bipolarity of *'atzvut* (sadness) and *simḥah* (joy) thus structures early and later discussions of religious joy in Judaism, even as the discussions shift from hortatory counsels to a consideration of the divine and human implications of such psychological states. As a religious phenomenon, this bipolarity is both widespread and has wider significance, as is evident in William James's pioneering examination of *The Varieties of Religious Experience*.[58] In this work, the great psychologist of religion delineated several structures of sensibility which exfoliate into distinct religious temperaments or types. Among them is the healthy-minded person, on the one hand, for whom the goodness and divine vitality of existence is an ever-present and dominant feature of consciousness; and, on the other, the so-called sick soul, who is obsessed by evil and sin, and dwells on the fragmentariness of things as an inner and outer reality.[59] Clearly, these polar types permit a wider perspective on the Jewish materials examined thus far. For the overall structure of joy as a religious modality in Judaism is characterized by a bountiful devotion and vitality of focus on divine realities, like the healthy-minded type in

James's construction, as against the sick-soul type, which is characterized by sadness, depression, and a devitalizing sense of sin.

There is a further Jamesian correspondence to the repeated notion in the Jewish sources that the joyous performance of the commandments transfigures this-worldly actions and gives them a sacred if not supernatural dimension. In his discussions of the phenomenon of conversion especially, William James gave voice to processes of spiritual transformation—for in his view the event of conversion involves a convergence of "personal energy" ("actuated by spiritual enthusiasms") towards a "religious centre," such that one's "previous carnal self" is doubly transformed: both as a matter of self-awareness and in terms of potential performance. Indeed, as the wholly earthly self surrenders to a divine Source, the human will is typically regenerated in and through emotional effusions that partake of transcendental reality. According to many testimonies, the gravity of the natural is lifted at such moments by a lightness of being that radiates divine grace. The so-called divided self which James also considers is, then, a person that not only swings between the extremes of religious healthy-mindedness and sickness, but who bears the two in his conflicted soul—yearning for rebirth through a convergence of his parts towards one centre, forever.[60]

No Jewish saint exemplifies these psycho-spiritual poles more fully than Rabbi Naḥman ben Simḥah of Bratzlav (1772–1810). Indeed, in his being the tensions and mood swings between joy and depression gave expression to profound teachings and powerful outbursts.[61] The imperious and heart-rending demands: *Du zollst nokh zayn in der moroh sheḥoroh; du bist meḥuyyav meshuneh freylikh tzu zayn!* ("Are you again in depression? You must be particularly joyful!"), and *Man tor zikh nisht meya'esh zayn. Gevald! Zayt aykh nisht meya'esh* ("You must not despair; O woe! Don't despair") are addressed as much to his companions as to himself.[62] He calls out of the depths in an effort to raise the fallen spirit to new life. The possibilities of joy required the most steadfast focus and effort. Quite exemplary is the following teaching, in which Rabbi Naḥman retells a parable transmitted from his maternal great-grandfather, Rabbi Israel Ba'al Shem.

> Concerning joy [*simḥah*], [consider this] parable: Sometimes when people are rejoicing and dancing, they grasp a man from outside [the circle]—one who is sad [*be-'atzvut*] and depressed—and press him

> against his will into the circle [*maḥol*] of dancers, and force him to rejoice with them. So it is with joy: for when a person is happy, his depression and sufferings stand off to the side. But the higher level is to struggle and pursue that very depression, and bring it also into the joy, until the depression is transformed into joy . . . For [indeed] there are [types of] sorrow and woe that are [manifestations of] the [demonic] Other Side, and do not want to be bearers of holiness; hence they flee from joy, and one must force them into [the sphere of] holiness—namely, joy—against their will, as [I] just said.[63]

We will analyze this parable at length in the next chapter, together with an extended discussion of the relationship between joy and dance in the spiritual counsels and theology of Rabbi Naḥman.[64] Here, mention of the particularly innovative features of this teaching on joy must suffice. Of these, perhaps the most striking is the emphasis on acts of joy unrelated to religious duties. Indeed the emphasis of the passage is on raw psychological states of sadness or depression, and the need to treat them aggressively and transform them into joy. Sometimes this transformation is against one's will, and one must forcibly integrate the depressed qualities into the self. This is hardly a spiritual therapy of sublimation or repression, but of active transformation of the realities of sorrow through the activation of joy. And since these negative states are regarded as manifestations of external demonic powers, the acts of spiritual aggression against depression are all the more important and potentially redemptive. Joy is thus a triumph of the religious will, a catalytic transformation of the evils of sorrow that jolts the self into a new spiritual state.

At its deepest core, then, joy is a divine dynamism that may fuse the fragments of one's inner being and transmute demonic decay into holiness and health. As Rabbi Naḥman understands it, the power of joy lies in its capacity to heal the divisive depletions of depression. But a joy that goes unredeemed, a joy which does not integrate the inner demons into a higher wholeness, does not truly transform the person into a bearer of divine holiness. Therefore Naḥman goes on to say that it is a "great commandment" or "obligation" *(mitzvah gedolah)* to be "in joy always" *(be-simḥah tamid)*,[65] resisting the sickness *(ḥol'at)* of sadness with an ever-expanding joy.[66] Then will the *Shekhinah* descend upon the sick *(ḥoleh)* soul as a whirling sphere *(ḥolah)* of dance *(maḥol)* and heal its divisions.[67] Rabbi Naḥman does not hesitate to call this a redemptive repair *(tiqqun)*.

Although the depiction of dancing in the parable is not halakhic, there is no doubt that for R. Naḥman "the essence of joy arises through the commandments."[68] This principle remains for him the core of true religious praxis. Nevertheless, because religious performance can be undermined at the deeper psychic levels of will, desire, or ego by the forces of depression, self-alienation, and despair, the renewal of observance must be preceded by a regeneration of spiritual energy and focus. Such an inner arousal is of the essence of joy—a precious uplifting of the spirit that must be strengthened with great psychological perspicacity. Rabbi Naḥman therefore provided counsels of a non-halakhic order. Of primary importance among these *hanhagot* (or spiritual practices) is *hitboddedut,* the practice of physical withdrawal or self-isolation. For a portion of every day the seeker should withdraw to a place of sensory isolation and there open his heart to God in an uninhibited confession of his naturalness and distance from God. This deep broken-heartedness *(lev nishbar)* will act upon the soul by stilling the passions of the imagination and stimulating the roots of joy that link the worshipper—as by an inflamed charge—to God.[69]

A complex circuit of energy thus leads from troubled desire, through tears and talk before God, to a joy which heals the broken heart and stimulates wholehearted worship—and thence back to deeper moments of *hitboddedut.*[70] The process is a purification of inwardness and the development of a simplified service that overcomes (through joy) intellection and ego. It is indeed a liberation (or *herut*), as Naḥman says, from one's all-too-human nature. A remarkable exegesis makes the point. Taking up the verse from Isaiah 55:12, which predicts that the people "will leave [Babylon] in joy [*be-simḥah*] and be led [homeward] secure [*be-shalom*]," the master teaches a personal path of renewal. If one works to leave one's inner "Babylon" of natural desire and confusion of thought *through* the joyous performance of the Sabbath and other commandments, then a harmonious wholeness *(shelemut)* of mind will result—and with it true liberation. With his substitution of the older prophetic word, Rabbi Naḥman converts the divine promise into a saintly condition: joy is now the spark of freedom, the first flame of a purified consciousness.[71] "When the mind is linked to joy, it is taken out of bondage and becomes free."[72]

The highly privatized practice of *hitboddedut* is complemented by other, more interpersonal possibilities for the arousal of joy. Some of these have a striking resonance with teachings in *Reshith Ḥokhmah,* but now with the unique psychological and pedagogical "Bratzlav" twist.[73] Thus where de Vidas stresses the value of seeing the face of a sage, Rabbi Naḥman naturally replaces this figure with the saint or righteous master (the Hasidic *Tzaddiq*), who radiates a higher joy that shines through him.[74] The result of this illumination is the stimulation of joy in the dormant spirit and the activation of energized service *(zerizut)* in the fulfillment of the commandments.[75] The process of this return to inwardness by the Hasid (pious disciple) begins by journeying to the Tzaddik on Holy Days. This pilgrimage serves as an outward manifestation of the worshipper's progressive divestment of naturalness, and is complemented by acts of charity and gift-giving.[76] So prepared, the seeker may properly receive the radiant joy of the Tzaddik's face through his eyes—whence they penetrate his inmost being and induce repentance.[77] The light of the saint's face thus opens up a space for introspection in the penitent. Revising the psalmist's cry "I will sing to the Lord as long as I live [*be-'odi*] . . . [Yea] I will rejoice [*'esmaḥ*] in the Lord" (Psalm 104:33–34), Rabbi Naḥman taught that one must begin one's song of spiritual renewal with whatever residue *(be-'odi)* of goodness can be found in the self, and devote that "good point" *(nequdah ṭovah)* joyfully to God.[78] With this rebirth of inner light, one may go out into the world and rejuvenate the heart of each neighbor.[79] Hereby the circuit of energy is a current of ethicized light. In Naḥman's hands, de Vidas's teachings have been boldly psychologized.

The struggle for joy must thus begin with whatever inner resources remain with the depressed or despairing self—be this the will to transform the sorrow through acts of joy or the courage to rebuild oneself from the residues of self-affirmation. At its nadir, all that may remain is a sense of one's facticity as a creature of God. And this too may be enough, as Rabbi Naḥman once taught in a tale that speaks indirectly of his own struggles. According to the brief summary preserved by a disciple, the narrative described a Tzaddik whose perfect service of God was destroyed by a fall into depressive impotence, in which he wallowed until he was able to arouse himself through the simple sense of gratitude to God for creating him a Jew.[80] The catalyst is a fragment from the morning prayer service in which the worshipper gives thanks to Heaven "that You did not create me a gentile" *(she-lo 'asani goy).* In Naḥman's mind and circumstances this phrase evoked a renewed sense of chosenness and capacity to serve God that charged his consciousness with the force of an inner revelation. It served as the spark for spiritual regeneration.

An even more jolting version of this teaching is conveyed in the following instruction. Its power rests in the assertion that the mere awareness of being a Jew—and here it is the sorrowing commoner that is meant, not the Tzaddik—is the psychic root of joy and primary to any expression of joyous observance of the commandments. Indeed, with simple directness the teaching reveals the most basic of moral states—gratitude for life—to be the most profound core of creaturehood.

> Sadness is no sin; but the depression that sadness can bring about goes beyond the worst sin [*'atzvus iz dokh keyn 'aveyreh; ober dem ṭimṭum halev vos 'atzvus fershtelt ken nit farsteyn di grubste 'aveyreh*] . . . When I speak of the need for joy [*simḥah*], I don't mean the joy of doing a commandment [*simḥah shel mitvah*], since this is itself a [spiritual] level [*madregeh*] . . . I only mean no sadness [*nit keyn 'atzvus*]. Put plainly: a Jew who does not rejoice in his being a Jew is an ingrate before God [*iz a kafui ṭovah dem himmel*]. It is a sign that he has never [truly] understood the [morning] blessing, *she-lo 'asani goy* ["that You did not create me a gentile"]![81]

With these words, spoken to simple peasants in the harsh physical and historical reality of nineteenth-century Eastern Europe, the old Talmudic adage concerning the primacy of joy in doing divine service is set aside for the mere gratitude of being a Jew (and thus chosen by God for His service). Indeed, this attitude is not even deemed a spiritual achievement, but rather the most primary level of creaturely awareness. In this formulation the lofty teachings on joy in the spiritual heritage of Judaism are condensed to their rudimentary core. Joy is now seen as the most basic recognition of embodied difference, and of thankfulness for the fact of being. In this teaching, "no sadness!" is the great commandment—reverberating beyond Sinai, and before it.

11

The Mystery of Dance According to Rabbi Naḥman of Bratzlav

What happens when we dance? What really happens when the Omaha Indians circle a ritual pole, the Wanyamwezi pitch in ecstasy, or the Basques perform their fox dance? What happens in these patterns of movement, these convoluted leaps and revolutions? Can one really dance the corn out of the ground or ensure the rhythms of heaven? It depends on whom you ask. Euripides and Lucian of old had their theories; and modern anthropologists divine in dance encoded dramas of class and crisis, emotional release, or rites of transformation. Philosophers naturally propose their own perspectives about form and motion, and physiologists feel the pulse of altered states of consciousness.[1]

Dance plays a role also in textual tradition. Rabbi Moshe Ḥayim Ephraim of Sudlikov (1737–1800), received the following teaching from his grandfather, Rabbi Israel Ba'al Shem (the Ba'al Shem Tov, founder of modern Hasidism). It is found in his great work *Degel Maḥaneh Ephraim*, and it developed as a comment on the biblical verse "And all the nation saw the *voices*" (*qolot;* literally, the "sounds" or "thunderclaps"; Exodus 20:18)—a passage that describes the experience of the nation during the theophany at Mount Sinai. In his teaching, the master attempts to explain the oxymoron of seeing sounds. He offers this parable.

> There was once a musician who performed on a very fine instrument with great sweetness and pleasantness, and all who heard it could not restrain themselves and danced [*roqedim*] with great abandon. The closer one stood to the music the greater his pleasure and the more enthusiastic was his dancing. [Now] amidst the tumult came a deaf person who could not hear any sound [*qol*] of the pleasant instrument.

Seeing the people dance mightily, he thought them mad, and wondered "What can joy [*simḥah*] accomplish?" Truly, were he wise and understood that all this was due to the great pleasure and loveliness of the instrument's sound, he too would have begun to dance then and there.

Now the meaning [of the parable] is clear, and one may apply it to the verse "And all the people saw the sounds [*qolot*]." They saw that the Holy One, blessed be He, appeared before all (the people) in the unity of His divine light, which they all together perceived. When they saw the great joy [roundabout them]—for "the angels of the hosts were dancing about" [Psalm 68:13]—they understood that it was because of the sweetness and loveliness of the light of the holy Torah, and strained forward to hear its sound [*qol*]. For though they were still deaf, and did not "hear" the sounds, their minds and eyes were illumined when they saw the great happiness and joy [of the angels]. They then understood that this was due to the sounds [*qolot*]; that is, to the loveliness and pleasantness of the sound [*qol*] of the Torah. Thus: even though they did not perceive the loveliness of the Torah, they understood from the joy [expressed by the angels] that this was due to the great loveliness of the Torah—and so they pressed forward to hear the sound itself, in the hope that they might even perceive and understand the loveliness of the light of the Torah. The enlightened will understand.[2]

The image of a musician who played with such sweetness that all who heard drew close and leaped in joy—all, that is, except for a deaf man—is compared to the scene in Sinai, when God appeared before the nation in a great light, and those assembled perceived the joy of the heavenly hosts as they jumped for joy, enthralled with the sweet light of the Torah and its sounds.[3] In their own lower spiritual state, the people only saw this joy; but since they were also blessed with some wisdom, they pressed forward to try to hear the sounds of the Torah and bask in its holy light.

The first notable point about this teaching is the striking discordance between the parable and its application. In the former, the deaf man comes to a negative judgment about joy and does not achieve any deeper understanding. In the latter, the people first perceive a limited, visual truth, and then desire a deeper (aural) understanding. From this difference we may infer that the parable was formulated independently of the biblical verse and its interpretation. In fact, we may infer that the Ba'al Shem's parable was originally intended to ridicule the opponents of early Hasidism (the Mitnaggedim), who aggressively criticized their counterparts' ecstatic movements in prayer.[4] The Hasidic counterthrust here is that such rebuke is devoid of religious insight. The deaf man's query, "What can joy achieve?" (from Ecclesiastes 2:2), underscores this jibe—for through it the debunkers are made to condemn themselves as spiritually deaf, and able to perceive only the external aspects of religious expression.[5] In contrast, the true believers, or Hasidim, penetrate to hidden realms of Divinity. Rabbi Moshe Ḥayim makes this point by a bold application of the parable to the opening scriptural verse, concerning the sounds seen at Sinai (Exodus 20:18). In his interpretation, the nation is shown to transcend an original "deafness" by its readiness to see beyond the dancing angels to the source of their joy—the holy Torah and the sweet sound of God's word. And if the angelic dance is an act of supernatural joy, so too, we reason, is the dance of true believers also an ecstatic expression of transcendence. Indeed, the discourse instructs that through joy one may transcend his earthly nature and connect with the inner light of Scripture, whose splendor is a facet of God Himself.

The movements of dance thus express a desire for divinity—even the pull of transcendence upon the spiritually awakened soul. Human nature is thereby transformed, but not through an act of will or external compulsion. For this we must turn again to Rabbi Naḥman's radical teaching of our parable.

> Concerning joy [*simḥah*], consider this parable: Sometimes when people are rejoicing and dancing, they grab a person from outside [the circle]—one who is sad [*be-'atzvut*] and depressed—and press him against his will into the circle [*maḥol*] of dancers [*meraqqedim*], and force him to rejoice with them. So it is with joy: for when a person is happy, his depression and sufferings stand off to the side. But the higher level is to strive and pursue that very depression, and bring it into joy . . . For [indeed] there are [types of] sorrow and woe that are [manifestations of] the [demonic] Other Side, and do not want to be bearers of holiness; hence they flee from joy, and one must force them into [the sphere of] holiness—namely, joy—against their will . . .[6]

This revision of the parable is remarkable—for in it the social and nomistic aspects of the earlier versions have been thoroughly psychologized.[7] The image of two circles, of the dancers and nondancers (whether the holy troupe versus the scoffer, or the angelic ensemble vis-à-vis the people of Israel), now turns into a dramatic contest within a psychic division, whereby the joyous celebrant temporarily cuts himself off from his own depressive deadness. Significantly, Rabbi Naḥman affirms this momentary emotional revitalization and does not reduce it to religious observance. That is not to deny or demote the joyous observance of the commandments. Indeed, Naḥman repeatedly stressed that: *'iqqar ha-simḥah min ha-mitzvot* ("the essence of joy arises through the commandments")[8]—a principle which derives ultimately from the Talmud (*b. Shabbat* 30b) and its Zoharic reformulation (*Vayeḥi*, I. 216a).[9] It is rather that he was also aware that (religious) joy may be generated from the most natural and seemingly frivolous of acts *(ve-'afilu be-milei de-sheṭuta)*.[10] Hence simple dance—when performed in the service of religious ends and not purely private passions *(hitlahavut ha-yetzer)*—may induce a catalytic catharsis in the individual and lead to a higher healing. But this requires the celebrant to direct the energies so elicited toward the divisive and depressive dimensions of the self. Accordingly, Rabbi Naḥman instructs his followers to work for psychic wholeness—urging a psychological activism that pursues the agents of one's depression in all their guises, and transforms them through the agency of joy.

Dance is thus both the arch-act and arch-metaphor for this cathartic process. In another, related teaching, Rabbi Naḥman goes on to stress how depression is an illness, a *ḥola'at,* when the cords of joy are snapped and one is put in a bad temper, so to speak.[11] The antidote *(refu'ah)* is the joy of dance, or *maḥol*. Its circular swirl draws the heavenly *Shekhinah* (or feminine gradation of supernal Divinity) down to the earthly realm, where it may alight upon the sick soul *(ḥoleh)* in healing union.[12] This spiritual therapy gives a new mystical application to a passage in the Jerusalem Talmud: "In the future the Holy One, blessed be He, will be at the head of every dance troupe [*ḥolah*], for the righteous ones [*tzaddiqim*] in the future."[13]

Struck by the similarity of sounds between *ḥolah* (dance troupe) and *ḥoleh* (sick person), Naḥman interprets the passage as God's descent that effects a therapeutic transformation of the sick into *tzaddiqim,* or righteous saints. Indeed, by virtue of the contrast established hermeneutically between the words *ḥoleh* and *tzaddiqim,* the sick and the healthy, Naḥman depicts a ritual process whereby dance *(maḥol)* transforms the depressed person *(hola'at)* into a righteous one *(tzaddiq)* through its power to engender joy and a conjunction with the heavenly realm. What is more, Naḥman's substitution of the feminine epithet, *Shekhinah,* for the masculine "Holy One, blessed be He" not only gives an erotic valence to this Holy Union—whereby the supernal masculine gradations of *Yesod* (Foundation), also called *Tzaddiq* (Righteous One), and the feminine gradation of *Malkhut* (Kingdom), also called *Shekhinah* (Indwelling), are unified in Divinity and in the dancer[14]—but also points to the psychosomatic process whereby the fragmented self is regenerated as a whole and healthy being. At once, the dancer is both male and female; a whirling circle *and* its axis of rotation; the engendering foundation *and* the orbit of eros. Given the language of Naḥman's exegesis (playing on *ḥola'at* and *maḥol*), and the fact that he elsewhere affirms the dictum that God will himself be a *maḥol* (dance) for the righteous in the future,[15] I would suggest that the whole hermeneutic is based on a calculated mishearing. To his Yiddishized ear, the Hebrew word *maḥol* was perceived as *moḥol,* that is, as having the overtone of spiritual healing and forgiveness *(meḥilah).* Naḥman concretized this (dialectal) convergence, deeming it a linguistic sign of supernal and spiritual truth. From this perspective, dance is a deep transformational grammar.[16]

The full messianic aspect of Rabbi Naḥman's teaching may be approximated in stages. As a first step, take his treatment of Isaiah 35:10—a verse which functions as the biblical prooftext for several instructions. Speaking to the nation in exile, the prophet had said: "The redeemed of the Lord will return [*yeshuvun*]: they shall come rejoicing to Zion, with eternal joy on their head [*simḥat 'olam 'al rosham*]; they shall attain [*yasigu*] gladness and joy, while sorrow and despair flee." Naḥman reads this promise psychologically and gives it a more activist character. Joy is not simply rendered by divine grace but must be aggressively pursued; for with the arousal of joy the forces of sadness flee *(boreḥim), and must therefore be forcibly seized (yitpesu)—in order that the self may be integrated and perfected as a true "chariot of holiness."*[17] This is clearly a complex and paradoxical doctrine, whereby personal redemption requires the self to absorb (and not just neutralize) negative energies. The deeper mythic dimension is indicated by Naḥman's designation of despair as the demonic Other Side.[18]

In Rabbi Naḥman's worldview, which derives ultimately from features in the book of *Zohar* as mediated through Lurianic belief and practice, the Other Side *(Siṭra Aḥra)* originates as negative "judgments" *(dinim)* in the divine attribute of Understanding *(Binah).*[19] In the conception of the supernal hierarchy imagined as Anthropos, this gradation corresponds to the heart *(lev)*. From here the deposits of *dinim* descend through the thighs and feet of the Divine Body (identified with the divine gradations of *Netzaḥ* (Eternity) and *Hod* (Splendor), and become lodged in the lowest extremities, the heel(s).[20] Significantly, Naḥman says that the means to force these negative extrusions *(ḥitzonim)* "to flee" *(le-havriaḥ)* the lower part of the divine Corpus is to "draw down" *(mamshikh)* joy from its source in the inner root of Understanding. This theurgical "action" *(pe'ulah)* is effected on earth through a psychosomatic activation of energy *(hitlahavut)*, which results in the movements of dance *(riqqudin)*.[21] Indeed, the arousal of human feet in holy (divinely directed) dance releases the fluids of joy from the heavenly heart; and as they course through the Divine Body and its earthly image, the demonic deposits are leached and purified. Thus are the thighs *(birkayim)*, for example, transformed into a blessing *(berakhah)* and a birthright *(bekhorah)*.[22]

The patriarch Jacob exemplifies this supernatural process. For though he was born holding on to the "heel" *('aqev)* of his brother Esau (Gen. 25:26), and indeed has that very fact inscribed in his own name *(Ya'aqov)*, the hidden reality is that his name is a complex multiple of the divine Name Elohim, which symbolizes the powers of "judgment," and through that identity he perceived that the source of these powers is in *Binah*, whose essence is joy.[23] Accordingly, says Naḥman, when Jacob perceived that the thighs of the divine hierarchy (*Nezaḥ* and *Hod*) were invaded by destructive judgment, he went to his father Isaac (who symbolizes the divine gradation of Power) and brought him wine to drink (Gen. 27:25)—knowing that "Wine makes the heart of man rejoice" (Psalm 104:15). That is, through his mystical understanding that wine stands for the spiritual stimulus which opens the heart of the Divine Anthropos to the blessed energy of joy, Jacob brought wine to his earthly father, so that he, Isaac, might rejoice and infuse the "(heavenly) Man" (through himself) with supernal bounty.[24] In this way, both upper and lower worlds were blessed.

On another occassion, Jacob effects this therapy on the Cosmic Corpus with his own body—for Rabbi Naḥman interprets the phrase "And Jacob raised *(va-yissa')* his legs" (literally, when Jacob set forth [for Padan Aram]; Gen. 29:1) to mean the truth of dance, whereby one's bodily movements of raising the legs may (with the right intention) "draw down" *(le-hamshikh)* joy from the inner recesses of the divine heart to the lower limbs.[25] What Rabbi Naḥman means is that Jacob's physical action of raising the legs symbolizes the mystical "raising" or healing of the lower extremities of the divine Corpus. By high-stepping, so to speak, the lower forces of judgment in the legs are purified and raised upwards to their source in the heart. This interfusion of energy also elicits the manifestation of the most hidden Mother and Bride *(Binah)*, and thus activates a psychological healing of Jacob and a mystical marriage within Divinity itself.[26] Moreover, when Jacob married (*nasa'*; that is, raised or healed) Leah (who symbolizes the divine gradation of Bride), he created another conjunction of the corresponding hierarchies in heaven. This mystical moment was celebrated by the dancers at Jacob's marriage feast, according to Naḥman's theosophical interpretation of an ancient midrash.[27] It may also be induced through joyous dance at any Jewish wedding, and is thus the mystical purpose of *meraqqedim lefnei ha-kallah*, of dancing before the bride.

Dance is thus a deep process of human and divine transformation whereby the gravity of sin and depression is suspended, at least momentarily, and the dancer raises himself to a higher plane and jumps in and through the joy which animates the whole body. Indeed, in Rabbi Naḥman's view, human sin and depression secrete negative judgments through the blood of the body, and these coagulate, like clots, in the lower extremities, preventing the proper circulation of blood to the heart, which is the source of healthy life and joy.[28] This results in corresponding blockages in the arteries or "channels" of the divine Corpus, and these can only be thinned or "sweetened" when the individual "judges himself" and corrects his behavior in the light of the Torah and its teachings. Then the weight of sin is lifted and one is blessed with the lightness of dance—which is the pulse of joy, down to one's heel *('eqev)*. Rabbi Naḥman found this truth encoded in the biblical verse, "And it shall be if *('eqev)* you heed these judgments *(mishpaṭim)* and observe them carefully" (Deut. 7:12). He interprets it to mean that if one enacts self-judgment (and its corresponding behavioral corrections) one will merit the fullness of joy throughout one's body.[29]

These ideas have roots in rabbinic lore. One ancient midrash taught a deep homology between the totality of 613 divine commandments and the human body, to the effect that the 248 positive commandments of Scripture correspond to the sum of bodily parts (even as the 365 negative commandments correspond to the number of arteries and to the days of the solar year).[30] One implication of this correspondence is that the ritual performance of divine duties has both anthropic and cosmic implications—such that the positive and negative duties fulfill the human self as a whole, while the latter ones also preserve the natural order. Add to this the midrashic teaching that fulfillment of the commandments "adds strength" to the divine order, while sins diminish or "weaken" its power, and the mythic ground of rabbinic ritual comes into view, against the background of a heavenly Anthropos.[31] What one does has effects above and below. In this light, the old midrash on Deuteronomy 7:12, which interpreted the phrase "if *('eqev)* you heed the commandments" as an exhortation to be on guard lest even a minor commandment lie hidden under one's heel *('aqev)*, has rich mythic possibilities—since even those sins may debilitate man and God alike.[32]

The theosophic worldview appropriated by Rabbi Naḥman had long since maximized the mythic potential of such speculation. For from the period of the *Zohar* itself, in the thirteenth century, the divine Anthropos was the ultimate beneficiary of the various commandments which were enacted by the human individual (with all his mind, body, and means). One need merely recall the pertinent passages in the *Zohar* itself, where "the commandments of the Torah are all connected with the supernal, holy King";[33] or in such works as *Sefer Ha-Rimmon,* by Moshe de Leon;[34] or the commentary on the commandments *(Sefer Ṭa'amei Ha-Mitzvot)* attributed to Rabbi Yitzḥaq ibn Farḥi, in order to prove the point.[35] This conception pervades the whole Lurianic corpus and its derivatives.[36] What is more, the theosophical notion that precipitates of evil from human sin lodge in the heels of the Cosmic Man is also found in thirteenth-century Castillian sources and in the school of Safed three centuries later. Rabbis Yitzḥaq Luria and Ḥayim Vital provide numerous ways for the worshipper to participate in the mythical drama of divine purification—and gave special attention to the flaws of the feet.

Rabbi Naḥman absorbed these teachings and reformulated them in light of his psychosomatic theories of joy.[37] As he says, when one sins with any limb or organ and breaks any one of the 613 commandments of the Torah, a "defect" (or *pegam*) is inflicted upon the Torah and the sinner, such that the joy inherent in God's word is blocked and the human being is not only cut off from its holy energy but left with the depressive deadness of a wholly natural being.[38] For "The commands of the Lord are upright, rejoicing the heart" (Psalm 19:9); and how can these agents of divine vitality act on the heart if they are not absorbed through the limbs which perform the commandments with joyful intent?[39] Accordingly, each and every commandment has a structure of joy inherent in it, and one must activate that joy in its proper manner—the hands, say, through gift-giving or holding the *lulav* and *etrog* correctly; the mouth, through pure prayer and honest speech; and of course the sexual organs, through the holiness of matrimonial union and procreation. The feet or legs also have their ideal functions, such as walking on the Sabbath, going on a pilgrimage, or dancing before the bride—both divine and human.

The full activation of the entire body in holy actions is thus a therapy of total joy, whereby the currents of divine energy enliven and integrate the human being in all 613 parts. As Naḥman says:

> Joy [*simḥah*] is a total structure [*qomah shelemah*], comprised of 248 limbs and 365 arteries, and therefore when one rejoices or dances, he must be certain that he activates [*ya'avor*] the entirety of joy, from head to heel; for sometimes joy is only in the feet, or only in the heart, or only in the head, as alluded to by the verse, "and eternal joy on their head" [Isaiah 35:10]. But the essence of joy is that one activate the entirety of joy; that is, through the whole structure that joy comprises. And for that one needs many *mitzvot:* for the roots of the points of the *mitzvot* are in [the gradation of] joy; and "the commands of the Lord rejoice the heart" [Psalm 19:9]; and every one of the 613 commandments has a specific limb [in the structure of joy]—each one according to its type.[40]

Accordingly, he concludes, if one sins in any way one causes a defect in the entire bodily structure *(qomah),* and this must be "repaired and rebuilt" *(le-taqqen u-libnot)* through confession and the proper actions.

All this is clear enough. But to fully grasp Rabbi Naḥman's theology of dance we must, I think, penetrate the micro- and macro-systems which the human body mediates. Let me begin with the macro-system, following up the reference to the *qomah* which must be maintained or rebuilt. This nomenclature seems to point beyond the human body to the Cosmic *Qomah*—or the full structure of the Heavenly Anthropos, whose limbs and arteries contain in their hidden depth the roots of the divine commandments which the human *qomah* may activate through joyful performance of the halakhic duties associated with them. Other indications support this claim. Among these is the repeated emphasis in Naḥman's sermons and prayers that "feet" are the divine gradations of *Netzaḥ* and *Hod,* and that their elevation in holy joy may purify these pillars of truth and "bring" them to their "holy Source [on high]."[41] At the other pole is the micro-structure of dance, which is, in fact, the deep structure of each and every commandment. For Rabbi Naḥman not only identifies the core of each *mitzvah* with joy, as discussed earlier, but, precisely because each commandment replicates the anthropomorphic structure (or *qomah*) of the whole,[42] he understands the lower or imperfect level of each commandment to be its "feet."[43] He thus teaches that all "the lower levels which are called 'feet'" *(ha-madregot ha-taḥtonot ha-mekhunot raglayim)*—like evil speech, or money, or barrenness—may be elevated through the holy actions requisite for their transformation. Indeed, even faith *('emunah)* has forms called "feet" that may be re-established upon a firm foundation.[44] Accordingly, since joy rises through the raised feet of dance, the perfect performance of a *mitzvah* is an elevation of its base levels (the "feet" of a commandment, so to speak) to their divine or holy root. Confession or charity or kindness may heal the aforementioned defects—even as simplicity and humility may raise up faith when it falls through pride or cleverness. Such ritual rectifications are dance-like in their dynamism, filling the structure (or *qomah*) of each commandment with a joyous energy. In turn, their perfected performance repairs and perfects the limbs which perform them, as well as the corresponding members of the *Qomah* on high. Accordingly, from the micro- to the macro-levels the *mitzvot* have messianic potential—and dance is their catalyst.

Let me conclude this point with reference to a third genre (alongside the teachings and prayers) in the Bratzlav corpus, the tales, and in particular to his "Tale of the Seven Beggars." The multifacted messianic message of this narrative is well known, and its early commentators have not failed to note that the appearance of the seventh beggar "without feet" *(vos on fees)* on the seventh day of the wedding celebration symbolizes the seventh and final gradation of the divine hierarchy, whose perfection, so necessary for all higher unifications, is clearly marred. Indeed, Rabbi Naḥman himself explicitly indicates the truncated messianic potential of this image when he says that the tale of the crippled beggar will only be heard in messianic times, *shoyn nit herrn biz moshiaḥ vet kumn.* Yet the "beggar without feet" is preceded by six other messengers, each of whom has an obvious defect in his eyes, ears, mouth, neck, back, and hands, respectively. That is, each beggar is associated with a specific part of the body, and together they symbolize the anthropomorphic structure of the divine hierarchy that may be perfected when humans purify their limbs through holy deeds and commandments. For Naḥman, this is the messianic core of this last of 13 *mayses* (or tales), which clearly alludes to the supernal cosmic structure.[45]

Rabbi Naḥman's suggestion that the messianic truth cannot now be heard *(shoyn nit herrn)* brings us back to the high state of hearing alluded to in the teaching of Rabbi Moshe Ḥayim Ephraim, at the beginning of this chapter. He tells us that the people at Sinai only saw the dancing angels—as the earthly animation of God's voice. They themselves did not yet merit the higher level of actually hearing it. Naḥman, who so profoundly personalized the parable of dance in that earlier teaching, also has a remarkable instruction concerning hearing itself.

Rabbi Naḥman says that one must work hard and persistently to enter the holiness of joy, which is of the nature of the deepest affirmation of God's truth in deed and hearing. Hence when the people of Israel at Sinai said *na'aseh ve-nishma'* ("Let us do and hear"; Exodus 24:7) they achieved a blissful moment of transcendence, when myriads of angels crowned each and every one with both the manifest or exoteric meaning of Torah, the level of *na'aseh* (doing), and with its hidden or esoteric truth, called *nishma'* (hearing). Thus through the proper performance of the commandments, in their exoteric aspect, the Jew will be enveloped by their mystical aura and drawn to their secret sound in his heart. Here transpires the highest level of divine worship, a mystical "service of the heart" whereby the natural self is totally annihilated through attachment to the Infinite *(biṭṭul u-devekut la-'ein sof)*.[46]

Now this highest of all levels is not attained without great spiritual work, whose very dialectic is itself of the nature of *na'aseh ve-nishma'*. That is, there is at every "level" of this world, and "in every world," a dynamic process of moving from *na'aseh* (doing) to *nishma'* (hearing) in continual progressions and spirals—for each attainment of *nishma'* is but a level of *na'aseh* for the ongoing quest.[47] The true adept must thus struggle onward with ceaseless honesty and perseverance, since deceptions and demands are repeated at every level with ever greater subtlety. And yet Rabbi Naḥman gives hope that eventually one may attain the "beginning of (the) divine emanation" where, for the first time, the seeking soul will perceive the *torat ha-Shem be-'emet*, "the Divine Torah in (its essential) truth." That is, it is only at this consummate rung of *na'aseh* where one realizes that all previous perceptions of God's Torah were but derivative and metaphorical *(mush'al)*, owing to the representational nature of human consciousness. Beyond this, there is nothing more to say. For when one passes over to the level of *nishma'* in this dyad, the seeker "merits to be utterly absorbed into the Infinite Divine, [wherein] truly his Torah is the actual Torah of God, and his prayer the actual prayer of God" *(ukhishe-zokheh le-hikkalel be-'ein sof, 'azai torato torat ha-Shem mamash, u-tefillato tefillat ha-Shem mamash)*.[48]

Rabbi Naḥman believed that his teachings and reproof, which functioned (as he says) as the "feet" of his generation, might heal the soul of those who listen, and raise them to ever higher levels of faith.[49] Indeed, he believed that his stories had the power to catalyze his followers to the very heights of ecstasy, and to give them, in one moment, the ultimate bliss of God. Or as he said, in what may be the most astonishing word of an astonishing master: "The world has not yet tasted me at all; for if they were to hear but one torah that I say, *with its (proper) melody and dance*, they would all attain complete spiritual annihilation *(hayu beṭellim be-viyṭul gamur)*"—*zey zolln mikh herrn eyn toyroh mit dem nign un mit eyn tanz, vollt di ganze velt oys gegangen* (the whole world would 'expire')."[50]

This completes a cycle of answers to my initial question of what may happen when we dance. For Rabbi Naḥman of Bratzlav, as interpreted here, the structure of dance activates a series of homologies that coordinate the human world of action and the divine worlds of blessing. Indeed, through dance, the de-vitalized natural self absorbs transcendental powers which, in turn, energize the supernal Being vitiated by human sin. But in closing we have learned more: even the very teachings of the master, like those discussed here, have each an ideal configuration or conjunction of content, sound, and movement. When these are perfectly realized, as a verbal *torah* (teaching) performed with its requisite and unique dance-like gestures (or energy), the hearer may be seized in one fell swoop by a transcendental ecstasy. How much more so may the speaker himself? It is thus hardly surprising (though no less startling) to learn that, immediately after Rabbi Naḥman spoke of "the dance of instruction," he turned to his disciple and scribe, Rabbi Noson, and asked: *Vos hob ikh gezokt* ("What did I [just] say")?![51]

Notes

Credits

Index

Notes

1. Midrash and the Nature of Scripture

1. In the edition of Louis Finkelstein (New York: Jewish Theological Seminary of America, 1969), 399.
2. See *Mekhilta de-Rabbi Ishmael, Yitro,* 9; in the edition of Hayim Horowitz-Israel Rabin (Jerusalem: Bamberger and Wahrmann, 1960), 235. The first of the anonymous traditions in the *Sifre,* dealing with the arm, is attributed to R. Shim'on bar Yochai, in *Songs Rabba,* I.2:2; in this midrashic corpus the aforenoted Akiban tradition is presented by R. Berekhia, in the name of R. Ḥelbo, and the fire is said to have come directly to God's right hand.
3. *De Decalogo,* sec. 19, and 154; also *De Specialibus Legibus,* I, sec. 1.
4. *Sifre Deuteronomy,* 313.
5. This text adds that the Israelites were also informed of the judgments, punishments, and rewards consequent to obedience to the Law.
6. A classic formulation of this paradox is *Targum Onqelos'* elaboration of the biblical statement that God spoke only the Decalogue at Sinai "and no more *(ve-lo yasaf)*" (Deut. 5:19) into the rabbinic truth that God's voice resounded "without end"; and cf. Rashi's gloss, *ad loc.*
7. I have discussed such matters at length in my *Biblical Interpretation in Ancient Israel* (Oxford: Clarendon Press, 1985).
8. For the relationship between *langue* and *parole,* see Ferdinand de Saussure, *Cours de linguistique générale,* 3rd ed. (Paris: Payot, 1967). For these terms in the wider context of structural poetics (and such issues as relational identity and binarism), see Jonathan Culler, *Structuralist Poetics* (New York: Cornell University Press, 1975), chap. 1.
9. The "Book of Moses" in 2 Chronicles 35:12 refers to the traditions mentioned from the books of Exodus and Deuteronomy in v. 13. See my discussion in *Biblical Interpretation,* 134–37.
10. See my discussion of Scripture as a *Sondersprache* in *The Garments of Torah: Essays in Biblical Hermeneutics* (Bloomington: Indiana University Press, 1989), chap. 3.

11. For the relationship between oracular inquiry and exegesis, see my *Biblical Interpretation*, 245.
12. Cf. *Genesis Rabba* 1.4; see *Bereshit Rabba*, Juda Theodor and Chanoch Albeck, eds. (Jerusalem: Wahrmann Books, 1965), I, 6–7.
13. See the commentary of *Minḥat Yeḥudah*, in *Bereshit Rabba*, Theodor and Albeck, eds., 108, and the gloss in the *Liqqutin*. Solomon Buber, *Midrash Shoḥer Tov* (Vilna, 1891), par. 114, p. 471 (note, *ad loc.*) which renders "livelihood" or "sustenance," following Alexander Kohut, ed., *Aruch Completum* (Vienna: Menorah, 1926), s.v., *byyh*, II, 45a. William Braude, *The Midrash on Psalms* (New Haven: Yale University Press, 1959), II, 520 (n.7), renders "power" (Greek *bia*), so that God is "He who wields power" *(biastes)*. Braude adduces the observation of Saul Lieberman that this term is equivalent to Latin *defensor civitatis* or *defensor loci*. This would link *bia* to other juridical functions mentioned in the text (see below). Daniel Sperber, *A Dictionary of Greek and Latin Terms in Rabbinic Literature* (Jerusalem: Bar Ilan University Press, 1984), 68–69, has adduced evidence to render "justice."
14. Greek *ekdikos;* see *Minḥat Yehudah* in *Bereshit Rabba*, Theodor and Albeck, eds., 108; and lexical evidence in Sperber, *A Dictionary*, 32.
15. Greek *ekbibastēs* (one who executes justice); see Saul Lieberman, *Tarbiz* 36 (1967), 401, and Sperber, *A Dictionary*, 31 f.
16. For the text and variants, see *Genesis Rabba* 12.10, in *Bereshit Rabba*, Theodor and Albeck, eds., 107–109.
17. I have followed the *editio princeps* of Theodor and Albeck, pp. 107–109. For manuscript variants and other suggestions concerning the names of the regents, see the *varia lectiones* and the commentary of *Minḥat Yehudah* on p. 108.
18. A striking example occurs in *Genesis Rabba* 56.4, in connection with the phrase "God will show him the lamb *(ha-śeh)* for the offering" in Gen. 22:8. Deepening the irony of the father's answer, the sages played on the Greek pronoun *se* ("you"). This pun sneaks back into the vernacular in *Targum Jonathan* II (and cf. *Pirqei de-Rabbi Eliezer*, 31). The conceptual basis for such puns is found in the teaching that every one of God's commandments at Sinai "was divided into 70 languages" (see *b. Shabbat* 88b).
19. Cf. *Genesis Rabba* 1.5.
20. Cf. *biyya' biyya'* in *b. Yebamot* 97b; and the explanation of Yelammedenu Leviticus 13:24 in Kohut, ed., *Aruch Completum*, II, 44b–45a. There is an obvious pun as well on Hebrew *biv.*
21. See the interpretation of Jer. 23:29 in *b. Sanhedrin* 34a, and the reading of R. Samuel in the *Tosafot, ad loc.*, s.v., *Mah.*

22. *Songs Rabba* 1.10:2. According to traditions in *b. Ḥagigah* 14a and *yer. Ḥagigah* 2.1, a fire descended as Rabbi Eleazar ben Arakh dealt with mystical matters. However, also in the last source there is an account of fire which descended while Rabbi Eleazar and Rabbi Yehoshua "were engaged" in studying Scripture and conecting verses one to another. This tradition is stylistically similar to that in *Songs Rabba* (but correct *ḥozrim*) in the *yerushalmi* passage to *ḥorzim,* "linking" or "enchaining."
23. *Songs Rabba, ibid.*
24. *Midrash Shoḥer Ṭov* 9.1; Solomon Buber, ed. (Vilna, 1891), 79–80. In these cases *laben* is construed as *libban*—an Aramaic noun with third person masc. pronoun suffix, corresponding to Hebrew *libbam.*
25. *Ibid.*, 9.4; p. 82.
26. See *Genesis Rabba* 1.14. I have followed the sequence of interlocutors as reconstructed by the *Minḥat Yehudah.* See this discussion in *Bereshit Rabba,* Theodor and Albeck, eds., 12.
27. The opposite of such exegeses are the praiseworthy *haggadot meshubba*. *hot;* cf. *Mekhilta de-Rabbi Ishmael, Vayissa'* 1, Hayim Horovitz and Israel Rabin eds. (Jerusalem: Bamberger and Wahrman, 1960), 157.
28. In the *Mekhilta de-Rabbi Ishmael, Beshalaḥ* 6, p. 112, and many other places. On this tradition, see the important manuscript evidence that Menahem Cahana has reviewed and presented in his study, "Mahadurot ha-Mekhilta de-Rabbi Yishmael le-Shemot be-Re'iy Qiṭe'ei ha-Genizah," *Tarbiz* 55 (1987), 499–515. His arguments are compelling.
29. I have woven together similar accounts in *yer. Ta'anit* IV.4; *Tanḥuma, Ki Tissa'* 26 and 30. Cf. also *Avot de-Rabbi Nathan,* A. Solomon Schechter, ed., 3rd corrected ed. (New York: Phillipp Feldheim, 1967), 11; and Pseudo-Philo 12.5.

2. "The Holy One Sits and Roars"

1. Compare Isa. 11:11–16; 27:1; 51:9–11; and Ps. 74:12–14; 89:10–11, among others. Overall, see the seminal contribution of Umberto Cassutto, "The Israelite Epic," in *Biblical and Oriental Studies* (Jerusalem: Magnes Press, 1975), II, especially pp. 71–102 (originally published in *Kenesset* 8, 1943). For some particularly striking correspondences with Ugaritic mythology, see Cyrus H. Gordon, "Leviathan—Symbol of Evil," in *Biblical Motifs: Origins and Transformations,* Alexander Altmann, ed. (Brandeis Texts and Studies; Cambridge, Mass.: Harvard University Press, 1966), 1–9.
2. See Louis Ginzberg, *The Legends of the Jews* (Philadelphia: Jewish Publication Society, 1925), V, 17–18, 26–27, 41–50; and his discussion in *Jewish*

Law and Lore (New York and Philadelphia: Meridian and Jewish Publication Society, 1962), 63, where he refers to these mythological elements as "faded fragments" of non-Jewish antiquity. For a full analysis and appreciation of the vitality of *b. Baba Bathra* 74b–75a, see below, Chapter 3.

3. See Cassutto, "The Israelite Epic."
4. See the study by Jefim Schirmann, *The Battle between Behemoth and Leviathan According to an Ancient Hebrew Piyyut,* Proceedings of the Israel Academy of Sciences and Humanities (Jerusalem, 1970), IV, no. 13.
5. *Ibid.*, 355, 1.76.
6. See Moshe Spitzer, ed., *The Bird's Head Haggada of the Bezalel National Art Museum in Jerusalem,* intro. vol. (Jerusalem, 1967), pl. 32.
7. For Qallir's statement, "He [Leviathan] encircles the Great Sea like a ring," see Schirmann, *The Battle between Behemoth and Leviathan,* 355, 1.77.
8. Max Müller, "The Philosophy of Mythology," appended to his *Introduction to the Science of Religion* (London, 1873), pp. 353–55. See also his *Lectures on the Science of Language,* 2nd ser. (New York: Scribner, Armstrong, 1873), 372–76.
9. Johann Herder, "Abhandlung über den Ursprung der Sprache," in *Herders sämmtliche Werke,* Bernhard Suphan, ed. (Berlin: Wiedmannsche Buchhandlung, 1877–1913), V, 53 f.
10. See Joseph Aistleitner, *Wörterbuch der Ugaritischen Sprache* (Berlin: Akademie Verlag, 1967), 63 (no. 612).
11. On the expression *sefer ha-hagu* in the Damascus Document (CD X.6 and XIII.2), see Moshe Goshen-Gottstein, *Vetus Testamentum* 8 (1958), 286 ff. Cf. also Ps. 123:4, reading with the *Qere.*
12. A similar tradition recurs in Joel 4:16. The link between a divine roar and earth tremors is made explicit in this passage (note: *ve-ra'ashu,* "will shake"); it is more implicit in Amos 1:2, where a future oracle ("will roar") follows the notice (v. 1) that Amos prophesied two years before the earthquake *(ha-ra'ash).*
13. This understanding of the noun *naveh* is implicit in Exod. 15:13, and explicit in the *Mekhilta de-Rabbi Ishmael, Shirata,* Ḥayim Horovitz and Israel Rabin, eds. (Jerusalem: Bamberger and Wahrman, 1960), 146 (also quoting Ps. 79:7). This is also the explanation of the Targum, and is followed by Rashi and Kimḥi.
14. See also the versions in *Midrash Shoḥer Ṭov,* Solomon Buber, ed. (Vilna, 1891), 18.12 and 104, which apparently derive from this Talmudic tradition. Also see next note.
15. I have translated the word *'apiylon* as "threatens," assuming it to reflect the Greek participle *apeilōn,* (from *apeileo,* "to threaten punishment").

The form is translated in the *Shoḥer Tov* as *biqqesh,* "to decide" (to destroy it, *le-haḥarivo*).

16. Benjamin M. Lewin, ed., *'Otzar ha-Ge'onim. Thesaurus of the Geonic Responsa and Commentaries* (Haifa and Jerusalem, 1928–43), *Berakhot* 2. R. David Kimḥi likewise apologizes for the expression "roar" in Jer. 25:30, saying that "He roars from on high" is *'al derekh mashal,* "a figurative expression."
17. Lewin, ed., in Appendices to *'Otzar ha-Ge'onim, Berakhot,* 62–63. See now *Peirushei Rabbenu Ḥananel bar Ḥushiel le-Masekhet Berakhot,* R. David Metzger, ed. (Jerusalem: Lev Sameaḥ Institute, 1990), 130.
18. See *Sefer 'Arugat ha-Bosem,* Ephraim E. Urbach, ed. (Jerusalem: Mekitze Nirdamim, 1962), III, 108–109.
19. *Diologus Petri, cognomento Alphonsi, ex iudaeo christiani et Moysi iudaei,* Migne, *Patrologia Latina* CVII, 553.
20. *Ibid.*
21. *Ibid.,* 550–51.
22. According to Israel Davidson, *Sefer Mikhamot ha-Shem* (New York: Jewish Theological Seminary of America, 1934), 3. The work was written before 942, C.E.
23. *Ibid,* chap. 14, p. 108 (11. 5–18).
24. See Raphael N. Rabbinovicz, *Diqduqei Soferim. Varia Lectionis in Mischnam et in Talmud Babylonicum* (Munich, 1881), *Berakhot,* p. 4, n. 5 (Ms. Munich), and 337 (Ms. Paris). For other sources, see Saul Lieberman, *Shiqiin,* 2nd ed. (Jerusalem: Wahrmann, 1960), 70.
25. Migne, *Patrologia Latina* CLXXXIX, 622. See the comparison in Lieberman, *ibid.,* 28–29.
26. The comment of Rashi (eleventh century) on the divine roar in Jer. 25:30, "He [God] mourns [*mit'abbel*] over His Temple" seems to indicate that he also knew the Talmudic reading *'oy li.*
27. See Leon Nemoy, "Al-Qirqisani's Account of the Jewish Sects," *Hebrew Union College Annual* 7 (1930), 352.
28. Thus Salmon refers to (1) the bodily form of God (the *Shi'ur Qomah*); (2) divine tears and Israel's exile; (3) God wearing phylacteries (cf. *b. Berakhot* 6a); and God's prayer that His mercy overcome His anger (cf. *b. Berakhot* 7a). See n. 22. These topics are all mentioned by Petrus; cf. *Patrologia Latina* CVII, 543, 550–551.
29. Yizhak Baer, *The Jews in Christian Spain* (Philadelphia: Jewish Publication Society, 1978), I, 151.
30. Solomon Buber, ed., *Midrash Eikha Rabba* (Vilna: Romm, 1899), 13 a–b.
31. For the theme of the gradual ascent of the *Shekhinah* after Adam's sin, and its descent culminating in the completion of the Tabernacle, see *Pesiqta*

de-Rav Kahana 1.1, Bernard Mandelbaum, ed. (New York: Jewish Theological Seminary, 1962), I, 1–2; and *Tanhuma, Pequdei* 6. Cf. *Bereshit Rabba* 19.7, Juda Theodor and Chanoch Albeck, eds. (Jerusalem: Wahrmann Books, 1965), 176–177. Hence the ascension after the destruction is a return, as our *petihta'* says.

32. See *Midrash Eikha Zuṭṭa,* Solomon Buber, ed.(Vilna: Romm, 1925), 32b, the *Yalquṭ* to *Eikha* is appended thereto; see 43b, para. 4 in the traditional text, no. 996. The words *'oy li* are omitted twice.
33. *Synopse zur Hekhalot-Literatur,* Peter Schäfer, ed. (Tübingen: J. C. B. Mohr, 1981), par. 68–70 (Mss. Munich 40 and Vatican 228, respectively), 34–35.
34. 3 Enoch 48 A:1–4=Schäfer, par. 68.
35. I have taken up in detail in this midrashic topic my essay "Arm of the Lord: Biblical Myth, Rabbinic Midrash and the Mystery of History," in *Language, Theology, and the Bible,* Samuel Balentine and John Barton, eds. (Oxford: Clarendon Press, 1994), 271–292.
36. The prohibition of *'arayot,* so strongly condemned in the Talmud (cf. *b. Sanhedrin* 74a), is given various mystical interpretations in the *Zohar;* see especially the cluster in *Zohar* III.74a–75b, and the *Tiqqunei Zohar,* Tiqqun 34 (77b) and 56 (89b). Also cf. *Zohar* 1.27b (from *Tiqqunei Zohar*).
37. Cf. *Midrash Esther Rabbati, petiḥta'* VI; and *Eicha Rabba* I.31.
38. For the letter *yod* and its relation to the *membrum virile* and circumcision, see the midrashic tradition recorded in *Midrash Tanḥuma, Tzav* 14, and the clarification in Al-Naqawa's *Menorat ha-Ma'or,* edited by Hyman Enelow (New York, 1932), III, 470 (Jerusalem, 1961; p. 183). Note the ritual comment in R. Abraham b. Nathan Ha-Yarḥi's *Sefer ha-Manhig,* Yitzḥak Raphael, ed. (Jerusalem: Mosad ha-Rav Kook, 1978), II, 579. For a wide-ranging discussion, see Elliot Wolfson, "Circumcision and the Divine Name: A Study in the Transmission of Esoteric Doctrine," *The Jewish Quarterly Review* 78 (1987), 77–112.

3. The Great Dragon Battle and Talmudic Redaction

1. See the discussion and plate reproduced in Henri Frankfort, "God and Myths on Sargonid Seals," *Iraq* 1 (1934), 8 (and Plate I*a*); the seal was found in the temple. A seal impression of a coiled serpent with seven heads was also found in the Early Dynastic layer. Cyrus H. Gordon, "Leviathan: Symbol of Evil," in *Biblical Motifs. Origins and Transformations,* Alexander Altmann, ed. (Brandeis University Texts and Studies, III; Cambridge, Mass.: Harvard University Press, 1966), 4, also notes the first

example and gives a number of other textual sources pertinent to this theme.

2. A. Herdner, *Corpus des tablettes en cunéiformes alphabétiques* (Paris: Imprimerie Nationale, 1963), text 5.1.1–5; Anat slays a seven-headed monster named Tannin *(tnn)* according to 3.3. 35–39. On this see also Samuel Loewenstamm, "Anat's Victory over the Tunnanu," *Journal of Semitic Studies* 20 (1975), 27.
3. The Greek in 12:3 reads: *drakōn megas . . . echōn kephalas hepta*); the last phrase recurs in 13:1.
4. In view of the use of the verb *shibber* in Psalm 74:13 in a context of battle, it would appear that one should emend *tishabḥem* ("You praise them") in Psalm 89:10, where it makes no sense, to *tishabrem* ("You crush them," that is, the waters). The Targum reads *tam'ikhinun*. Alternatively, we have a second form of the stem *shabeaḥ*. Thus already Rashi proposes here and in Psalm 65:8 that the verb means "bring low" *(tashpilem)*. Cf. Ibn Ezra: "silence" *(tashqitem)*. Significantly, the verb *išbḥnh* occurs in the Anat cycle parallel to *ištbm tnn*, "I indeed muzzled Tannin." See Mitchell Dahood, *Psalms II. 51–100* (Anchor Bible 17; Garden City, N.Y.: Doubleday, 1968), 112, and in *Orientalia* 34 (1965), 392.
5. Or "to the place of the sea-monster"; so Rashi. The mythic allusion remains. *Tannim* is a biblical variant for *Tannin*. Cf. Ezek. 29:3.
6. See Samuel R. Driver and George B. Gray, *The Book of Job* (International Critical Commentary, 1921; rpt. Edinburgh: Clark, 1977), 71; and Naftali H. Tur-Sinai, *The Book of Job*, rev. ed. (Jerusalem: Kiryat Sefer, 1981), 140 (but correct the reference). In the Babylonian myth the limit refers to the heavenly waters. For limits imposed on the earthly waters, cf. Jer. 5:22; Ps. 104:9; Job 38:10–11.
7. See R. Du Mesnil du Buisson, "Le Bas-Relief du Combat de Bel contre Tiamat dans le Temple de Bel a Palmyre," *Les Annales Archéologiques Arabes Syriennes* 26 (1976), 83–100.
8. See James A. Montgomery, *Aramaic Incantation Texts from Nippur* (Philadelphia: University Museum, 1913), Text 2.
9. See Charles E. Ruelle, *Damasciou diadochou aporiai kai luseis peri tōn prōtōn archōn* (Paris, 1889), I, 321–322.
10. See the version of Eusebius in *Eusebi chronicorum libri duo*, Alfred Schoene, ed. (Berlin, 1875), I, cols. 14–18. On Berossus and his traditions, see P. Schnabel, *Berossos und die babylonisch-hellenistische Literatur* (Leipzig, 1923.)
11. The terms *bariaḥ* and *'aqallaton* are an old crux, found first in Ugaritic myth (UT 67:I:1–2=CTA 5.1.1–2; and 'nt:III:38=CTA 3.3.38). I have followed the translation of Old Jewish Publication Society here. The first

term is difficult. Many medieval commentators interpreted it to mean "stretching"; compare Ibn Bal'am (citing Ibn Janaḥ), Ibn Ezra, and Kimḥi. The root *b-r-ḥ,* in "flee," seems to explain the New Jewish Publication Society rendering of "elusive." For the second term, compare Ibn Ezra and Metzudat David. R. Yoḥanan clearly understands the terms to refer to *two* serpents, not one with synonomous epithets (as the plain sense suggests).

12. That is, the sexual urge was diminished; compare *Bereshit Rabba* 87.4, Juda Theodor and Chanokh Albeck, eds. (Jerusalem: Wahrmann Books, 1965), III, 1072–103, and *yer. Horayot* III, 46d.
13. For a modern argument that the recipient of the waters is Leviathan, see Tur-Sinai, *The Book of Job* 557–558 and 562–563 (comments on vv. 15, 23, and 25).
14. Raba b. 'Ulla and R. Abba b. 'Ulla are probably the same person, with the abbreviations of his title R(abbi) being run together by copyists, thus contracting R' Abba into Raba. Also see Wilhelm Bacher, *Die Agada der babylonischen Amoräer,* 2nd ed. (Frankfort, 1913), 139–140.
15. For R. Yoḥanan, see Ms. Hamburg 165 (19); for R. Yonatan, see *Midrash Ha-Gadol, ad* Gen 1:21; *Yalquṭ Shim'oni,* Isaiah, #361; and Raphael N. Rabbinovicz, *Diqduqei Soferim* (Munich, 1881), XI, 234.
16. Compare Rashi, *ad loc.* (also citing *b. Ḥullin.* 60b; *Arukh ha-Shalem,* Alexander Kohut, ed. (Vienna, 1926), VII, 132. The term in Greek is *kunēgia* (compare this topos in *Sibiline Oracles* 3.805–807, where the synonym *kunēgesia* is used). In *Pesiqta de-Rav Kahana,* Sup. 2, Bernard Mandelbaum, ed. (New York: Jewish Theological Seminary, 1962), 456, the event is a "war" waged by the angelic host.
17. The phrase "He [Leviathan] makes the sea into a spiced jar/broth [*merqaḥah*]" is reinterpreted to mean that somewhere the dragon immersed himself in perfume. For this sense of *merqaḥah,* cf. Exod. 30:25.
18. See *M. Avot* V.21.
19. The emphasis on a "banquet [*se'udah*]" for the righteous linked to Tabernacles is undoubtedly the result of the eschatologization of a halakhic theme. Cf. *M. Sukkah* II.6: "Rabbi Eliezer says: A person is obligated to have 14 meals [*se'udot*] in the booth, one by day and one by night; and the sages say: There is no fixed number, except for the first night of the festival [when a meal is required]." For other halakhic influences on this section, see n. 21, below.
20. Songs 8:13 is cited, using *ḥaberim* as regular companions. But the rabbinic identification of the term goes back to early Tannaitic groups of ritual fellowship and had a wider application in later periods. Cf. *Songs Rabba* VII.13:2, where the *ḥaberim* are "engaged in a halakhic matter."

21. The reading of the difficult *tzaltzal* as "covering" or "shading" as the reward for the second most meritorious is undoubtedly influenced by rabbinic rules regarding the building of tabernacles, where the "shade" *(tzel)* of the roof covering must predominate. See *M. Sukkah* I.1.
22. The word *tzaddiqim* is missing in Ms. Hamburg 165 (19) and other mss.; but this does not affect the overall theme.
23. This view differs from the one in *Bereshit Rabba* 7.4, Theodor and Albeck, eds., I, 52, where R. Idi states that neither Leviathan nor Behemoth was paired; according to Resh Laqish, Behemoth had a mate but was without desire. In my view, Rav gives a novel interpretation to Gen. 1:27b. Following v. 27a, which states that God "created him" (namely, the human) in His image, the ensuing clause that "male and female He created them" begs interpretation; Rav has presumably related it to *all* living things.
24. Namely, reading *yifqod* to mean that God will "appoint," "account," or "set aside" the monster for the righteous.
25. The verb used is *ba'aṭ*, though the prooftext from Job 26:12 is *raga'* (presumably a variant of *raqa'*, "beat down"). In Job 9:8, God "treads" *(dorekh)* on Yam; while other rabbinic myths of origins state that God "trampled" *(kabaš)* the ancient waters at the beginning. *Tanḥuma, Ḥuqqat*, 1 (and *Numbers Rabba* 18:22) use all three terms. In a wonderful play, *Tanḥuma, Bereshit* 1 states that God "conquered" or "suppressed" the Tehom *(kabaš 'et ha-tehom)* with the Torah. The full mythic undertone emerges by comparison with *Enuma elish* IV.129 (*ikbus-ma belum ša Tiamtum išidsa;* "The lord [Marduk] trod on the legs of Tiamat").
26. According to *Midrash Alpha Beitot, v"h d"g*, in Shlomo Wertheimer, *Batei Midrashot*, 2nd ed., with additions by Avraham Wertheimer (Jerusalem: Ktav Va-Sepher, 1968) II, 438, God slaughters the monster ritually. By contrast, *Pesiqta de-Rav Kahana*, Mandelbaum, ed., has God direct a final battle between Leviathan and Behemoth; while in *Tanḥuma, Shemini* 7, this double death is a mutual ritual slaughter.
27. The word *'ilmale'* occurs twice in Part I, but without the other key phrases that mark the relationship between II and V.
28. Cf. n. 7; and also Jefim Schirmann, "The Battle between Behemoth and Leviathan According to an Ancient Hebrew *Piyyut*," *Proceedings of the Israel Academy of Sciences and Humanities* vol. 4, no. 13 (Jerusalem, 1970), 350–359.
29. *Pesiqta de-Rav Kahana* adds mythic interpretations to Job 41:8, 9, 18, 19, 20, 21. For a mythic reading of v. 17, see *Bereshit Rabba* 4.4; for a different midrash on v. 19, see below.
30. For the text, see Benno Landsberger and J. V. Kinnier Wilson, "The Fifth Tablet of 'Enuma Eliš,'" *Journal of Near Eastern Studies* 20 (1961), 160 f. (I

have also examined the critical edition being prepared at the University of Chicago, courtesy of Prof. Walter Farber.) The image of the rivers emerging from the monster's eyes also appears in a late commentary to the myth; see E. Ebeling, *Tod und Leben nach den Vorstellungen der Babylonier* (Berlin: Walter de Gruyter, 1931), I, 35:3.

31. It seems to me that the prooftext *in this context* has activated a latent biblical myth—for were this mythologem altogether lacking, it is hard to imagine its invention from this verse. The sequence of Ps 89:11–12 (slaying Rahab and creating cosmic order) is suggestive in this regard; so, too, is the midrash that "the world was created *on* Leviathan" (cited by Ibn Ezra in the introduction to his Torah commentary). This myth is developed in *Zohar, Bo'* (II. 34a–35b) in profound ways.
32. See *Enuma elish* I. 133–146 (with parallels in II and III). According to Wilfred Lambert, the number 11 is part of a mythic revision of Ninurta mythology (where 8 monsters occur); see his "Ninurta Mythology in the Babylonian Epic," *Keilschriftliche Literaturen. Ausgewahlte Vorträge der XXII. Rencontre Assyriologique Internationale* 1985, K. Hecker and W. Sommerfeld, eds. (Berlin: D. Reimer Verlag, 1986), 56 f., 57 n. 6.
33. I am fully cognizant of the difficulties posed by named traditions in rabbinic sources. For the present subject, cf. n. 6; and in general, see now the discussion of S. Stern, "Attribution and Authorship in the Babylonian Talmud," *Journal of Jewish Studies* 45 (1994), 28–51 (with literature cited). Nevertheless, the clusters in our pericope suggest some real or constructed tradition which cannot be dismissed outright.
34. Rav Yehudah even consulted with Rabbi Yoḥanan on occasion; see *b. Qiddushin* 39a.
35. On the basis of various textual and analytical considerations, Daniel Sperber, "Ha'im 'alah Rabba le'eretz yisra'el?" *Sinai* 71 (1972), 140–145, rejects the possibility that Rabba actually sat before Rabbi Yoḥanan (even though he followed this master's methods; see *b. Shevi'it.* 10b). Many manuscripts read Rabbah bar Bar Ḥana (instead of Rabba, as tradent of Rabbi Yoḥanan) in *b. Baba Bathra* 75a (see *ibid.*, 141), but this does not undermine my overall argument, since Bar Ḥana was a student of Rabbi Yoḥanan, spent time in Pumbeditha, and met with Rav Yehudah (see *b. Shabbat* 148a; *b. Pesaḥim* 53b).
36. See *b. Berakhot* 50a; *b. Shabbat* 72a; and *b. Qiddushin* 12a.
37. See the discussions on traditions *II* and *IV*, above. The themes of killing and cleaving the sea monster seem to have been combined in Ugaritic myth as well; compare Charles Virolleaud, *Le Palais Royal d'Ugarit* (Imprimerie Nationale: Paris, 1957), II, 12 (who links 'nt III:33–43 to *UT* 1003:3–10), and the discussion of Samuel Loewenstamm, "Mitos ha-Yam

be-kitvei 'Ugarit ve-Ziqato 'el Mitos ha-Yam ba-Miqra'," *Eretz Israel* 9 (1969), 99 f. On the combination of the motifs of splitting the sea, divine kingship, and temple-building in ancient Israel, compare Exodus 15 and the comments of Samuel Loewenstamm, *Massoret Yetzi'at Mitzrayim Be-hishtalshelutah* (Jerusalem: Magnes Press, 1965), 114–115.

Western aspects of the *Enuma elish* have been pointed out by Thorkild Jacobsen, "The Battle between Marduk and Tiamat," *Journal of the American Oriental Society* 88 (1968), 104–108. Given the shared traditions, it may not be accidental that the myths of creation in *Tanḥuma, Ḥuqqat* 1 include reference to the "sweet" and "salt waters" and their intermingling. In the Babylonian tradition, these waters are personified by Apsu and Tiamat, respectively.

38. For example, in VIII the righteous benefit maximally from the skin of Leviathan; while others partake of smaller pieces in descending degrees, depending on merit. The other nations of the world are lowest on the hierarchy, and only benefit from the radiance of the skin, which serves as an eschatological beacon to Zion.
39. This myth does not deal with human origins, only their perfected end. According to another exegetical tradition, the skin of the sea dragon is used much earlier. In the medieval commentary of Ḥizquni, we are told that Adam's "garments of skin" in Gen. 3:21 are "from the skin of the mate of Leviathan, which the Holy One, Blessed be He, slaughtered and salted the remainder for the righteous for the future to come." This interpretation is also found in *Sefer Da'at Zeqenim* (Livorno, 1783); in the commentary of the Rosh on the Torah, in *Sefer Hadar Zeqenim* (Livorno, 1840); and in the pentateuchal glosses of R. Yehudah b. Eliezer and R. Obadiah mi-Bertinoro, in *Ba'alei ha-Tosafot 'al Ḥamishah Ḥumshei Torah* (Warsaw, 1876)—all in the name of a (lost) "midrash."

4. The Measure and Glory of God in Ancient Midrash

1. For the need for methodological care in dealing with "the reciprocal relationship pertaining between the world of rabbinic mysticism and the world of the 'Aggadah," see D. Flusser, "Scholem's Recent Book on Merkabah Literature," *Journal of Jewish Studies* 11 (1960), 68.
2. In his paraphrase, Rashi clearly understood the verb *rokheb* ("rides") in the second verset to have a double function; that God rides through the heavens *and* the high vaults in His majesty to help Israel.
3. The well-known epithet of Ba'al, "Rider of the Clouds" *(rkb 'rpt)* in *UT* 'nt: II-39–40 is paralleled by the divine epithet *rokheb ba-'arabot* in Ps. 68:5. Later in the psalm, there is also mention of the majesty *(ga'avato)* of God

and "His might in the high vaults *(sheḥaqim).*" We are thus dealing with an old descriptive cluster adapted by Israelite poets. The ancient Semitic imagery even spread to Greek literature. See M. Weinfeld, "'Rider of the Clouds' and 'Gatherer of the Clouds,'" *The Journal of the Ancient Near Eastern Society of Columbia University* 5 (1973), 421–26.

4. The juxtaposition of the divine command "Destroy!" (v.27) with the chariot imagery is striking. Also notable is the fact that the settlement mentioned in v.28 has already occurred.
5. Cf. the use of meteors, lightning, and thunder as divine weapons in Judg. 5:20; Josh. 10:11; 1 Sam. 7:10; and 2. Sam. 22:14–15 (=Ps. 18:14–15).
6. My translation follows the Hebrew syntax here; for just this sequence underlies the ensuing dialogue.
7. Instead of "O Jeshurun." While the Hebrew reads *'el yeshurun,* both context and sense suggest that the sages construed *'el* as *'el[ah],* "except" (a type of *'al tiqre* construction). In fact, the *Midrash ha-Gadol, Devarim,* ed. S. Fisch (Jerusalem: Mosad ha-Rav Kook, 1972), 775, has this very reading. For *'el* as "God," see below.
8. Hebrew has *nikhnas,* "entered"; but in light of the sequel to the parable, the man is clearly only at the entrance to the city.
9. Following the *editio princeps* of Louis Finkelstein, *Siphre ad Deuteronomium,* 2nd ed. (Berlin, 1939; rpt. New York: Jewish Theological Seminary of America, 1969), 422–423.
10. The Greek rendition is *hosper ho theos,* a construct form ("like the god of Jeshurun"). That such a reading was still known in Jewish circles in the late Middle Ages is attested by the fulminations of the Gur Aryeh.
11. See n. 7, above, where this same reading is adduced from the *Midrash ha-Gadol.*
12. This formulation even hints at the relative divinization of Israel-Jeshurun. A partial parallel can be found in the divinization of the patriarch Israel-Jacob. See *Midrash Bereshit Rabba* 77. 1, Juda Theodor and Chanokh Albeck, eds. (Jerusalem: Wahrmann Books, 1965), II, 910. This point is even justified by correlating descriptions of God and the ancestor, as in our *Sifre* passage. For Jacob as an "angel of God," see Origen, *In Ioannem* I.31, which is quoting the "Prayer of Joseph." See the text and comments of Jonathan Z. Smith in *The Old Testament Pseudepigrapha* (Garden City, N.Y.: Doubleday, 1985) II, 699–714. This text also speaks of Jacob as "minister before the face of God," a tradition known from Gnostic sources (cf. Smith, 702) and rabbinic tradition (*b. Ḥullin* 91b). As is well known, the face of Jacob was also a figure on the heavenly Merkabah (divine Chariot), cf. *Midrash Bereshit Rabba* 73. 12–14, and also Adolph Jellinek, *Bet Ha-Midrash* (rpt. Jerusalem: Wahrmann Books, 1967), V, 63.
13. Cf. *Midrash Eikha Rabba, petiḥta* 24, Solomon Buber, ed. (Vilna: Romm,

1899), 38. Alternatively, the pun may be with the Hebrew particle *hen,* "if" (Jer. 3:1; cf. also Hag. 2:12–13, where it is parallel to *'im*).

14. Cf. *Midrash Pesiqta Rabbati, Va-Yehi Ba-Yom* V, Meir Ish Shalom, ed. (Vilna: Kaiser, 1900), 18b. In this homily it is said that the righteous *(tzaddiqim)* bring the *Shekhinah* earthward throught their deeds. The prooftext, from Prov. 2:21, adduces the word *yesharim,* as in our *Sifre* text. The phrase *ki yesharim yishkenu 'aretz,* "for the righteous will dwell in the land," was thus reinterpreted (on the basis of this theurgic theology) to mean: "for the righteous will cause the *Shekhinah* to dwell [reading as if: *yashkiynu*] on the earth." The prooftext in *Midrash Bereshit Rabba* 19. 7, Theodor and Albeck, eds., 176–177, is Ps. 37:29, which includes both the noun *tzaddiqim* and the verb *vayishkenu.*
15. The most famous case is found in *b. Menaḥot* 29b, where Moses sees God adding coronets to the letters of the Torah scroll (for future exegesis).
16. See the extended depiction of Moses' incursion in *Midrash Pesiqta Rabbati* 20, 96b–98b. Indeed, some cases even represent Moses as attacking the angels like a goring ox *(Exodus Rabba* 41.7). Midrashic echoes of this idea also occur in Aramaic hymns. Cf. Moses Ginsburger, "Les Introductions Araméennes à la Lecture du Targoum," *Revue des Études Juives* 73 (1921), 15–16. The whole purpose of this awesome ascent, of course, was to receive divine wisdom. As Moses notes: "I participated in battle with the angels and received a Law of fire . . . I defeated the heavenly host and revealed their secrets to mankind" (*Deut. Rabba* XI. 10). The issue of angelic resistance has been discussed by Joseph Schultz, "Angelic Opposition to the Ascension of Moses and the Revelation of the Law," *Jewish Quarterly Review* n.s. 61 (1970–71), 282–307; and Peter Schäfer, *Rivaltät Zwischen Engeln und Menschen* (Berlin: Walther de Gruyter, 1975). See also the psychological proposal by David Halperin, "Ascension or Invasion: Implications of the Heavenly Journey in Ancient Judaism," *Religion* 18 (1988), 47–67.
17. For this topos see Sabine MacCormack, *Art and Ceremony in Late Antiquity* (Berkeley: University of California Press, 1981), chap. 1.
18. Cf. Arthur Marmorstein, *Studies in Jewish Theology* (London: Oxford University Press, 1950), 8–9.
19. So in *Yalquṭ Shimoni,* and with a slight variant in the *Yalquṭ Shimoni,* Ms. Oxford (Neubauer-Cowley 2637, Heb. b. 6). Both are cited in Finkelstein's critical apparatus in *Siphre,* 422, l. 16 (the verb *zun* also recurs in the continuation of the passage).
20. See *Hekhalot Rabbati* VIII. 3, in Jellinek, *Bet ha-Midrash,* III, 90; and in Peter Schäfer, *Synopse zur Hekhalot-Literatur* (Tübingen: J.C.B. Mohr, 1981), § 160.
21. Cf. *Pesiqta Rabbati* 41, Ish Shalom ed., 80*a; and Pesiqta de-Rav Kahana,* 6,

Bernard Mandelbaum, ed. (New York: Jewish Theological Seminary, 1962), I, 110.

22. See *Pesigta Rabbati,* Ish Shalom, ed., 184a. R. Yitzhak was variously involved in esoteric lore; see, *inter alia, b. Sanhedrin* 95b. He belonged to the same school as R. Abbahu, who was also versed in mystical matters (see *b. Ḥagigah* 13a), and who transmitted the tradition that at the beginning, "the upper realm was sustained *(nizonim)* by the splendor of the Shekhinah" (*Bereshit Rabba* 2.2, Theodor and Albeck, eds., 15).
23. The verb *nikhnas* also suggests an esoteric allusion. As noted earlier (n. 10), the term is oddly placed in the parable; but its use there makes sense in light of its technical usage in various mystical traditions (cf. Schäfer, *Synopse,* §§ 248, 338–339, 398, 441).
24. In the edition of Solomon Buber (Cracow: Fischer, 1903), 15–16; but see now Burton Visotsky, *Midrash Mishle: A Critical Edition Based on Vatican Ms. Ebr. 44* (New York: Jewish Theological Seminary of America, 1990), 86.
25. Note the variant *ge'ut,* preserved in *Peirush ha-Aggadot le-Rabbi Azriel* [*Commentarius in Aggadoth auctore R. Azriel Geronensi*], Isaiah Tishby (Jerusalem: Mekitze Nirdamim, 1945), 62, p. 27. The hypostasis of *ga'avah* is further confirmed by a Hekhalot text, where the expression *ro'eh ga'avah,* "sees the Majesty," occurs. See Ithamar Gruenwald, "Qeṭa'im Ḥadashim mi-Sifrut ha-Hekhalot," *Tarbiz* 38 (1969), 360.
26. For discussion and texts, see Martin Cohen, *The Shi'ur Qomah. Liturgy and Theurgy in Pre-Kabbalistic Mysticism* (Lanham, Md.: University Press of America, 1983), and *The Shi'ur Qomah: Texts and Recensions* (Tübingen: J.C.B. Mohr, 1985).
27. For a comparable sequence, see *Pesiqta Rabbati* 20, Ish Shalom, ed., 98b; and see the discussion below. The combination of throne, beauty *(yofi),* and stature *(to'ar)* also occurs in the hymns preserved in *Hekhalot Rabbati;* see chap. 24 in Jellinek, *Bet ha-Midrash,* III, 101, and Peter Schäfer, *Synopse,* § 253. On this point, see also Gershom Scholem, *Jewish Gnosticism, Merkabah Mysticism and Talmudic Tradition* (New York: Jewish Theological Seminary, 1965), 61–62.
28. Note also the first-person divine designation of Glory in *Midrash Wayyikra Rabba,* 2.8, Mordecai Margulies, ed. (Jerusalem: Wahrmann Books, 1972), I, 46–47. Here, "after [God] showed him [Ezekiel] the entire Merkavah, He said to him: 'Son of man, this is my Glory *(zehu kebodi)* . . .'" Cf. *Seder Eliahu Rabba,* Meier Ish Shalom, ed. (Vienna, 1904), chapter 7, p. 34.
29. *Midrash ha-Gadol* 776 (lines 14–17).
30. See Schäfer, *Synopse,* § 692.

31. Cited by Peter Schäfer in his *Konkordanz zur Hekhalot-Literatur* (Tübingen: J. C. B. Mohr, 1986), I. 132. Thanks to Elliot Wolfson for recalling the reference.
32. The prayer is a *silluq* for *parashat Sheqalim,* conveniently found in the *Seder Abodat Yisrael,* Salomon Baer, ed. (Rödelheim, 1868; and in the new and corrected edition, Schocken, 1937), 653–654.
33. On this theme, see the wide-ranging discussion of Elliot Wolfson, "Female Imaging of the Torah: From Literary Metaphor to Religious Symbol," in *From Ancient Israel to Modern Judaism: Intellect in Quest of Understanding. Essays in Honor of Marvin Fox,* Jacob Neusner, eds. (Atlanta, Ga.: Scholars Press, 1989), II, ch. 30.
34. In *Sefer Ḥayim Schirmann,* Ephraim E. Urbach, ed. (Jerusalem: Schocken Institute for Jewish Research, 1970), 1–25.
35. See the discussion in Moshe Idel, *"Tefisat ha-Torah ba-Heikhalot uba-Kabbalah," Meḥaqarei Yerushalayim be-Maḥshevet Yisrael* (1981), 40 ff.
36. *Sefer ha-Bahir,* Reuven Margulies, ed. (Jerusalem: Mossad ha-Rav Kook, 1978), par. 98.
37. See Gershom Scholem, *Origins of the Kabbalah,* edited by R. J. Z. Werblowsky (Philadelphia and Princeton: Jewish Publication Society and Princeton University Press, 1987), 55 n. 10. Scholem believed that the terminology in the *Bahir* had "ancient sources." His views is confirmed by the evidence below. The text is printed in Reuven Margulies, par. 98, and in Gershom Scholem, *Das Buch Bahir* (Leipzig: W. Drugulin, 1923; Darmstadt: Wissenschftliche Buchgesellschaft, 1970), par. 67 (p. 70).
38. *See Papyri Graecae Magicae. Die griechischen Zauberpapyri,* K. Preisendanz, ed. (Leipzig-Berlin: Teubner, 1931), vol. II: xiii. 270–77 (esp. I. 272). The text also appears in R. Reitzenstein, *Poimandres. Studien zur griechisch-ägyptischen und frühchristlichen Literatur* (Leipzig: Teubner, 1904), 22.
39. See *The Nag Hammadi Library,* James M. Robinson, ed. (San Francisco: Harper and Row, 1977), 166.
40. See the full discussion of N. Séd, "Les Douze Hebdomades, Le Char de Sabaoth et Les Soixante-Douze Langues," *Novum Testamentum* 21 (1979), 156–84, and the independent observations of M. Idel, "Le-Be'ayat Ḥeqer Mesorot shel Sefer ha-Bahir," in *Reshit ha-Mistiqah ha-Yehudit be-Eiropah, Meḥqarei Yerushalayim be-Maḥshevet Yisrael* 7 (1987), 57–63. Scholem's *Origins* also adds a reference to the 72 *morphai* in the Gnostic source.
41. Cf. Margulies, par. 95; Scholem, *Das Buch Bahir,* par. 63 (p. 65).
42. Thus Idel, "Le-Be'ayat"; cf. Séd, "Les Douze," 182 ff.
43. Cf. the observation of W. Schoedel, "Scripture and the Seventy-Two Heavens of the First Apocalypse of James," *Novum Testamentum* 12 (1970),

128–129. For this text and its bearing on the present discussion, see below.

44. See Idel, "Le-Be'ayat," 61–63. The texts have been published by Carol Newsom, *Songs of the Sabbath Sacrifice: A Critical Edition* (Atlanta, Ga.: Scholars Press, 1985), 293.
45. See my discussion in "Some Forms of Divine Appearance in Ancient Jewish Thought," in *From Ancient Israel to Modern Judaism,* Jacob Neusner, et al, eds., II, 261–270.
46. See A. Böhlig, *Koptisch=gnostische Apokalypsen aus Codex V von Nag Hammadi* (Halle-Wittenberg, 1963), 29–54.
47. See the English translation in Schoedel, "Scripture," 121; also in *The Nag Hammadi Library,* Robinson, ed., 243.
48. See *Coptic Dictionary,* 609a; also *Nag Hammadi Codices,* V-VI, Bentley Layton, ed. (Leiden: E. J. Brill, 1979), 72–73. Layton notes that *shoshou* is a pan used for liquid measures, and thus also for human measurement.
49. *Abot de-Rabbi Nathan* A, 37, Solomon Schechter, ed. (New York: Feldheim, 1945), 110 (55b).
50. Cf. Scholem, *Origins,* 82, where the hypostatic aspect of these potencies is also noted.
51. Note also that the word for "peace" in the text is *'emet,* whereas *'emunah* (lit., "faithfulness") is the term used in Hosea.
52. See also Ps. 97:2–3, where righteousness and justice also support the throne and where a fuller storm imagery is found. Note that in this tradition the vision of God's enthronement is not reserved for the elite. Upon the divine advent, "all peoples see His *kabod*" (v. 6).
53. See RS.24.271 A l.14 (= Ugaritica V: 1968, 610 l.14).
54. See in Eusebius, *Praeparatio Evangelica* I, 10,13. See now the critical text and translation by Harold W. Attridge and Robert A. Oden, *Philo of Biblos: The Phoenician History* (CBQMS 9; Washington, DC: Catholic Biblical Association of America, 1981), 44–47. Also note the remarks of Samuel A. Loewenstamm, "Philon mi-Gebal," in *Peraqim* 2 (1971), 319.
55. Other traces exist in 4Q 403 1 i 38 (cf. 1. 27). Cf. Newsom, *Songs of the Sabbath Sacrifice,* 209; noted also by Joseph Baumgarten, "The Heavenly Tribunal and the Personification of Sedeq in Jewish Apocalyptic," in *Aufstieg und Niedergang der Römischen Welt,* ed. W. Haas (Berlin: Walther de Gruyter, 1979), II, 223, with more wide-ranging speculations on pp. 227–229.
56. In *Batei Midrashot,* Shelomo Wurtheimer, ed., expanded with notes by Avraham Wertheimer (Jerusalem: Ketav ve-Sefer, 1980), I, 88; and Schäfer, *Synopse* § 172 of N 8128 and V 228 (variants read *kise' ha-kabod*).

See also Peter Schäfer, *Geniza-Fragmente zur Hekhalot-Literatur* (Tübingen: J. C. B. Mohr, 1984), 105.

57. In "How Much Greek in Jewish Palestine," in *Biblical and Other Studies,* Alexander Altmann, ed. (Brandeis Texts and Studies, 1; Cambridge, Mass.: Harvard University Press, 1963), 141.
58. An exegetical method known as *serus.* The stem *ḥ-l-q* would yield *ḥillaqta,* "you gave" or "distributed."
59. According to H. St. J. Thackeray, *The Relation of St. Paul to Contemporary Jewish Thought* (London, 1900), 182.
60. See 5:10–11, reading *dōsei.* This was already observed by Jean Danielou, *Théologie du Judéo-Christianisme* (Tournai, 1958), 265.
61. This mythologoumenon can be found in other texts in the Pauline corpus; for example, Rom. 12:4–8 and 1. Cor. 12–27–28. See the important discussion by Guy Stroumsa, "Form(s) of God: Some Notes on Metatron and Christ," *Harvard Theological Review* 76 (1983), 281–283, where these texts are proposed as traces of old Jewish *Shi'ur Qomah* speculation. Significantly, like Eph. 4:7–16, these texts also speak of the mystical body of Christ and the tasks or graces of various individuals in building up this body. These elements were thus a fixed topos of ancient Christology.
62. The stress on full knowledge *(epignōsis)* of Christ in this context has the same gnostical ring as the knowledge *(da'at)* of God mentioned in the Jewish sources discussed earlier.
63. See above for examples.
64. According to Gershom Scholem, *On the Mystical Shape of the Godhead* (New York: Schocken Books, 1991), 278 n. 19.
65. See *The Gnostic Scriptures,* ed. and trans. by Bentley Layton (Garden City, N.Y.: Doubleday, 1987), 337 (no. 40).
66. See the comments of W. C. Unnik, "The Notes on the 'Gospel of Philip,'" *New Testament Studies* 10 (1963–64), 456–69; and the same observations made by Yehuda Liebes, "Ha-Mashiaḥ shel ha-Zohar," in *Ha-Ra'ayon ha-Meshiḥi bi-Yisrael* (Jerusalem: Israel Academy of Sciences and Humanities, 1982), app. 6, 232 n. 16, and Layton, *Gnostic Scriptures,* note d.

5. Midrashic Theologies of Messianic Suffering

1. See *Midrash Psalms,* Solomon Buber, ed. (Vilna, 1891), Psalm 31.8, p. 240. The reference is to the seventh benediction of the *'Amida* prayer. The eulogy *go'el yisrael* is in the participial form, based on Isa. 49:7. See Ben Sira 51:25. The language is also found in *M. Ta'anit* 2.4 as the conclusion to the plea for divine intervention connected with the salvation of

Abraham. The position of benediction no. 7 has long been a puzzle, since one would expect a plea for deliverance from personal difficulties at this point; accordingly, some have suggested that the origin of the benediction was in the supplementary petitions for fast days, formulated in *Mishnah Ta'anit*. Samuel David Luzzato suggested that benediction no. 7 was originally composed "for the redemption of individuals in captivity or prison," which would make good sense in the present for the *'Amida*. See Luzzato, *Mabo' le-Maḥzor ke-Minhag benei Roma'* (Leghorn, 1856), 18; and in the edition of E. Daniel Goldschmidt (Tel Aviv: Devir, 1966), 18. The participial form also concludes the evening *'Emet ve-'Emunah* prayer.

2. For these expressions, see *Midrash Psalms,* Buber, ed., 45.3, p. 269; *b. Sanhedrin* 96b, 98a, and 99a.
3. *Bereshit Rabba,* Juda Theodor and Chanokh Albeck, eds. (Jerusalem: Wahrmann Books, 1965), 2.4, pp. 16–17.
4. *Ibid.*, pp. 3–4. The *editio princeps* and other mss. read *sheriy* for the Massoretic reading *sherei'*.
5. Both traditions are presented in *Bereshit Rabba* 3.4, Theodor and Albeck, eds., pp. 19–20. The first tradition about primordial light is presented as an esoteric secret transmitted by R. Shemuel bar Naḥman, and ultimately made public by R. Yitzḥak, according to the testimony of R. Berekhiah. The second tradition follows this same chain, and is reported by R. Berekhiah in the name of R. Yitzḥak. According to the parallel version in *Vayira' Rabba* 31.7, Mordecai Margulies ed., *Midrash Wayyikra Rabbah* (Jerusalem: Wahrmann Books, 1972), II, 725–726, R. Berekhiah is missing in the first tradition, and R. Yitzḥak in the second. The two explanations for the origins of light obviously constituted mysteries of the creation, known as *Ma'aseh Bereshit*. The first tradition is found in many sources. For the second tradition that the Temple was one of the primordial creations, see *Bereshit Rabba* 1.4, p. 6.
6. *Pugio Fidei,* B. Carpzov, ed. (1687; rpt. Farnborough, 1967), 862.
7. I have found this view anticipated by Abraham Epstein, *Mi-Qadmoniyot ha-Yehudim,* A. M. Haberman, ed. (Jerusalem: Mosad Ha-Rav Kook, 1957), 101. For other authentic midrashim in the *Pugio Fidei,* see Saul Lieberman, *Shekiin,* 2nd ed. (Jerusalem: Wahrmann Books, 1970), 52–67.
8. However, he cites it in the name of "our Rabbis." Clearly, the manuscripts varied. The *Aruch Completum,* Alexander Kohut, ed. (Vienna: Menorah, 1926), III, 353a, s.v. *hvvr* has "School of Rabbi Yishmael" for "School of Rabbi." This is undoubtedly a mistake in construal of *raby* as an abbreviation for *rab(bi) y(ishmael)*. See the note, *ad loc.*
9. Cf. *Songs Rabba* I.6, "the nations of the world afflict *(monin)* Israel." See *Aruch Completum,* IV, 140b.

10. See *Maḥzor le-Yamim Nora'im,* vol. 2, *Yom Kippur,* Daniel Goldschmidt, ed. (Jerusalem: H. Koren, 1970), 410. The word *yinnon* occurs twice: in l. 1, where his existence is "before creation" along with the Temple; and in the final l. 12, referring to the advent of the Messiah (following Isa. 11:11). The term itself derives from Ps. 72:17, understood as follows: "May his name be eternal, before the sun [existed] Yinnon is his name." In context the name refers to the king. Its preexistence was already noted in the *Targum.* Medieval commentators understood the overt sense of *lifnei shemesh* to refer to the duration of the existence of the sun (Rashi, Kimḥi) and the verb *yinnon* to be a *nif'al* based on the stem *nyn,* and having the sense of continuity (Rashi, Ibn Ezra, Kimḥi).
11. See ll. 7–10
12. See Meir Ish Shalom, ed., *Pesiqta Rabbati* (Vienna, 1880), 146b. Presumably, this suffering is endured in heaven.
13. Gustav Dalman, *Die leidende und der sterbende Messias der Synagogue* (Berlin, 1888).
14. Arnold Goldberg, *Erlösung durch Leiden: Drei rabbinische Homilien über die Trauernden Zions und den leidenden Messias Efraim (PesR 34. 36. 37)* (Frankfurter Judaistische Studien 4; Frankfurt am Main, 1978).
15. Adolph Jellenik, *Bet ha-Midrash,* 3rd ed. (Jerusalem: Wahrmann Books, 1967), III, 70, 73.
16. Abraham Wertheimer, *Batei Midrash* (Jerusalem: Ketav ve-Sefer, 1980), I, 117–133.
17. *Me'or 'Einayim le-'Azzariah min ha-'Adumim,* D. Cassel, ed. (Vilna, 1864–66; rpt. Jerusalem, 1969–70), 231–32.
18. *Kitvei Nahman Krochmal,* Simon Rawidowicz, ed. (London, 1961), 254–255.
19. The entire cycle was formed for the Sabbaths between the 17 of Tammuz and Tabernacles. Overall, see Lewis Barth, "The 'Three of Rebuke and Seven of Consolation': Sermons in the *Pesikta de-Rav Kahana,*" *Journal of Jewish Studies* 33 (1982), 503–515, with bibliography.
20. *Pisqa* 34, the fourth *haftarah* of consolation, begins with Zech. 9:9; *pisqa* 35, the fifth one, begins with Zech. 2:2. The treatment of messianic themes here is significant, along with allusions to Isaiah 53 (see below). But equally significant is the *explicit* omission of references to this text, which had taken a central place in Christian literature. The omission is quite glaring in the cycle of consolation in the *Pesiqta de-Rav Kahana.* There, the fourth *haftarah* is Isaiah 51:12–52:12, and the fifth begins with Isaiah 54:1. Thus Isaiah 52:13–53:12 is missing from the sequence—and this is precisely the central passage dealing with the suffering servant of God! This significant gap was noted by Raphael Loewe, in his Prolegome-

non to the reprint of *The Fifty-Third Chapter of Isaiah According to the Jewish Interpreters,* with texts comp., ed., and tr. by Samuel R. Driver and Adolph Neubauer (1876; rpt. Library of Biblical Studies, New York: Ktav Publishing House, 1969), II, 21.

21. See *Aramaic Papyri of the Fifth Century* C.E., ed. with tr. and notes by A. Cowley (Oxford: Clarendon Press, 1923), 112 (Papyrus 30; from 408 B.C.E.).
22. See *Tosefta Soṭa* 15, in *Tosefta. Seder Nashim* (New York: Jewish Theological Seminary, 1973), 242–244; and see also the instructive teaching of Rava in *b. Soṭa* 31a.
23. The group mentioned in the midrash has often been linked to the Karaite group of the same name that gathered in Jerusalem in the tenth century. This linkage is not necessary; and in any case it is important to stress that the preservation of these chapters in a rabbinic document must presuppose a time before the decisive split between the communities. Some have found indications of earlier historical events in our text; see Bernard Bamberger, "A Messianic Document of the Seventh Century," *Hebrew Union College Annual* 15 (1940), 425–431. For an even earlier proposal, see the study by Arthur Marmorstein, n. 24 below. The Karaite group itself has recently been discussed by Ḥayim Hillel Ben-Sasson, "The Karaite Community of Jerusalem in the Tenth-Eleventh Centuries," *Shalem* 2 (1970), 1–18 [in Hebrew].
24. I follow the reading of the Parma ms., *mi-yisrael,* against the reading *le-yisrael* by Friedmann. Arthur Marmorstein long ago observed, correctly, that only *mi-yisrael* makes contextual sense; see his "Eine messianische Bewegung im dritten Jahrhundert," *Jeschurun* 13 (1926), 18.
25. The midrash appears in *pisqa* 29, Ish Shalom, ed., 139a; it also occurs in the *Pesiqta de-Rav Kahana, pisqa* 16.1 *(Naḥamu),* Bernard Mandelbaum, ed. (New York: Jewish Theological Seminary, 1962), II, 265.
26. See especially *Mekhilta de-Rabbi Ishmael,* in Ḥayyim Horovitz and Israel Rabin, eds., (Jerusalem: Bamberger and Wahrmann, 1960), *Bo, parashah* 14, p. 51.
27. Reading *ḥibbiytem,* with the Parma ms.
28. See *Pesiqta Rabbati* 31, Ish Shalom, ed., 144b. A highly condensed and de-mythologized version is reported in *Pesiqta de-Rav Kahana* 17, I, 286.
29. See above, n. 22.
30. The phrase *meshiaḥ tzidqi* recalls the aforenoted *piyyuṭ* by Kallir, where the messianic figure is called *meshiaḥ tzidqenu.* See *Maḥzor,* ed. Goldschmidt, l. 7. This led Bamberger to conclude ("A Messianic Document," 426, n. 4) that the latter is "an unmistakable echo" of our *pisqa.* This is possible, but

not necessary. It may well be an independent construction, drawing on the epithet *tzidqenu* in Jer. 23:6, used with respect to the royal shoot of David (v. 5), and combined with the idiom *meshiaḥ YHWH* in Lam. 4:20.

31. Cf. *Bereshit Rabba,* Theodor and Albeck, ed., 6, l. 9, "The name of the Messiah entered [God's] mind, as it is written, 'before the sun [was created], Yinnon is his [the Messiah's] name' [Ps. 72:17]."
32. *Pugio Fidei,* 598. As in our midrash, the Messiah triumphs over Satan.
33. See Ad. Posnanski, "Le Colloque de Tortose et de San Mateo (7 Fevrier 1413—13 Novembre 1414)," *Revue des Études Juives* 74–75 (1922), 160–161.
34. The language of "will" and "joy" are part of the technical vocabulary of legal volition clauses; see the important study by Yoḥanan Muffs, "Love and Joy as Metaphors of Willingness and Spontaneity in Cuneiform, Ancient Hebrew, and Related Literatures," part I in his *Love and Joy: Law, Language and Religion in Ancient Israel* (New York: Jewish Theological Seminary, 1997), chap. 7, and especially Excursus III; the author doesn't bring the present example from *pisqa* 36.
35. See *ibid.*, 144; and part II, chap. 8, especially pp. 180, 186 (with combinations of *'ahavah* and *ratzon*).
36. Presumably, under the divine throne; alternatively, within the Cosmic Body *(guf)*, out of which the soul emerges to be incarnated on earth, and which must be depleted before the Messiah can come (cf. *b. Yebamot* 62a, 63b; *b. Niddah* 13b).
37. Rabbi Ḥiyya's statement in *yer. Shabbat* (chap. 16, *kol kitvei,* hal. 1, at the beginning), to the effect that Rabbi Yehudah's sufferings were for the sins of the nation, and that this had a messianic dimension (see the prooftext from Lam. 4:20), would be a middle position (suffering for the sins of others, but not *all* others).
38. Cf. v. 11b, *ve-'avonotam hu' yisbol,* "he bears their sins" (meaning their punishments, the consequences of the sins; cf. Gen. 4:13).
39. *Pugio Fidei,* 866.
40. See Saul Lieberman, *Shkiin,* 2d ed. (Jerusalem: Wahrmann Books, 1970), 65. Martini cites it from the *Sifrei.* The text is also referred to in the Debates at Tortosa; see Posnanski, "Le Colloque," 163.
41. I have used the *Sifra* edition of Louis Finkelstein (New York: Jewish Theological Seminary, 1983), II, 206–207. The sin of *piggul* is an "offensive thing" related to misuse of the sacrifice. According to Lev. 7:19, the sacrifice of well-being (presented as a vow or votary offering) was edible on the day of sacrifice or the day after, but any flesh "remaining," *notar,* was to be burnt; however, if it was not burnt and was eaten on the third day after the sacrifice, the act was deemed *piggul.* The sages expanded the

concept, so that it came to include all sacrificial flesh that the offerant (during the slaughter itself, or acts related to the draining, gathering, or sprinkling of the blood) intended to eat on the third day (see *Sifra, Tzav,* chap. 12, *parashah* 8). Such an intention made the flesh *piggul* from the moment of its sacrifice.

42. Lieberman, *Shkiin.*
43. *Ibid.,* 67–72, has reviewed the materials ascribed to Rabbi Rachmon and speculated that he was one of Martini's "helpers who gathered material from the Talmud" (p. 69). No doubt Martini had a helper; but I would suggest that the name Rachomon was chosen as a Hebrew play on his own name Raimundo, and perhaps even as a messianic allusion (*Raḥman* meaning "Merciful One").
44. See *Dial. c. Tryphone* 36,1; 68,9; 99,1. A. J. B. Higgens, "Jewish Messianic Belief in Justin Martyr's *Dialogue With Trypho,*" *Novum Testamentum* 9 (1967), 298, speculated that for apologetic purposes Justin Martyr put a mixture of Jewish and Christian views in the mouth of Trypho. But as seen from earlier examples his argument is not convincing; moreover, even the designation of the Messiah figure as "Lord" (68,9) is found in authentic Jewish sources (cf. *b. Baba Bathra* 75b).
45. See Ish Shalom, ed., *Pesiqta Rabbati,* 161b.
46. According to Hulsius, *Theologia Judaica,* p. 328; conveniently available in *The Fifty-Third Chapter of Isaiah* (see n. 20), I, 9 (g).
47. The text is Oxford MS. Heb. f. 21, leaves 24–31+Bodl.2727, published by Adolph Büchler in *Jewish Quarterly Review* o.s. 6 (1894), 39–42; see especially p. 40 (and pp. 13–14). The text was reprinted by Jacob Mann in *The Bible as Read and Preached in the Old Synagogue* (published 1940; rpt. Library of Biblical Studies, New York: Ktav Publishing House, 1971), I, 565–574; see especially pp. 565–566 and notes 70–71, and the discussion on pp. 298–299.
48. For a review of some possibilities, see Jacob Klausner, *Ha-Ra'ayon ha-Meshiḥi be-Yisra'el,* 289–95; G. H. Dix, "The Messiah ben Joseph," *The Journal of Theological Studies* 27 (1926), 130–143; Charles Torrey, "The Messia, Son of Efraim," *Journal of Biblical Literature* 66 (1947), 253–277. Louis Ginzberg, *An Unknown Jewish Sect* (1922; New York: Jewish Theological Seminary, 1970), 237, proposed that Ephraim was chosen so that the eschatological end would balance events during the Exodus. In my view, this interpretation totally by-passes the theme of atoning suffering; it could be because he wondered if texts like *Pesiqta Rabbati* 36 were not "perhaps under Christian influence?"; see *ibid.,* 236, n. 113. I think that this approach impoverishes the Jewish theological tradition.
49. See Ephraim E. Urbach, *The Sages* (Cambridge, Mass.: Harvard University Press, 1987), 687.

50. See the end of *pisqa* 34; Ish Shalom, ed., *Pesiqta Rabbati,* 159b.
51. Cf. *musar shelomeinu 'alav,* "he bore the chastisement that made us whole" (Isa. 53:5); and *ḥoloyeinu hu' nasa',* "he bore our wounds" (v. 4; cf. v. 12). Obviously, the focus of the Jeremian source would have been exegetically revised, since there Ephraim is chastised for sin. But such transformations would directly follow the assumed link to Isaiah. As an example, I would assume that the phrase "bear the disgrace of my youth [*ne'uray*]" would have been understood, if my approach is correct, as "bear the disgrace of my sons"—and in the light of Isaiah, "bear" would also assume its connotation of atoning for sins.
52. This in fact is the concluding prophecy in *pisqa* 34, where Ephraim is named for the first time.
53. See at *b. Baba Bathra* 12a. The ensuing discussion neutralizes the neutralization.

6. Five Stages of Jewish Myth and Mythmaking

1. The subject is vast; for a broad overview of opinions see J. W. Rogerson, *Myth in Old Testament Interpretation* (Beihefte zur Zeitschrift für die alttestamentlich Wissenschaft 134; Berlin: Walter de Gruyter, 1974). The idea of a total conceptual break has been advanced forcefully by Yehezkel Kaufmann, in *The Religion of Israel,* tr. and abridged by Moshe Greenberg (Chicago: University of Chicago Press, 1960), 24–34, 60–73; James Barr has given a more nuanced argument for shifts away from mythic features in "The Meaning of 'Mythology' in relation to the Old Testament," *Vetus Testamentum* 9 (1959), 1–10.
2. Note the formulation of Umberto Cassutto, "The Israelite Epic," in *Biblical and Oriental Studies* (Jerusalem: Magnes Press, 1975), II, 82.
3. See Gershom Scholem, *On the Kabbalah and its Symbolism* (New York: Schocken Books, 1965), chap. 3 ("Kabbalah and Myth").
4. A revised perspective has been emerging, focusing especially on the continuity and vitality of mythic images. See Moshe Idel, *Kabbalah. New Perspectives* (New Haven: Yale University Press, 1988); Yehuda Liebes, *Studies in Jewish Myth and Jewish Messianism* (Albany, N.Y.: SUNY Press, 1993), especially chap. 1 ("*De Natura Dei:* On the Development of the Jewish Myth"); Elliot Wolfson, *Through a Speculum that Shines. Vision and Imagination in Medieval Jewish Mysticism* (Princeton: Princeton University Press, 1994); and Arthur Green, *Keter. The Crown of God in Early Jewish Mysticism* (Princeton: Princeton University Press, 1997).
5. Cf. the linguistic perspective of Hermann Usener on "momentary" and special gods in *Götternamen. Versuch einer Lehre von der religiösen Begriffsbildung* (Bonn: F. Cohen, 1896); Ernst Cassirer, in *Sprache und My-*

thos. Eine Beitrag zum Problem der Götternamen (Leipzig, 1925) continues this orientation from a philosophical perspective. My approach is not focused on divine names as such but on the primary fabulations that result from naming things.

6. Johann Herder, "Abhandlung über den Ursprung der Sprache," in *Herders sammtliche Werke,* Bernhard Suphan, ed. (Berlin: Weidmannische buchhandlung, 1877–1913), V, 53f.
7. The polemical nature of this text has not been missed; cf. Frank M. Cross, *Canaanite Myth and Hebrew Epic* (Cambridge, Mass.: Harvard University Press, 1973), 194.
8. The traditions are found in *b. Berakhot* 59a; see my analysis in Chapter 2, above.
9. I have adapted the term "momentary" from Usener's discussion of momentary gods; see his *Götternamen* (n. 5 above).
10. On the *Enuma elish,* see simply the analysis of Thorkild Jacobsen, *The Treasuries of Darkness* (New Haven: Yale University Press, 1976), chap. 6; and also the materials collected and analyzed by Richard J. Clifford, *Creation Accounts in the Ancient Near East and in the Bible* (Catholic Biblical Quarterly Monograph Series, 26; Washington, D.C.: Catholic Biblical Association, 1994), chap. 3 ("Creation Accounts in Mesopotamia: Akkadian Texts").
11. Compare, for example, the language in Psalm 74:13, Isaiah 27:1, and 51:9–10 with the stanza in *Corpus des tablettes en cunéiformes alphabétiques,* A. Herdner, ed. (Paris: Imprimerie Nationale, 1963), 5.1.1–5.
12. See Moshe Weinfeld, *Deuteronomy and the Deuteronomic School* (Oxford: Clarendon Press, 1971), 116–123.
13. See *Midrash Bereshit Rabba,* Juda Theodor and Chanokh Albeck, eds. (Jerusalem: Wahrmann Books, 1965), 1.6, p. 4, where Rabbi Yehuda bar Simon refers to passages in Genesis 1 as hidden mysteries, revealed but "not explicated" there. The mythic explications are found in non-pentateuchal passages.
14. *Ibid.,* 5.1, pp. 31–33.
15. See in the edition of Solomon Buber (Vilna, 1885), *Huqqat,* 1.
16. On the fundamental valence of justice and mercy, see the discussion of Liebes, *Studies in Jewish Myth.*
17. For a full analysis, see my study, "Arm of the Lord: Biblical Myth, Rabbinic Midrash, and the Mystery of History," in *Language, Theology, and the Bible. Essays in Honour of James Barr,* Samuel Balantine and John Barton, eds. (Oxford: Clarendon Press, 1994), 271–292.
18. For a kabbalistic elaboration of Gen. 1:9, touched on earlier from the perspective of midrashic myth, see Chapter 7, below.

19. Ḥayim Bialik, "From the Winter Songs" *(Mishirei ha-Ḥoref)*, in *The Penguin Book of Hebrew Verse*, ed. and trans. by T. Carmi (New York: Penguin Books, 1981), 510–12.
20. Cf. Dan. 7:9 and *Zohar* II. 122b–123a.
21. *b. Ḥagigah* 14b. The master counsels other adepts not to confuse the "alabaster stones" in heaven with water, despite appearances.

7. The Book of *Zohar* and Exegetical Spirituality

1. In a penetrating exploration, Yehuda Liebes, "Zohar ve-Eros," *'Alpayyim* 9 (1994), 67–119, considers the multifaceted aspects of Zoharic creativity, and its sources of inspiration. This study is an important first step towards an *ars poetica* of the *Zohar.* My point here is to stress the primacy of the spiritual desires that generate this creativity through exegetical forms.
2. For considerations of this medieval dating, see the classic discussion of Gershom Scholem, *Major Trends in Jewish Mysticism* (New York: Schocken Books, 1946), Lecture 5, in which a case for individual authorship by Rabbi Moses de Leon is made; and the compelling analysis of Yehuda Liebes, "Keitzad Nithaber Sefer Ha-Zohar?", *Jerusalem Studies in Jewish Thought* 8 (1989), 1–71, on which a case for a circle of authors is advanced. An English rendition, "How the Zohar Was Written," appears in the author's *Studies in the Zohar* (Albany, N.Y.: SUNY Press, 1993), 85–138, pp. 194–227].
3. For two explorations of exegetical renewal in the *Zohar,* see Daniel Matt, "Matnitin di-lan: Tekhniqah shel Ḥidush be-Sefer ha-Zohar," *Jerusalem Studies in Jewish Thought* 8 (1989), 123–145; and "'New-Ancient Words': The Aura of Secrecy in the *Zohar,*" in *Gershom Scholem's Major Trends in Jewish Mysticism. 50 Years After,* Peter Schäfer and Joseph Dan, eds. (Tübingen: J. C. B. Mohr, 1993), 181–207.
4. Cf. *Zohar* III. 152a; also III. 149a/b.
5. *Zohar* III. 202a.
6. *Song of Songs Rabba* I.2:ii.
7. Regarding the Hebrew Bible, see my *Biblical Interpretation in Ancient Israel* (Oxford: Clarendon Press, 1985), on various forms of later Jewish spirituality, see my *The Kiss of God. Spiritual and Mystical Death in Judaism* (Seattle: University of Washington Press, 1994).
8. See Moshe Idel, *Kabbalah: New Perspectives* (New Haven: Yale University Press, 1988), 222–229, for this idea in the context of kabbalistic symbolism.
9. See *Zohar* III. 200b–202b.
10. Literally, "its tree."

11. The verb "to instruct," *le-'izdaharah,* provides a multi-level pun; for it evokes both the Hebrew nouns for legal warning *('azharah)* and spiritual illumination *(zohar)*. The Torah scholar is associated with both qualities in this homily.
12. *Zohar* III. 202a.
13. The change of addressee required no change to Scripture; the reconception of the siege as an act of destruction did. It assumes that the verb *tatzur* was midrashicaly construed as meaning "(when) you act as an enemy"—from the same stem *(tz-w-r)*. This virtual change is implied by the thematic shift from human warfare to divine doom.
14. For the semantic survey of tree symbolism in the *Zohar,* see Yehuda Liebes, *Sections of the Zohar Lexicon* (Jerusalem: Akadamon Press, 1976), 107–131; and this instance, p. 118 no. 69 [Hebrew].
15. *b. Ta'anit* 7a.
16. For a wide-ranging characterization, see Gershom Scholem, *On the Mystical Shape of the Godhead* (New York: Schocken Books, 1991), chap. 4.
17. This is due to a play on *tzar* or *metzar,* "narrow place."
18. *Zohar* III. 202b.
19. See *Zohar* II. 182a.
20. *b. Pesaḥim* 118a; and see *b. Makkot* 23a; *yer. Ḥagigah,* ch. 3, 1. According to Rabbeinu Baḥye, the juxtaposition refers to the divine attributes of judgment and mercy; see *Rabbeinu Baḥye. Be'ur 'al ha-Torah,* Ḥayim Chavel, ed. (Jerusalem: Mosad Ha-Rav Kook, 1982), II, 356.
21. Significantly, the *Zohar* does not develop a theosophical explanation nor interpret the passages in terms of the heavenly gradations of Judgment and Mercy. This line was taken by the contemporary commentator Rabbeinu Baḥye ben Asher on Exodus 34:17; see *Rabbeinu Baḥye,* Chavel, ed., 356.
22. On this power, see Scholem, *On the Mystical Shape,* chap. 2.
23. R. Shim'on calls the evil inclination *ḥamir ba-'isah,* thus giving an Aramaic rendition of the common idiom *śe'or sheba-'isah* in rabbinic literature; cf. *b. Berakhot* 17a. His rendition draws on the *Targum* to Exodus 12:15; and cf. *b. Pesaḥim* 5a.
24. The teaching continues through *Zohar* II. 182 a/b.
25. *b. Berakhot* 14a. On this theme of blessing God before greeting men, see *Zohar* I. 228a.
26. The prooftext used is from Proverbs 27:14, "He who greets his fellow loudly early in the morning shall have it accounted for him *(teḥashev lo)* as a curse." This proof fits well thematically and verbally with Isaiah 2:22 (cf. *neḥshav lo,* "will he be accounted?"). See also *Zohar* II. 226b. R. Moses de Leon cites mystical explanations received for both passages; see *R.*

Moses de Leon's Sefer Sheqel ha-Qodesh, critically edited and introduced by Charles Mopsik (Los Angeles: Cherub Press, 1996), fol. 36b, p. 42 (in Hebrew).

27. *Nefesh* and *neshamah* occur with nostrils in Genesis 2:7; *ruaḥ* and *neshamah* occur with nostrils in Genesis 7:22.
28. The triad parallels, in ascending order, *Malkhut* (Dominion; the lower Mother, *Shekhinah*); *Tiferet* (Splendor; the Husband of the Bride, the Holy One, blessed be He); and *Binah* (Supernal Wisdom; the upper Mother).
29. See *b. 'Eruvin* 65a.
30. *Zohar* I. 18a.
31. This tradition is also found later in the present passage, where the verb *yiqavu* is glossed by the hyper-phrase: *medidu de-qav u-meshiḥta',* "the measurement of the measuring-line and the measurement."
32. See *Midrash Bereshit Rabba* 5.1 and 28.2, Juda Theodor and Chanokh Albeck, eds. (Jerusalem: Wahrmann Books, 1965), I, 32 and 260. In both cases the noun *middah,* "measure," is used.
33. The letter *vav* usually symbolizes the middle column of the line, known as *Tiferet* (splendor), and when it suits exegetical purposes, the lower gradation of *Yesod* is called a small *vav.* Since *Tiferet* is regularly symbolized by "heaven," "under the heavens" would symbolized the next lower gradation, *Yesod.* The fact that the letter *vav* is spelled with two *v(av)*s marks this esoteric point orthographically.
34. In some printed editions the four letters of the Tetragram are variously marked in the first four words of the Gen. 1:9. Cf. the annotation of the Derekh Emet in the margin of *Zohar* I. 18a.
35. See the fine formulation in *Zohar Ḥadash* 105c, where it is said that "those who are engaged in Torah [study], and contemplate the words of Torah with intention and deliberation . . . do not contemplate the word alone, but rather the [supernal] place upon which the word depends; for there is no [scriptural] word that is not dependent upon another supernal mystery". For the passage and a discussion, see Elliot Wolfson, *Through a Speculum That Shines: Vision and Imagination in Medieval Jewish Mysticism* (Princeton: Princeton University Press, 1994), 390–391.
36. The phrase is given there as an eschatological promise; the *Zohar* cites it as a theological reality.
37. I prefer the reading *'itbesis,* "established," to *'itbesim,* "perfumed" (or purged of the dross of judgment).
38. *Zohar* I.18a.
39. See *Zohar* I. 18a/b. All the classical sources are cited: Exodus 24:10; Numbers 14:10; 17:7; Isaiah 6:1; and Ezekiel 1:28. In a brilliant addition, the teaching supplements this series with a citation from Genesis 35:16, "and

Rachel was in childbirth, and had difficulty *(va-tiqash)* in her labor." With this verse the letters of *qeshet* (rainbow) are inverted as the teacher makes the esoteric point about the manifestation of the lower gradation of *Malkhut* (in which the bow of the upper world is revealed) through the arousal of the left side (the side of judgment, limitation, and hence restriction or difficulty).

40. It would appear that these colors symbolize the supernal triad of Grace *(Ḥesed)*, Power/Judgment *(Gevurah/Din)*, and Splendor *(Tiferet)*. If so, this configuration is understood to be reflected in the manifestation of the divine Glory in *Yesod* (the upper unity) and *Malkhut* (the lower unity). For the color symbolism of the bow, see also *Zohar* III. 215a, and the comment of R. Baḥye ben Asher (*Rabbeinu Baḥye*, I, 122), on Genesis 9:13. Our passage is considered within a wider framework by Gershom Scholem, "Colors and Their Symbolism in Jewish Tradition and Mysticism," *Diogenes* 109 (1980), 69–71.

41. The imagery of the bow in the cloud has commonly been understood as a symbol of sexual conjunction (the union of the final masculine gradation of the upper world, *Yesod*, with the receiving feminine gradation in the lower world, *Malkhut*), insofar as the *qeshet* (bow) is an old rabbinic euphemism (based on Genesis 49:24) for the *membrum virile*; see *b. Soṭah* 36b. For this passage, see Scholem, "Colors," 70–71; and more broadly (based on *Zohar* II. 99a), Idel, *Kabbalah* 227. A strong reading of the symbolism in terms of the unveiling of the "androgenous phallus" in the lower gradation, as "the basic phenomenological presupposition of theosophic kabbalah and zoharic kabbalah in particular" is presented by Elliot Wolfson, *Through a Speculum*, (n. 30), 336–45. I would nuance the matter at hand differently—despite the erotic valence—since the bow is called here the "appearance of the semblance of the divine Glory"; that is, despite the metonymic aspect of the bow as symbolic of male sexual potency, this arc of colors is perceived as the *whole* divine Glory in a form like a Man. It is this anthropomorphic configuration as a whole that enters the Kingdom *(Malkhut)* of the beloved, symbolized by the cloud.

42. This rotation of the closed eye is called here *gilgula' de-ḥeizu de-'eina'*; for an analysis, see Liebes, *Sections of the Zoharic Lexicon*, 291–293. Among other formulations of the praxis, note the instruction *'asḥar galgalakh* in *Zohar* II. 23b.

43. For other modes of color visualization in prayer, see Moshe Idel, "Kabbalistic Prayer and Colors," in *Approaches to Judaism in Medieval Times*, David Blumenthal, ed. (Atlanta, Ga.: Scholars Press, 1988), III, 17–27.

44. There is reason to suppose that the triune assertion of YHVH-Eloheinu-YHVH has been influenced by Christianity; see the analysis of Yehuda

Liebes, "Christian Influences on the Zohar," *Jerusalem Studies in Jewish Thought* 2 (1983), 40–45 [Hebrew]; English translation in his *Studies in the Zohar,* 140–145. Liebes cites a passage from Moses de Leon's *Sheqel ha-Qodesh* that, like our *Zohar* passage, deals with the mystery of unity of the three Names in Deuteronomy 6:4 and adduces Zechariah 14:9; see *R. Moses de Leon's Sefer Sheqel ha-Qodesh,* Mopsik, ed., 103. An extended discussion there (82 f) is very similar to our Zoharic formulation, and the language of the unity of the three Names is similar to *Zohar* II. 43b. On this text, see already Adolph Jellinek, "Christlicher Einfluss auf die Kabbalah," *Der Orient* 12 (1851), 580–583.

45. *Zohar* I. 18b.
46. The verse is recited aloud only on Yom Kippur. It is derived from Psalm 72:19 and 145:11, and was the response formula in the Temple to the recitation of the ineffable Name by the high priest on Yom Kippur. See *M. Yoma* III.8. The phrase was transferred to the recitation of the *Shema'* at an early date. Its silent recitation in conjunction to the *Shema'* is presented with an aggadic anecdote in *b. Pesaḥim* 56a. *Zohar* II. 133b–134b is an extended parallel to our discussion; the author says there that the silent recitation of the phrase is for this world alone, not the eschatological world to come. See also the brief formulation, but linked to Genesis 1:9, in the third *Piquda'* in *Zohar* I. 12a. On this genre, see Ephraim Gottlieb, "Ma'amarei ha-'Piqudin' sheba-Zohar," *Kiryat Sefer* 48 (1972–73), 499–508.
47. This version of the episode follows *b. Berakhot* 13b; but I read R. Zeira' here as per the *yer. Berakhot,* chap. II. hal. 1, since R. Jeremiah was R. Zeira' pupil, as also in this piece. The mss. of the Babylonian Talmud vary; see Raphael N. Rabbinovicz, *Diqduqei Soferim,* (Munich, 1881), *Berakhot, ad loc.*
48. *M. Berakhot* II.2 (the verb there is *yiqabbel,* "receive"; "accept").
49. On Rabbi Zeira and certain ritual practices, see Abraham Goldberg, "Rabbi Zeira u-Minhag Bavel be-'Eretz Yisra'el," *Tarbiz* 36 (1966–67), 319–41.
50. See *b. Menaḥot* 62a and *b. Sukkah* 37b–38a, respectively, and the illuminating discussion of Meiron Bialik Lerner, "Ba-shamayim uva-'Aretz uva-'Arba' Ruḥot ha-'Olam," in *Sefer Zikaron le-Binyamin de-Vries,* Ezra Zion Melamad, ed. (Jerusalem: University of Tel Aviv Press, 1969), 101–109.
51. See in the edition of Shalom Albeck (Jerusalem: H. Vegshel, 1984), I, 14. For al-Barceloni's discussion, see his *Peirush le-Sefer Yetzirah,* S. J. Halberstam, ed. (Berlin: Mekitze Nirdamim, 1885), 204. The letter *dalet* is numerically "four," and thus deemed fitting to indicate divine totality. A comprehensive review of the sources of this head gesture appears in

Yitzhak Zimmer, "Tenuḥot ve-Tenu'ot ha-Guf be-Sha'at Qeri'at Shema'," *Asufot* 8 (1994), 359–362.

52. This spark is the *botzina' de-qardinuta'* which is mentioned in this creative capacity in the opening myth of creation, *Zohar* I. 15a (also II. 133b). The spark is sometimes referred to as *botzina' de-qadrinuta'*, "spark of darkness." On these terms, see Liebes, *Sections of the Zohar Lexicon,* 145–151, 161–164, respectively [Hebrew].
53. On this comprehensive figure, see Scholem, *On the Mystical Shape,* chap. 1.
54. The passage concludes with one further correlation between Scripture and liturgy: a correlation between a tripartite reading of Genesis 1:9 and the *trishagion* formula (from Isaiah 6:3) recited during the Kedushah recitation.
55. See *Zohar Ḥadash, Midrash Shir ha-Shirim,* 70d.
56. Cf. the famous exposition on this subject in *Zohar* I. 4b–5a. This passage is emphasized by Yehuda Liebes in his explorations of the imaginative impulses of the Zoharic creativity. See "Zohar ve-Eros," 71, and the wider discussion in 70–80. See his comprehensive treatment of this passage in "The Messiah of the Zohar" [in Hebrew], in *The Messianic Idea in Jewish Thought: A Study Conference in Honor of the Eightieth Birthday of Gershom Scholem* (Jerusalem: Israel Academy of Sciences and Humanities, 1982) 182–187.
57. This observation is indebted to the discussion of Yehuda Liebes in "Zohar ve-Eros," 104–112. He rightly stresses the highly eroticized dimension of the fellowship's relation to Rabbi Shim'on as a manifestation of the *Shekhinah* through the kiss (cf. *Zohar* III. 59a and 201b); indeed, the love of friends is deemed fundamental to the eros of creativity. Powerful sublimations are clearly involved. The issue of the "latent homoeroticism" of the fellowship has been taken up by Elliot Wolfson in a distinctive manner; see *Through a Speculum That Shines,* 368–372.

8. Substitutes for Sacrifice in Judaism

1. The literature on sacrifice is vast. In my view, the classic study by Hubert Hubert and Marcel Maus, "Essai sur la nature et la fonction du sacrifice," *L'année sociologique* 2 (1899), 29–138 remains a benchmark for its perception that sacrifice modifies the agent who accomplishes it and for its recognition of the many functions of sacrifice. Among recent discussions of terms and theory, with pertinent bibliographies, see J. van Baal, "Offering, Sacrifice and Gift," *Numen* 23 (1976), 161–178, and Th. P. van Baaren, "Theoretical Speculations on Sacrifice," *Numen* 11 (1964), 1–12.

2. *Abot de-Rabbi Nathan,* Solomon Schechter, ed., 3rd corrected ed. (New York: Phillipp Feldheim, 1967), A, IV, p. 19. This statement is justified by a strong and tendentious reading of Deuteronony 11:13. Starting from the older teaching in *M. Avot* I.2 that the world "stands" on the Temple "service" *('avodah),* this teaching asserts that the world is sustained through the rains which Temple service effects, by a reading of the biblical exhortation to "serve" *(la'avod)* the Lord with total devotion. The religious ideology of sacrificial efficacy undoubtedly preceded this Scriptural proof.
3. *Inter alia,* this teaching is repeated in *Pesiqta de Rav Kahana,* Bernard Mandelbaum, ed. (New York: Jewish Theological Seminary, 1962), I, 5.17 *(Ha-Hodesh ha-Zeh),* 106–107; 6.4 *(Qorbani Laḥmi),* 120–121; 15.7 *(Eikha),* 257. The prooftext is Isaiah 1:21, "and righteousness (read as "a righteous one") shall dwell therein." Cf. Rashi, *ad loc.*
4. A fragment of a mythic assertion of this reality is found in *Pesiqta de-Rav Kahana,* Mandelbaum, ed., 309 *(Anokhi Anokhi),* where the divine promise "to plant the heavens and make firm the earth" (Isaiah 51:16) is linked to "the sacrifices."
5. See Julius Lewy, "Julianus Caesar u-Binyan ha-Bayit," in *'Olamot Nifgashim* (Jerusalem: Bialik Institute, 1969), 221–254.
6. For this post-destruction situation, see *Tosefta Soṭa* XV.10–12, in *Tosefta, Mo'ed,* Saul Lieberman, ed. (New York: Jewish Theological Seminary, 1973), 242–244. For an elaboration of such groups of mourners, see the discussion in Chapter 5, above.
7. *b. Berakhot* 17a.
8. It is nevertheless notable that the usual expression of atonement in these priestly sources emphasizes priestly agency *(ve-khipper 'alav ha-kohen,* "and the priest shall make atonement/expiation"), while here the reflexive *u-mitkapper* is used. The same sources also stress that "favor" is the result of proper ritual performance (*ve-nirtzah lo,* "that it may be acceptable on his behalf"), while here favorable acceptance is requested assertively (*va-tirtzenni,* "and do Thou favor me"). In Psalm 19:15 the formulation is more circumspect ("May the words of my mouth . . . be acceptable" *(yiheyu le-ratzon).*
9. *b. Soṭah* 5b.
10. The verb *ḥafetz* ("want") is often used in polemics against sacrifices (in general or as improperly performed). Cf. 1 Samuel 15:22; Isaiah 1:11; Hosea 6:6.
11. *b. Yoma* 86b.
12. *Abot de-Rabbi Nathan* A IV, p. 21.
13. A trace of this notion occurs in Psalm 89 itself (vv. 10–12), where cosmogony follows from the slaughter of a primordial monster of chaos. This

biblical tradition has been discussed earlier (see Chapter 3). Of course slaughter is not (necessarily) identical with sacrifice; nevertheless, the idea that the world is founded upon death and destruction is thoroughly different from its foundation upon loving kindness. This latter is the rabbinic point, which turns on the biblical term *ḥesed* (meaning favorable acts of divine power; see Psalm 89:2), with the foundational character of loving kindness.

14. *Abot de-Rabbi Nathan* A IV, p. 8.
15. The topos of reciting *(qore'in)* the biblical laws of sacrifice as a substitute for sacrifices and the divine gift of forgiveness occurs in *b. Ta'anit* 27b and b. *Megillah* 31b. In *Tanḥuma, Tzav,* 14, the concern to be occupied with the recitation of the sacrifices precedes a divine statement to Ezekiel that if the people are occupied with the details of the new temple when in exile, "the reading thereof is as great as its [re]building . . . and the reward for [the people's] studious preoccupation with it is that I shall account this for them as if they were occupied with the building of the temple [itself].
16. See *The Guide of the Perplexed* III.32, tr. with an introduction and notes by Shlomo Pines (Chicago: University of Chicago Press, 1963), 526–527. For a trace of this notion that sacrifices are an institution accomodated to the mentality of idolatry, see already in *Leviticus Rabba* 22.5, Mordecai Margulies, ed., 2nd ed. (Jerusalem: Wahrmann Books, 1962), III, 517–518. Margulies also notes the similar aetiology of biblical sacrifice in this ancient midrash and in Maimonides' thought. For the biblical transformation of pagan sacrifices, see Maimonides, *Guide* III. 46 (pp. 581–92).
17. Cf. *Zohar* III. 48a, where it is directly stated that sacrifice sustains the upper and lower worlds.
18. See *Zohar* II. 20a–20b *(Midrash Ha-Ne'elam).*
19. *Zohar* II. 218b–219a.
20. This refers to the tradition cited earlier (from *Pesiqta de Rav Kahana,* 15, among others), to the effect that all of Jerusalem residents' sins would be expiated by the daily evening and morning offerings.
21. *Zohar* I. 191a–191b.
22. *Zohar* III. 252b–253a *(Ra'aya' Mehemna').*

9. Contemplation of Death in Jewish Piety

1. For a full discussion see my book, *The Kiss of God: Spiritual and Mystical Death in Judaism* (Seattle: University of Washington Press, 1994). The broader ideal of love of God in Judaism has been discussed by Georges

Vajda, *L'amour dieu dans la theologie juive du moyen age* (Paris: Librarie Philosophique J. Vrin, 1957).

2. See *Sifre on Deuteronomy,* Louis Finkelstein, ed. (New York: Jewish Theological Seminary, 1969), *pisqa* 32, p. 55.
3. This verse is also cited in the *Tosefta, Berakhot,* VI.7; see *Tosefta. Zera'im,* Saul Lieberman, ed. (New York: Jewish Theological Seminary, 1955), 35 (l. 37).
4. This verse is repeatedly used in the context of martyrdom; cf. in the *Mekhilta de-Rabbi Ishmael, de-Shira* 3; Ḥayim Horovitz and Israel Rabin, eds. (Jerusalem: Wahrmann Books, 1960), 127.
5. *Ibid.*
6. The combat motif is quite common. Compare the following two sayings of Rabbi Resh Lakish: "One should always incite the good inclination against the evil one [one that Rashi glosses: 'He should wage war against the evil inclination] . . . If he conquers him, fine, if not, let him study Torah . . . " (*b. Berakhot* 5a); and, "A person's [evil] *yetzer* gathers strength each day, and seeks to slay him . . .; and were it not that the Holy One, blessed be He comes to his aid, he would not overcome it" (*b. Qiddushin* 30b).
7. For *b. Menaḥot* 110a, see the citation above, in Chapter 8.
8. *Sefer ha-Manhig,* Yitzḥak Raphael (Jerusalem: Mosad Ha-Rav Kook, 1978), I (*dinei tefillah* 1), 35–36 (Hebrew pagination); the ruling follows *Sefer ha-Oraḥ* (par. 12): *qorban ḥashvinan le-hu* (noted ad 1.36). The scriptural citation from Hosea is notable; for while it accords with the main sense of the Massoretic text, the reading *peri* ("fruit") instead of *parim* ("bulls") is similar to the Septuagint *karpon* ("fruit").
9. See *Abudarham ha-Shallem* (Jerusalem, 1959), *Seder shaḥarit shel ḥol,* 48.
10. *Sefer Shibbolei ha-Leqeṭ ha-Shallem,* Solomon Buber, ed. (Vilna, 1886), 2. R. Zedekiah's brother, R. Benjamin, is said to have written "that the recitation of the *tamid*-service is obligatory [*ḥovah*]."
11. In *Perushei Siddur ha-Tefillah la-Rokeaḥ,* R. Moshe Hirschler and R. Yehudah Alter Hirschler, eds. (Jerusalem: Makhon Ha-Rav Hirschler, 1992), II, 16; on 35, R. Eleazer justified the custom by citations from Hosea 14:3 and b. *Megillah* 31B.
12. *Shulḥan 'Arukh,* 'Oraḥ Ḥayyim, 2.
13. *The Book of the Pomegranate: Moses De Leon's Sefer ha-Rimon,* Elliot R. Wolfson, ed. (Atlanta, Ga., 1988), 225–226.
14. So Jacob Katz, in his influential essay "Beyn TaTeNU le TaḤ TaT," in S. Baron, ed., *Yitzhak Baer Jubilee Volume* (Jerusalem: Historical society of Israel, 1960), 318–37. For my critique, see *The Kiss of God,* 74–77.

15. See, for example, R. Menaḥem Recanati, *Peirush 'al ha-Torah* (Venice, 1548), fol. 77 c-d. For a full discussion, see my *The Kiss of God,* chap. 1.
16. *Bayit Ḥadash* to *Tur, 'Oraḥ Ḥayyim,* sec. 61.
17. See the section *Mitzvot 'Asei min ha-Torah* (Positive Commandments of the Torah), chap. 9.
18. See the accounts in *b. Berakhot* 61b and *yer. Sota* 5. 20c, and the discussion in *The Kiss of God,* 66–73, where the historicity of this account is analyzed and its role as a mythic model considered.
19. *Yosef 'Ometz* (Frankfurt-am-Main, 1922), no. 482.
20. *Ibid.,* no. 485.
21. See *M. Baba Qama* VIII.6; *Tosafot Baba Qama* 91a, s.v., *ve-lo'; Pisqei Tosafot, Baba Qama,* no. 215; and Maimonides, *Mishneh Torah, Hilkhot Yesodei ha-Torah* V.6–7.
22. *Yosef 'Ometz,* no. 485.
23. For the text, see the citation in Chapter 8.
24. The *Yosef 'Ometz* was published in Frankfurt, 1723; the *Sefer Ḥaredim* in Venice, 1601.
25. In the first phrase "your soul" is in the (masculine) singular, and derives from Deut. 6:5; the second is in the (masculine) plural, and derives from Deut. 11:13. The two phrases are taken from the first two paragraphs respectively of the *Shema'* service that follow the recitation of the *Shema'* proclamation itself (Deut. 6:4).
26. The reference to earthly wealth alludes to the phrase "and with all your might" in Deut. 6:5, according to the traditional interpretation.
27. *Sefer Ḥaredim.*
28. *Yosef 'Ometz.*
29. Cf. the *Ascension of Isaiah* 8:14–15; 9:1–5, 36–40.
30. See *Zohar* I. 66a, 224a-b; III. 69a. On the whole subject, see Gershom Scholem, "Ḥaluqa de-Rabbanan," *Tarbiz* 24 (1955), 297–306.
31. *Shnei Luḥot ha-Berit,* vol. II, pt. 1 *(Torah She-Bekhtav)* 1 c-d.
32. For example, according to the halakhic norms, it is not possible to fulfill the laws of the sabbatical year outside of the land of Israel; and obviously not everyone can fulfill the commandment of a leviratic marriage.
33. See the discussion of this source and older sources in Arthur Green, *Devotion and Commandments: The Faith of Abraham in Hasidic Tradition* (Cincinnati: Hebrew Union College Press, 1989), 39–59.
34. It is found at the beginning of his *No'am Elimelekh* (Cracow, 1896) and in collections of spiritual practices.
35. The major "Standing" prayer of each service; the weekday form is also known as the *Shemonah 'Esreh,* the "Eighteen" benedictions. The first blessing refers to God as "the shield of Abraham." According to midrashic

lore, this patriarch was cast into a fiery pit in Ur of the Chaldees and was saved by God. See *Midrash Bereshit Rabba, Noaḥ,* 38.13, Judah Theodor and Chanokh Albeck, eds. (Jerusalem: Wahrmann Books, 1965), I, 362–364.

10. Joy and Jewish Spirituality

1. *Abot de-Rabbi Nathan,* ed. with an introduction by Solomon Schechter, 3rd ed. (New York: P. Feldheim, 1967), version A, chap. 34, p. 103 (52a). The Hebrew terms are: *sason, simḥah, gilah, rinah, ditzah, tzahalah, 'alizah, ḥedvah, tiferet, 'alitzah.* These terms all occur in the Hebrew Bible, but not all of them as nouns (for example, the rabbinic noun *ditzah* only appears in the Bible as a verb; cf. Job 41:14).
2. I follow here the treatment of *simḥah* as indicative of the joy of giving by Yochanan Muffs, *Love and Joy: Law, Language and Religion in Ancient Israel* (New York: Jewish Theological Seminary, 1992), chap. 8. This work continues the approach begun with his *Studies in the Aramaic Legal Papyri from Elephantine* (Studia et documenta ad iura orientis antiqui pertinenta 8; Leiden: E. J. Brill, 1973). Recently, Jeffrey Tigay, *Deuteronomy* (Jewish Publication Society Torah commentary; Philadelphia: Jewish Publication Society, 1996), 122, argued that here and in other instances in Deuteronomy the issue was rejoicing in the meal. Cf. Gary Anderson, *A Time to Mourn, a Time to Dance* (University Park, Penn.; Pennsylvania State University Press, 1991), 19–26. This approach ignores the clear references to the gifts to God and the issue of thankful celebration (stressed in Deut. 28:47, see below).
3. Muffs, *Love and Joy,* 133 n. 16 refers to the pair *simḥah* and *ṭuv lev* in Deut. 28:47 in this light; the technical meaning of the term *ṭuv lev* as volitional giving is established by Muffs for all cognate languages in his *Aramaic Legal Papyri.* Tigay, *Deuteronomy,* 268, paraphrases Deut. 28:47 as meaning "when you were joyful and glad because of abundance," but this forces the plain sense, quite apart from the present argument.
4. See my *The Garments of Torah: Essays in Biblical Hermeneutics* (Bloomington: University of Indiana Press, 1989), 70–71, for examples.
5. Rashi understood *sova' semaḥot* as "joy without end or diminishment"; and Ibn Ezra refers to the worshipper "enjoying the radiance of the Shekhinah," and his soul as seeing transcendental truth directly.
6. See *Sifre on Deuteronomy,* Louis Finkelstein, ed. (1939; rpt. New York: Jewish Theological Seminary, 1969), *pisqa* 141, p. 195. The dialectical exclusion there of birds and meal-offerings (since they are not derivatives of the *ḥagigah*-offering) reflects *M. Ḥagigah* I.4; see also *b. Ḥagigah* 8a.

7. The *Targum Yerushalmi* specified joy through celebrating the Beit ha-Sho'evah ritual with flutes. Verse 15 was also interpreted in terms of ritual performance; see *Sifre on Deuteronomy, pisqa* 142, p. 195. The teaching specifically adds the requirement of joy for the first night of the festival, but *yer. Ḥagigah* 76b applies this exegesis to the last day.
8. See *Midrash Wayyikra Rabba,* Mordecai Margulies, ed. (Jerusalem: Wahrmann Books, 1972), 30.2, p. 694; and *Midrash Shoḥer Ṭov,* Solomon Buber, ed. (Vilna, 1891), 16.12, p. 124 (62b).
9. *Ibid.*, 100.3, p. 426 (213b).
10. The other contradiction mentioned in the Talmudic passage is between the praise of anger in Eccles. 7:3 and the praise of joy in 2:2. The rabbinic expression for the the desire to withdraw the book is *biqshu lignoz;* cf. *b. Shabbat* 13b, and the concern to withdraw Ezekiel because of contradictions between it and the pentateuchal laws.
11. For a comprehensive study of the term Shekhinah, expressing the indwelling nearness and proximity of God, see Arnold Goldberg, *Untersuchungen über die Vorstellung von der Schekhinah in der frühen rabbinischen Literatur* (Berlin: Walther de Gruyter, 1969); and also Ephraim E. Urbach, *The Sages: Their Concepts and Beliefs* (Cambridge, Mass.: Harvard University Press, 1987), chap. 3.
12. Other uses of this prooftext focus on the inspiring presence of the Holy Spirit *(ruaḥ ha-qodesh)* during acts of joy: in *yer. Sukkah* ch. 5, halakha 1, Jonah ben Amitai receives the spirit during the Beit ha-Sho'evah regalia celebrations on Tabernacles (the parallel in *Yalquṭ Shimoni, Jonah,* par. 550, uses the term *Shekhinah*); and in *Midrash Shoḥer Ṭov,* Buber, ed., 24.3, p. 204, David receives the spirit while in a joyous state playing an instrument (the parallel in *Pesaḥim* 117a uses the term *Shekhinah*). The substitution of *Shekhinah* for Holy Spirit in the parallels and the use of *Shekhinah* in *b. Shabbat* 30b may be due to the gradual shift in terminology in Jewish late antiquity; cf. Goldberg, *Untersuchungen* 244.
13. The phrase *le-lamedekha* is a standard feature of the tradition, as it links an event with the dictum about inspired joy (see the sources in the previous note); I separate it from the dictum here only on formal grounds, but undoubtedly it was transmitted with it as a didactic introduction.
14. See Raphael N. Rabbinovicz, *Diqduqei Soferim, Shabbat* (Munich, 1881), p. 57, n. 4; also noted by Urbach, *The Sages*, 392, and n. 82.
15. The contrastive formula *'ein. . .'ella* (not *x* . . . but *y*) is an older lexical formula now used to frame an apodictic saying that something *only* occurs *when* something else is in effect.
16. Cf. *M. Avot* III.2, "[T]wo that sit together and are occupied with words of Torah [exchanged] between them have the Shekhinah among them

[*Shekhinah beineihem*]." Note that the language of inspiration (*Shekhinah shorah beineihem*) is not used here.

17. Goldberg, *Untersuchungen*, 244, speculates that the dictum is against acts of sorrowful asceticism by mystics; but this opinion isolates one term from the negative part of the dictum. It seems to me that the stress is best put on the second, positive part.
18. *Yad Ḥazaqah, Hilkhot Lulav*, ch. 8, hal. 12–15.
19. *M. Sukkah* 4.1, 8.
20. *Ibid.*, 5.2–4.
21. *Ibid.*, 5.1.
22. For some details of early merriment that was curtailed during the Beit ha-Sho'evah rite, see *Tos. Sukkah* IV. 1; see also the reference to activies in IV. 4–5. *M. Sukkah* V. 4 is cited somewhat confusingly at *Tos. Sukkah* IV. 2. See in *Tosefta Mo'ed*, Saul Lieberman, ed. (New York: Jewish Theological Seminary, 1962), 272–273.
23. *Hilkhot Lulav*, ch. 8, hal. 15.
24. It is not without irony, in my opinion, that Maimonides ends the halakha with the words: "And there is no greatness and honor other than to rejoice before the Lord, as is said, 'And King David leaped and danced before the Lord, etc.'" (2 Samuel 6:16). Granted that David later dismisses Michal's denigration of his behavior with an assertion of his disregard for social honor, and that he says that he is not ashamed to be humbled before God (v. 22)—even so, Maimonides' choice of this passage is striking, given its strong emphasis on ecstatic dancing. Presumably David is among those for whom such actions are not emotionally dangerous; but this halakha is a general statement for all Jews, and it is this that makes his citation so ironic.
25. The commentary of Rabbi Vidal Yom Tov of Tolosa (14th century) is printed in standard editions of Maimonides' *Mishneh Torah*.
26. *Zohar* III, *Aḥarei Mot*, 56a/b.
27. See the remarks of Yehuda Liebes, *Studies in the Zohar* (Albany, N.Y.: SUNY Press, 1993), 90–93, in a chapter entitled "How the Zohar Was Written."
28. See *Rabbeinu Baḥye 'al ha-Torah*, Ḥayim Chavel, ed. (Jerusalem: Mosad ha-Rav Kook, 1982), II, 346.
29. For the hermeneutical principle, see *yer. Berakhot*, ch. 9, hal. 5; and see Rashi's citation of it in Leviticus 23:27. Hillel is said to have learned the principle from Nahum Ish Gamzu.
30. *Ibid.*; and see also his religious lexicon *Kad ha-Kemaḥ*, in *Kitvei Rabbeinu Baḥye* (Jerusalem: Mosad ha-Rav Kook, 1970), s.v., *simhah*, 272–273, where part of this argument appears.

31. Baḥye's language of heavenly bliss echoes the combined comments of Rashi and Ibn Ezra on Psalm 16:11.
32. *Kad Ha-Kemaḥ* (see n. 30), 273.
33. *Zohar* I, *Vayehi*, 216b.
34. *Zohar* III, *Vayiqra'*, 8a/b. This text is cited and briefly discussed by Roland Goetschel, "Joie et Tristesse dans la Kabbale Espagnole," *Revue des Études Juives* 144 (1985), 64f; the other Zoharic texts adduced do not bear on the theme as I have developed it.
35. The Name YHWH recited as Elohim is the divine Name associated with *Binah*.
36. This Foundation is the principle of male potency, and is directly above the feminine potency of *Knesset Israel* in the divine hierarchy.
37. See R. Moshe Alsheikh's commentary on Psalm 100:2, in *Sefer Rommemut El. Be'ur Sefer Tehillim* (Vilna: Romm Press, 1903), *ad loc* (first published in 1605).
38. See for example *Sha'arei Qedushah*, II.2 and *Sefer Ḥeredim*, Introduction (to performing the commandments). Cf. the synopsis of these authors' views in Azriel Shoḥet, "'Al ha-Simḥah be-Hasidut," *Zion* 16 (1951), 31–36; and also his treatment of Rabbi Yeshaiah Horowitz's *Shnei Luḥot ha-Brit* (from the 17th century), pp. 36–38. Shoḥet's main concern is to locate prefigurations of 18–19th century Hasidic ideas.
39. For chap. 10 (of de Vidas's *Reshith Ḥokhmah*) all 50 sections are pertinent; for chap. 11 note especially sections 11, 26, and 33; and for chap. 12, see sections 20–26.
40. Chap. 10, section 1.
41. *Ibid.*, sections 3–14.
42. For the subject of angelic recitations in Jewish antiquity and the early Middle Ages, see John Strugnell, "The Angelic Liturgy at Qumran—4QSerek Širot 'Olat Haššabbat," *Congress Volume: Oxford, 1959* (Vetus Testatmentum Supplments, 7; Leiden: E. J. Brill, 1960), 318–45; Carol Newsom, *Songs of the Sabbath Sacrifice: A Critical Edition* (Harvard Semitic Studies, 27; Atlanta, Georgia: Scholars Press, 1985); Karl Erich Grözinger, *Musik und Gesang in der Theologie der frühen jüdischen Literatur* (Tübingen: J. C. B. Mohr, 1982), 13–16, 76–96, 281–329; Arthur Green, *Keter* (Princeton: Princeton University Press, 1997), chap. 2. More generally, see R. Hammerstein, *Der Musik der Engel* (Bern-München, 1962).
43. For the structure, complete with "Crown" above and "Kingdom" below, see *Zohar, Pequdei*, II. 232, cited by de Vidas.
44. *Reshit Ḥokhmah*, chap. 10, sections 14–27.
45. See *Zohar, Vayiqra'*, III. 8a-b, discussed earlier.
46. See *Reshit Ḥokhmah*, chap. 10, section 22.

47. *Ibid.*, sections 27–28.
48. *Ibid.*, sections 28–31.
49. *Ibid.*, sections 32–37; cf. sections 14–18.
50. *Ibid.*, sections 38–43. Section 41 is pivotal and quotes a long selection from chap. 9 of a 15th-century German pietist work known as *'Orḥot Tzaddiqim*—which de Vidas had in manuscript and cites as *Sefer ha-Middot,* the original title of this work, as can be shown from the Introduction.
51. See chap. 10, sections 44–54. Cf. section 44, especially.
52. See section 46, and compare section 4.
53. Chap. 10, section 49.
54. Chap. 11, section 33.
55. Chap. 12, sections 20–21.
56. *Ibid.*, section 22–23.
57. See *ibid.*, sections 24 and 26.
58. William James, *Varieties of Religious Experience* (Cambridge, Mass.: Harvard University Press, 1985).
59. *Ibid.*, Lectures IV–V and VI–VII, respectively.
60. See *ibid.*, Lectures VIII (on The Divided Self, and the Process of Its Unification) and IX–X (on Conversion).
61. References to periods of *'atzvut* and *marah sheḥorah* (sadness and depression) as well as *simḥah* fill the known episodes of his life. See the first-hand materials reported by Rabbi Naḥman's disciple Nathan of Nemirov in *Ḥayyei Moharan* (Jerusalem, 1985), *passim.* For a biographical contextualization and interpretation, see Arthur Green, *Tormented Master: The Life and Spiritual Quest of Rabbi Nahman of Bratzlav* (Woodstock, Vt.: Jewish Lights Publishing, 1992).
62. The first remark was to Nathan of Nemirov, as reported in *Ḥayyei Moharan,* no. 371; while according to *Ḥayyei Moharan*, 49, the second was said during his teaching on the Torah portion of *Ve'etḥanan,* found in *Liqquṭei Moharan, Tinyana'*, 78. However, the traditions differ. In the above citation reported in *Hayyei Moharan,* Rabbi Naḥman "drew out [the pronounciation of] the word *Gevald,* as one who warns and shouts from the depths of the heart." According to *Liqquṭei Moharan,* Naḥman's cry was *Kayn yeush iz gor nit far handin,* and he drew out these words "with great strength and astonishing and awesome depth" in order to strengthen the hearts of his listeners.
63. *Liqquṭei Moharan, Tinyana'*, 23.
64. See Chapter 11, below.
65. Naḥman's great-grandfather, the Ba'al Shem Tov, reportedly embodied this ideal. See especially in *Tzava'at ha-Ribash* (Brooklyn, N.Y.: Kehot, 1991), nos. 15, 44, 110, 137; and note the frequent correlations with sadness or depression. One may wonder whether Nahman's emphasis may not be

part of a family tradition, or his sense of reviving original values of the movement. Shoḥeṭ, "'Al ha-simḥah," 43, regards the emphasis on perpetual joy to be a *novum* of the Hasidic movement in Poland.

66. *Ibid.*, 24; see also *Liqquṭei 'Etzot,* s.v. *simḥah,* 29–31.
67. See the analysis below, Chapter 11.
68. *Liqquṭei 'Etzot,* s.v. *mo'adei ha-Shem,* 2.
69. See *Liqquṭei 'Etzot,* s.v. *hitbodedut,* 8, 13, 23; s.v. *simḥah,* 13, 15; and *Liqquṭei Moharan, Tenina',* 25, 95–98.
70. *Liqquṭei 'Etzot,* s.v. *simḥah,* 32.
71. *Liqquṭei Moharan, Tinyana',* 17.
72. *Ibid.*, 10. See Green, *Tormented Master,* 244, and n. 45, where he notes that the teachings in *Liqquṭei Moharan, Tinyana',* 10–17, were given in the summer of 1808, after Naḥman's return from Lemberg, and with the knowledge of his fatal illness in mind. See *Ḥayyei Moharan* (Jerusalem, 1985), 1:50 and 59. In 1:50 we are told that during this period the Master "spoke a great deal about joy, and strengthened us, and energized us to be always joyful [*be-simḥah tamid*]."
73. That Rabbi Naḥman drew from this work, cf. *Liqquṭei Moharan, Tinyana',* 17, on the subject of joy on the Sabbath and festivals.
74. *Liqquṭei Moharan,* I, 30.2
75. *Liqquṭei 'Etzot,* s.v. *simḥah,* 1.
76. *Ibid., Mo'adei ha-Shem,* 4–8.
77. *Ibid., 'Einayim,* 1.
78. See the important teaching in *Liqquṭei Moharan,* I, 282. See also *ibid., Tinyana',* 48 and *Liqquṭei 'Etzot,* s.v. *simḥah,* 28.
79. *Liqquṭei 'Etzot, simḥah,* 28.
80. See *Ḥayyei Moharan,* no. 65.
81. Published in *Kenesset Yisrael* (Warsaw, 1906), 145 (in an appendix).

11. The Mystery of Dance According to Rabbi Naḥman of Bratzlav

1. There is a rich bibliographical literature on the subject of dance. Pertinent for our inquiry are Geradius van der Leeuw, *Sacred and Profane Beauty: The Holy in Art* (Nashville: Abingdon Press, 1963), part 1; Janet L. Hanna, *To Dance is Human: A Theory of Nonverbal Communication* (Chicago: University of Chicago Press, 1979), and *Society and Dance,* Paul Spencer, ed. (Cambridge: Cambridge University Press, 1985), with bibliographies.
2. *Degel Maḥaneh Ephraim, parashat Yitro.*
3. For the dance of the angels, see *Midrash Song of Songs Rabba* 7.1, on Songs 7:6. Maimonides, in his *Epistle to Yemen,* relates this latter interpretation to the Sinai theophany; see his midrash in *Iggeret Teiman,* Abraham S.

Halkin, ed. (New York: American Academy of Religion, 1952), 23–33. See also *yer. Ḥagigah* 2.1, 77a.

4. Cf. Louis Jacobs, *Hasidic Prayer* (New York: Schocken Books, 1972), chap. 5, and the sources cited. Significantly, though the Ba'al Shem died in 1760 and thus began his teaching years earlier, the first polemic, entitled *Zamir 'Aritzim ve-Ḥarvot Tzurim,* appeared only in 1772. This work has been reprinted in Mordecai Wilensky, *Ḥasidim u-Mitnaggedim* (Jerusalem: Mosad Bialik, 1970), I, 27–69. On this matter, see Ze'ev Gries, *Sefer, Sofer, ve-Sippur be-Reshit ha-Ḥasidut* (Tel Aviv: Hakibbutz Hameuchad, 1992), 17–18, 69.
5. The citation of Ecclesiastes 2:2 may allude ironically to *b. Shabbat* 30b, where the verse serves to introduce a positive teaching about religious joy. See n. 7, below.
6. *Liqquṭei Moharan,* II, 23.
7. Cf. Arthur Green, *Tormented Master: The Life and Spiritual Quest of Rabbi Nahman of Bratzlav* (Woodstock, Vt.: Jewish Lights Publishing, 1992), 141–142f.
8. *Liqquṭei 'Etzot, Mo'adei ha-Shem, Shalosh Regalim,* 2; *ibid., Simḥah,* 2; and cf. *Liqquṭei Moharan,* I, 25 and II, 81.
9. The Talmudic passage builds on a contradiction between Eccles. 8:15, "Then I commended joy," and Eccles. 2:2, "And what does joy accomplish?" (see n. 3, above). The contradiction is resolved as follows. "'Then I commended joy'—this refers to the joy *(simḥah)* of (observing) a commandment *(shel mitzvah);* 'And what does joy accomplish?'—this alludes to joy that does not come from (the fulfillment) of a commandment. Thus Scripture teaches you that the Shekhinah [Divine Presence] does not rest [on a person] either when he is in a melancholy, or indolent, or frivolous mood . . . but only when he is inspired by something joyful *(davar simḥah).*" The standard edition of the Talmud now reads *shel mitzvah* ("of the commandment"), but this phrase is not found in the Mss. or in earlier editions. The words were apparently known to Rabbi Naḥman. For a further discussion of the Talmudic passage and its Zoharic and other developments, see my discussion above, Chapter 10.
10. *Liqquṭei Moharan,* II, 24.
11. *Ibid.*
12. For the transformation of the *Shekhinah* from Divine Presence in classical rabbinic sources to a supernal (feminine) hypostasis in kabbalistic texts, and a penetrating review of the subject, see Gershom Scholem, *On the Mystical Shape of the Godhead* (New York: Schocken Books, 1991), chap. 4.

13. *Yer. Megillah* II. 4 reads *rosh ḥolah* (literally, "head of the dance troupe"). *Midrash Wayyikra Rabbah* 11.9, Mordecai Margoliot, ed. (Jerusalem: Wahrmann Books, 1962), 240–241, reads *rosh ḥola'*, with a prooftext from Psalm 48:14 *(rosh ḥeylah)*; see further, *Midrash Shoḥer Tov*, Solomon Buber, ed. (Vilna, 1891), *ad loc.*.
14. For the supernal (masculine) gradation known as *Tzaddik*, or Righteous One, see Scholem, *Mystical Shape*, chap. 3.
15. *b. Ta'anit* 31a (this ends the tractate on a messianic theme; cf. the end of chap. 1, which also concludes with a promise to the righteous). This source is cited again in *Liqquṭei Moharan*, I, 65.4 *(ad fin.)*.
16. This seems to me the most convincing explanation, even if R. Naḥman was influenced by the teaching of R. Berekhiah on Psalm 81:1, where the expression *'al maḥalat* is interpreted as regarding *meḥilah* "forgiveness"); see *Midrash Shoḥer Ṭov, ad. loc.* See also the interpretation of Song of Songs 7:1, *meḥolat maḥanayim*, in *Yalquṭ Shimoni*, Song of Songs, 992. There are other instances where Rabbi Naḥman used puns. Noteworthy is the case where he refers to poetry "in their language" (German) as *Poesie*—a level one can attain if one is able to fulfill *feh zi* (i.e., it [sexual desire] is contemptible. See *Yemei Moharanat*, 36; noted by Mendel Piekarz, *Ḥasidut Bratzlav* (Jerusalem: Mosad Bialik, 1962), 45. On sexuality in Rabbi Naḥman's thought, see Yehuda Liebes, "Ha-Tiqqun ha-Kelali shel R. Naḥman Mi-Breslav ve-Yaḥaso le-shabta'ut," in his *Sod ha-'Emunah ha-Shabta'it* (Jerusalem: Mosad Bialik, 1995), 238–261, 429–444. Liebes also points to the aforenoted pun on p. 445, n. 125.
17. *Liqquṭei Moharan*, I, 23; for other uses of this verse, see *ibid.*, I, 22.9. The aggressive will required for integrating the forces of sadness is marked by Naḥman's language: in I, 24, he says one "must force *(le-hakhriaḥ)* them into [the domain of] holiness"; and this temerity is also called *'azut deqedushah* (I, 229).
18. *Ibid.*
19. A classic exposition of the theosophical teachings of the Zohar and Lurianic speculation is provided by Gershom Scholem, *Major Trends in Jewish Mysticism*, 2nd ed. (New York: Schocken Books, 1946), Lectures 6 and 7. See also Scholem, *Mystical Shape*, chap. 2, for a discusssion of the *Siṭra Aḥra*. The Zoharic source quoted by Nahman in *Liqquṭei Moharan* I, 41 says *binah dinim mit'arin minah* ("The judgments arise from *Binah*"; see *Vayiqra*, II. 10b). Biblical proof is adduced from Proverbs 8:14.
20. This is outlined in *Liqquṭei Moharan* I, 41, with thighs, feet, and heels brought into their correspondences in accordance with Lurianic teaching (in *'Etz Ḥayyim*, adduced at the beginning of Naḥman's discourse). Cf. the comment of R. Moshe Cordovero, *Pardes Rimmonim*, 23, *raglayim*, "*Malk-*

hut is called 'feet' in the mystery of the lowest aspect (of the supernal realm)."

21. The redemptive power of dance was already enunciated (albeit in different terms) by Rabbi Naḥman's great-grandfather, the Ba'al Shem. See *Keter Shem* \OS\T.\OS\ov, no. 179, 23a (regarding holy dancing before a bride).
22. See *Liqquṭei Moharan* I, 41 *(Ve-hu' loqeaḥ ha-bekhorah veha-berakhah she-zeh beḥinat birkayim).*
23. The sum *'a-q-b* is 172 + 10 for the initial *yod* = 182, which is twice the numerical value of Elohim. For this gematria, see as early as *'Etz Hayyim,* I (*Heikhal* 5, *Sha'ar* 22, *Pereq* 2); and among Hasidic sources, see the comments of Rabbi Jacob Joseph of Polonnoye, *Toledot Ya'aqov Yosef, parashat Noaḥ* (Warsaw, 1881), 16d.
24. *Ibid.*
25. See *ibid.*, I, 32; also I, 10.6, where the same technical terms appear.
26. *Ibid.*
27. It is stated in Genesis 29:25 that only in the morning, after the nuptials (v. 23), did Jacob realize that the woman "is *(hiy')* Leah." *Midrash Bereshit Rabba* 70.19, Juda Theodor and Chanokh Albeck, eds. (Jerusalem: Wahrmann Books, 1965), I, 818, interprets this phrase as the recitation of the celebrants who cheered "Yea *(hey)* Leah." Naḥman understood the cheer as the letter *he,* and as a sign to Jacob that Leah is *he'* (the 5th letter); that is, she is *binah* and *lev,* which are also the 5 alephs in the divine Name *'eheyeh,* and which form the healing source of *din* (judgment; and from there follows a whole further series of numerical equivalents which are 5 times *d-y-n*), and so the purification of the upper female (Leah) for the lower realms. See *Liqquṭei Moharan,* I, 32. For the relationship between *dam* (blood), and the purification of the feminine, see *ibid.*, I, 169 and 22.11.
28. See *Liqquṭei Moharan,* I, 169, especially. These "messengers of judgment" are called "runners" in the *Zohar* (I. 43) and "feet" in Rabbi Naḥman's corpus.
29. *Ibid.*
30. See *b. Makkot* 22b (R. Simlai); and in *Pesiqta de-Rav Kahana,* 12.1, Bernard Mandelbaum, ed. (New York: Jewish Theological Seminary, 1963), I, 203 (R. Judah b. Rabbi Simon).
31. *Pesiqta de-Rav Kahana,* 25.1, Mandelbaum ed., II, 380. And see the discussion of Moshe Idel, *Kabbalah: New Perspectives* (New Haven: Yale University Press, 1988), 157–160.
32. *Midrash Tanḥuma, parashat 'Eqev,* 1. The homily refers to the sum of 613 commandments, and mythicizes the metaphorical cargo of Psalm 49:6. See also the theme of the bodily microcosm in *Abot de-Rabbi Nathan,* A,

31, Solomon Schechter, ed., corrected ed. (New York, 1967), 91–92. Corresponding to the heavenly angel of death there is an angel of death in each person, and it is found in the heels.

33. See *Zohar* II. 85b (the passage continues: "some with the King's head, some with the body, some with the King's hands, and some with his feet—and none go beyond the body"); III. 136b *(Idra Rabba); Tiqqunei ha-Zohar, Tiqqun* 21, 60a, and 70, 130a-132a. Reciprocally, sins diminish the divine Body or block its channels; cf. *Zohar* I. 67a; 85b; II. 162b, 165b; III. 297a-b.
34. See the edition of Elliot Wolfson, *The Book of the Pomegranate: Moses De Leon's Sefer Ha-Rimmon* (Atlanta, Ga.: Scholars Press, 1988). Over 100 commandments are discussed by de Leon.
35. See Alexander Altmann, *Kirjath Sepher* 40 (1964/5), 256–276, 405–412.
36. Cf. *Sha'ar Ha-Mitzvot,* by Rabbi Hayim Vital (Jerusalem, 1872); and *Metzudat David,* by Rabbi David ben Shelomoh ibn Abi Zimra (Zolkiew, 1862).
37. For this theosophy in the context of "walking," see the valuable discussion (with earlier references) by Elliot Wolfson, "Walking as a Sacred Duty: Theological Transformation of Social Reality in Early Hasidism," in *Along the Path* (Albany, N.Y.: SUNY Press, 1995), 89–109, and 223–245.
38. *Liqquṭei Moharan,* I, 178; cf. II, 81. The idea derives from the *Zohar,* where it is frequently remarked how sin blocks the channels of the divine realm; cf. I. 67a and III. 297a-b.
39. *Ibid.,* I, 178.
40. *Ibid.*
41. Cf. *Liqquṭei Moharan,* I, 24.3; I, 81 specifically says that "feet *(ha-raglayim)* are *Netzaḥ* and *Hod,*" and goes on to identify them with the gradation of Prophet(s) *(naviy')*. An interpretation of Psalm 90:12, "and bring us *(naviy')* a heart of wisdom" is adduced to indicate how these supernal gradations may be brought (elevated) through dance to the heart of the sefirotic structure. *Liqquṭei Tefillot,* 10, *ad fin.,* speaks of raising the legs through dance to their supernal source.
42. See especially *Liqquṭei Moharan,* I, 277, "Every *mitzvah* is a complete *qomah;*" and II, 39, where Nahman speaks of "the form of the limbs *(tavnit ha-'evarim)* and the building and structure *(qomah)* and image, etc. of each and every thing *(kol davar ve-davar).*" The notion has its roots in the *Zohar,* where it is taught that each *mitzvah* contains all 613 commandments and replicates the anthropomorphic structure of the divine hierarchy; cf. *Zohar* III. 228b *(Ra'aya' Mehemna'), kol mitzvah 'ihiy sheqila' le-taryag.*
43. *Liqquṭei Moharan,* II, 81.

44. *Ibid.*, I, 22.11; cf. 10.6. Torah and prayer also have feet; see *ibid.*, I, 75.
45. The number 13 may refer to the 10 gradations plus the 3 pure lights above them; and also to the 13-petaled rose, which stands for the 13 attributes of mercy which emerge from *Binah* for the benefit of the Assembly of Israel (they flow down to surround and protect *Malkhut*). According to *Zohar* I. 1a, this rose or lily is the "cup of salvation(s)"—a clear messianic allusion. The 13 petals are linked there to the 13 "words" or references to the divine Name *Elohim* in Genesis 1:1–2:1.
46. *Liqquṭei Moharan,* I, 22.9.
47. *Ibid.*, 22.10.
48. *Ibid.*
49. *Ibid.*, end. According to *Zohar* II. 117b–118a *(Ra'aya' Mehemna'),* the righteous are "like the limbs of the Shekhinah"; and cf. *Tiqqunei ha-Zohar, Tiqqun* 70, 130b.
50. See *Ḥayyei Moharan,* no. 340, for the Hebrew and Yiddish versions. By the Yiddish expression *oys gegangen,* Rabbi Naḥman means a mystical death or expiry of the soul; an annihilation of self-consciousness. The idiom also appears in the *Kuntres ha-Hitpa'alut* ("Tract on Ecstasy") by R. Dov Ber of Lubavitch (1773–1827), a contemporary of R. Naḥman. Near the end of section 4 of the *Kuntres,* R. Dov Ber speaks of an "ecstasy of the whole essence [*hitpa'alut kol ha-'atzmiyut*], in which one is "so completely transported that nothing remains of him and he is without any self-consciousness." A Yiddish gloss immediately follows referring to "the very deep absorption of the whole of the soul to the extent that he leaves [or: dies to any sense of] the vessels of his mind or heart [*er kan oys geyn fun di keli ha-moaḥ veha-lev*]." See *Sefer Liqquṭei Bei'urim* (Jerusalem, 1974), 55. For R. Dov Ber's mystical experience in the context of Jewish spirituality, see my *The Kiss of God: Spiritual and Mystical Death in Judaism* (Seattle: University of Washington Press, 1994), chap. 3, especially pp. 117–20.
51. *Ibid.*, end.

Credits

Several chapters were originally published elsewhere. They have all been revised; most have been expanded; all are reprinted by permission of the publishers.

Chapter 1 first appeared as "'Orally Write therefore Aurally Right': An Essay on Midrash," in *The Quest for Context and Meaning: Studies in Biblical Intertextuality in Honor of James A. Sanders,* edited by Craig A. Evans and Shemaryahu Talmon (Leiden: E. J. Brill, 1997), 531–546.

Chapter 2 first appeared as "'The Holy One Sits and Roars': Mythopoesis and the Midrashic Imagination," in *The Journal of Jewish Thought and Philosophy* 1 (1991), 1–21; published by Harwood Academic Publishers.

Chapter 3 first appeared as "Rabbinic Mythmaking and Tradition: The Great Dragon Drama in *b. Baba Batra* 74b–75a," in *Tehilla le-Moshe: Biblical and Judaic Studies in Honor of Moshe Greenberg,* edited by Mordechai Cogan, Barry L. Eichler, and Jeffrey H. Tigay (Winona Lake, Ind.: Eisenbrauns, 1997), 273–283.

Chapter 4 first appeared as "The 'Measures' of God's Glory in the Ancient Midrash," in *Messiah and Christos: Studies in the Jewish Origins of Christianity Presented to David Flusser,* edited by Ithamar Gruenwald, Shaul Shaked, and Gedaliahu G. Stroumsa (Tübingen: J. C. B. Mohr, 1992), 53–74.

Chapter 9 first appeared as "The Imagination of Death in Jewish Spirituality," in *Death, Ecstasy, and Other Worldly Journeys,* edited by John J. Collins and Michael Fishbane (Albany: SUNY Press, 1995), 181–208.

Chapter 11 first appeared as "To Jump for Joy: The Rites of Dance According to Rabbi Nahman of Bratzlav," in *The Journal of Jewish Thought and Philosophy* 6 (1997), 371–387; published by Harwood Academic Publishers.

Index